HOW TO WRITE BIOGRAPHIES AND COMPANY HISTORIES

HOW TO WRITE BIOGRAPHIES AND COMPANY HISTORIES

Richard Sawyer

MOUNTAIN PRESS PUBLISHING COMPANY
Missoula — 1989

Cover Design by Janie Lowe

Library of Congress Cataloging-in-Publication Data

Sawyer, Richard V.
How to write biographies and company histories.

Bibliography: p.
Includes index.
1. Businessmen—Biography—Methodology. 2. Industrialists —Biography—Methodology. 3. Corporations—Historiography. I. Title.
HC29.S38 1989 808' .066338 89-9280

PREFACE

There is properly no history, only biography.

— Emerson

This book is being written because I have found a way for competent free-lance writers to control their work, their careers and the income they earn. It is no great sacrifice for me to share what I have developed and learned because there is enough work 'out there' for all of us. And, being a lazy fellow, I will be able to reach many more writers through this book than would be possible in seminars, workshops and private consultations. After years of presenting the material in this book piecemeal, to writers and writers *manque*, in such diverse settings as writers' conferences, my cluttered study at home and at symposia, I am doing what I should have done years ago—write this book. In 1973 I discovered a gold mine—a printing press that cranked out hundred-dollar bills—a writer's bonanza. And I want to share the treasure, no strings attached.

Every step in this book has undergone testing in the field—has endured trial by fire in the competitive marketplace and has proved workable and profitable. The following material is short on theory and long on practicability. *Biographies and Company Histories* is, then, a step-by-step how-to book which will allow you to take charge of your career and write your own ticket when it comes to income.

Working in an almost totally undeveloped area of writing, and in little more than a decade, I have created typescripts and privately published books (or helped to create the same) which have produced some $250,000 in income for myself and other free-lance biographers and corporate historians. While this kind of income doesn't put us in the same league as a Sidney Sheldon or a John McPhee, I am satisfied that any writer well grounded in nonfiction writing techniques can earn a full-time living from his craft.

There is a whole new industry waiting to be born, and ten thousand qualified writers could not handle all the potential business in this new field. Were I *not* to share what I have learned, I would feel like Aesop's dog in the manger. Just think! In every block of every hamlet and village, every town and metropolis in this (and every other) nation in the world, there is at least one story that is just bursting to be told. Add to these the tales of personal sacrifice, toil, and pertinacity—of failure and triumph—behind every family business, corporation or sole proprietorship in this nation, and one realizes that an army of writers couldn't document them all in several lifetimes.

Biographies and Company Histories then, provides writers with the key to a kind of scriveners' El Dorado—a mother lode of rich experience as well as money in the bank—all just waiting to be exploited.

It can be yours for the taking.

Richard Sawyer
Seattle, Washington—1989

To Carol, who urged me to *get going*;
to Cynthia, who urged me to *keep going*;
and to Archie, who catalyzed the whole
exercise so that at last, it *did go,*
this book is gratefully dedicated.

CONTENTS

INTRODUCTION

FIRST, YOU GET YOUR FEET WET

I was cold, wet, and scared spitless. The joyful rush of outrage and indignation which had compelled me to quit my job an hour before had deserted me. As I stood in the parking lot of the Seattle network-affiliate radio/TV station (where I had so recently been editorial manager), I felt terribly alone. The chill fog and drizzle of a typical Northwest March day seemed to suck the warmth of life right out of my body.

I unlocked my car and squished disconsolately into the driver's seat. Perhaps I had acted too hastily—perhaps I could have swallowed my pride and handled things differently. Perhaps.

"Idiot!" I shouted at an unresponsive steering wheel.

To this day, I don't remember the drive home through the rain.

At the time, I could not appreciate the importance of the moment. Only later did I realize that I had engineered an all-important turning point in my career, and that it had come with unintentionally precise timing at the very moment it was most needed. I was to have the luxury of some enforced leisure time during which I might examine the progress of my life's work. I could take a look at where I had been, and where I wanted to go in terms of writing. Just what did I want to do with the rest of my creative life?

As I ruminated, I was surprised at the dominance of a single thought. *I no longer wanted to be associated with any organization big enough to confuse me.* At age 47, and after having worked in the pharmaceutical, life insurance, nuclear, aerospace and electronic communication industries, I finally realized that I wanted to strike out on my own. After nearly three decades of working for someone else, I wanted to be my own boss.

My recent knee-jerk resignation from my job demanded that I make a decision, and my enforced vacation granted me the boon of time in which to sort things out. I would have to take inventory: what I had done, what I did well, what I most *liked* to do, and how to prime the pump of cash flow. And while I was going through this soul-searching, a kind providence prevented me from morbidly dwelling on the mortgage, car payments, the financial responsibilities of a household—all ongoing debits which had to be met without the benefit of my (until then) regular paycheck.

We were a two-income family, and my wife's salary was a godsend—but her income alone would not long sustain us. Whatever I was to do had to begin without delay. Within a few months, we would be feeling an uncomfortable pinch, and unless I was willing to again settle for second-best—once more working for wages—my new career directions would have to bear fruit quickly.

THE INVENTORY

If a merchant is to go into business, he must first take inventory of what he has to sell. And that is precisely what I had to do. For the entrepreneurial writer this must entail a cataloging of his skills in the various recognized fields of writing: fiction, nonfiction books, articles, technical writing, public relations, advertising, newspaper, etc. What skills can he bring to the marketplace? As I took inventory of my stock of wares—the skills I had to sell—I assigned a number rating, from 1 to 10, to each area of writing. This rating was based on two factors: the skills I brought to that particular branch of writing, and the enjoyment I derived from performing that kind of writing.

After having made an exhaustive list of all the things I enjoyed doing, and all the things I did well, my ballot was cast to a particularly unremunerative endeavor: writing the short personality profile of the kind usually seen in Sunday supplements and regional magazines. Writing the personality profile was one of my skills, and the format one which I enjoyed. The big catch lay in the compensation. At $50.00 to $350.00 per article, writing the little personality profiles simply wouldn't provide enough income. I had to earn more money—more than the small-format article could produce.

Could I expand the format? Pump it up some? Make it into a larger piece of work for which I could earn more money? Would it be possible to write longer articles for greater income? It seemed unlikely. The only markets purchasing such long articles on interesting or controversial subjects were the major magazines, and they were tough markets to crack. Even granted high productivity on my part and the great good fortune of selling a half-dozen of these pieces a year at, say, $2,000 each, the pickings would be mighty lean. There had to be another way.

The book-length biography came quickly to mind. But just as quickly came the realization that I had to have access to celebrities or mega-achievers. It was humbling to realize that I did not know one person whose life story would warrant the production of a trade book by a major publisher. Scratch the blockbuster biography—at least for the moment.

Then came the flash of insight—one for which I will remain thankful all of my days.

Why should only the great and near-great have books written about them? What about writing biographies on commission? Why not biography for *Everyman*? Could I not promote the concept of *Biography as Legacy*? Scratch the surface, and every man jack of us has a story to tell—a biographical heritage which our heirs should not be denied.

As I brainstormed, I expanded my thinking. Not only individuals, but companies and corporations had stories which should be recorded. I could write company histories as well! After all, every Ma-and-Pa store and every industrial giant began with a human vision. And documenting the human stories behind these visions was only biography of a different sort! As the possibilities seized me, I became quite overcome with a sense of mission. And I had to agree with Carlyle: "Biography is the only true history."

I had a product—and a ready-made market. Every sixty-year-old on the planet, and every company more than a few decades old automatically became prospects for my product!

The thoughts raced through my mind. I realized that this new concept—biography for *every*one—was something that could be sold. Instead of merchandising my ideas and my skills to editors and through the conduit of literary agents, I would be selling, not indirectly to the purchasers of magazines, newspapers and books, but directly to the consumer—the person who would pay my fees.

If I were to be successful, I would have to have near-total understanding of my subject—the rationale for the ideas I proposed, and counters to every objection I could imagine arising—to say nothing of knowledge about all printing, binding and production details for the books I proposed to write. I would have to be a one-man band, book all the engagements, write all the scores, play all the instruments and know all the orchestrations. But first, I had to get a solid grip on my ideas so that I might present them to others.

I determined that I would write *Biographies And Company Histories*, and become a storyteller commissioned to document the past for the benefit of future generations.

Surprisingly, my adventure into the unknown deeps of full-time free-lancing worked splendidly almost from the very beginning—as it can for you. From 1973 until the present, I have earned nearly all of my living from the free-lance writing of biographies and corporate histories, and I have yet to suffer the first pang of regret for having left the "safety" and "security" of big industry. I am convinced that for the writer possessed of industry, forthrightness, and the expected skills of his craft, a career in commissioned writing is within reach.

There is a whole new industry just waiting to be born, and the readers of *Biographies And Company Histories* will be in the forefront of what I hope, one day, will be a corps of thousands earning their livelihoods in this lucrative and rewarding field. It is realistic for me to share my ideas with every writer equipped to put them to use. Ten thousand writers could not handle all the potential business in this new field.

It is with a real sense of delight that I present these guidelines to you. If properly put to work, they will form the foundation for an entirely new American industry. These ideas will provide for their practitioners a sustained, dependable, monetarily rewarding, aesthetically fulfilling and dignified lifetime profession. And in their wake, these ideas will leave a succession of priceless documents of individual and corporate achievement, of sentiment and history, of family and personal triumph and tragedy. Collectively, the books and recorded tapes will proclaim our American heritage to the generations to come.

CHAPTER ONE

HAVE YOU THE "RIGHT STUFF" TO BECOME A BIOGRAPHER?

Those who take no pride in the accomplishments of remote ancestors are those least likely to do anything that will be viewed with pride by remote descendants.

— Thomas Macauley

WILL YOU BE ABLE TO DO THE WORK?

I don't know. That's for you to determine. In defining my audience for this book, I have considered only those writers who want to make money from their writing. It was, after all, no less a light than Samuel Johnson who said, "No man but a blockhead ever wrote except for money."

This book is dedicated to those writers who want to earn money from their writing and to those who are willing to *try* to make money from their writing. More importantly, perhaps, the information and direction contained in the following pages will permit those who faithfully follow "the recipe" (and embellish upon it) to become full-time professional writers earning their livings from the practice of their craft.

Several assumptions are made:

First: **You already have a good command of English grammar, syntax and vocabulary.** I don't mention spelling, because although I fancy myself to be a writer, I can't spell worth a damn. There is a word guide or dictionary at every typewriter in my house, upon the night stand, and beside my two favorite reading chairs. Besides, I take heart in Samuel Johnson's observation that knowledge is of two kinds. We know a subject ourselves, or we know where we can find information upon it. Spelling falls into the latter category.

Second: **You have the desire to be successful at writing, and to be adequately compensated for your experience and your work.** I find little merit in the romantic notion of the starving poet or playwright eking out a pittance by writing greeting-card verse in his unheated garret. Such sophomoric nonsense is best reserved for those determined dilettantes and dabblers for whom this book is specifically not intended. *Biographies And Company Histories* is written not for those who would like to be *known* as writers, so that they might share the mystical aura which is supposed to glisten, halo-like, about those in the creative community. No, this book is for those willing to learn new skills, redirect old ones, and serve the necessary apprenticeship to *become* well paid professional writers reaping the rewards for having finely honed their skills.

Third: **You are willing to be a one-man band and perform most of the work necessary in gathering the material and putting together a book yourself.**

In the following chapters we will explore, step-by-step, the proved formula by which you may become a successful biographer and a corporate historian. We will cover:

- defining the product which you will offer your client;
- explaining and promoting the product to your prospective clients by means of brochures and individualized letters;
- prospecting for potential clients;
- making initial contacts with those prospects by mail;
- securing the first, or "selling" appointment through the follow-up telephone call;
- answering (countering) objections to the initial interview;
- conducting the initial, or selling interview;
- providing the client with three options: tapes only, tapes and transcripts, or a book manuscript;
- determining the estimated cost of each option to the client, and determining your *own* rate of pay;
- securing the ten- or fifteen-percent retainer (your first paycheck) based on your estimates;
- explaining the billing procedure to your client;
- generating the interview questions;
- conducting the interviews;
- purchasing appropriate recorders, transcribers and typewriters/ word processors;
- likening the company history to the analogous, yet different, individual biography;
- establishing work habits; and
- packaging and delivering products to clients.

Even though you are an experienced writer, and much of the material looks to be oppressively familiar, please bear with me. You probably have not personally encountered or engineered your way through all the facets of the "work package" which are necessary in producing the finished personal biography or the corporate history.

As is proper with a "how-to" book, each new step succeeds the former. Following the instructions in *Biographies and Company Histories* is not unlike building a model boat from a kit or baking a batch of bread by adhering to cookbook directions—there is a well defined and quite predictable end product in sight.

If you will but "follow the simple directions" there is no doubt that you will one day soon hang out your shingle as a professional writer, command a suitable income, and achieve the independence most of us so ardently desire.

CHAPTER TWO

THE "ROOTS" OF THE MATTER:
Biography as Legacy

Each family, however modest its origins, possesses its own particular tale of the past—a tale which can bewitch us with as great a sense of insistent romance as can ever the traditions of kings.

— Llewelyn Powys

WHAT IS BIOGRAPHY?

The Merriam-Webster *Webster's Ninth New Collegiate Dictionary* defines biography as "a (usually) written history of a person's life." Houghton Mifflin's Second College Edition of *The American Heritage Dictionary* tells us that biography is "A written account of a person's life; life history." Under the notation "biographical literature," the redoubtable *Encyclopaedia Britannica* explains that biography is "one of the oldest forms of literary expression, includes all those works in which a writer seeks to recreate the life either of himself or of another, utilizing all the available resources of memory and research."

The writing of biographies, then, has been going on for centuries. And there was a time when we thought of biographies as books written about only the famous or the near famous. In short, nobody bothered about writing a book about a person's life unless the subject was someone illustrious whose life story could be expected to attract a wide audience of readers. It never occurred to most of us that the doings of *our* individual lives might prompt the writing of a book.

If we are to write biographies and corporate histories for others, and charge them substantial fees for our work, we must have a thoroughgoing and professional understanding of what we are about. Moreover, it is demanded of us that we have an uncompromising commitment to the value of the service we provide. We must be convinced of the *worth* of personal biographies before we can successfully promote and sell these services.

What is biography? The textbook definitions of biography are listed above. But I like to think of biography in far more personal terms. And I like to compare the biography to other familiar documents which pace our lives.

It is fit and proper to consider the biography as a companion document to the will. After all, if a will is a *legal* document concerned with objects and money, a biography is a *human* document concerned with people and ideas. *Both* are needed to transmit the tangible and *in*tangible riches of a lifetime to those of our family who are to follow us. And both documents, the will and the biography, are designed to safeguard that which we have found precious in our lifetimes. The will and the biography make certain that nothing is "lost" or "mislaid" along the way. These are the documents which distribute the wealth, memories, and wisdom of a lifetime.

LEGACIES

Legacies are gifts of money or property left by predecessors to those who follow. Some legacies are characterized as heirlooms—inseparable parts of the inheritance, or things of special value handed on from one generation to another. Wealth and property can best be passed from one generation to the next by means of the will, or a properly executed trust account handled by a financial institution.

But haven't we all heard of other kinds of legacies? We like to think of the United States as having a legacy of free speech and freedom of assembly. Western civilization has a legacy of knowledge derived from Greek philosophers, playwrights and poets. As a Northwesterner I have a legacy of reverence for the verdant forests and crystal waters—a legacy passed on to me by the culture of the Indians of Pacific Northwestern Coast.

Legacies, then, may be either tangible or intangible. Our lawyers and bankers have figured out how to pass on the tangible bequests of our lives, but what of the intangibles? How are these to be transmitted to their rightful recipients?

The biography comes quickly to mind as the instrument of choice for making certain that our legacies to our heirs are complete. In the selling interview, whose principles will be covered in a later chapter, I emphasize that entrusting the heritage which we leave to others entirely to the will and a financial instrument, such as a trust agreement, we have, in effect, created a two-legged stool. It is unstable, cannot stand by itself, and is insufficient for the job it is intended to do.

We must have the foresight to create a more substantial structure for our legatees—we must build that *three*-legged stool. For the disposition of our worldly goods, including our houses and business properties, jewelry, furniture, automobiles, crystal, and the bric-a-brac of life, we need the will. For the investment of capital and the regular disbursement of funds, the trust instrument is ideal. But for the passing on of family history, genealogies, personal recollections, accounts of relationships with others, philosophies of living, reactions to the issues and controversies of history, and the high points and depressions of our individual lives, the biography is the only vehicle which fills the bill.

It is our high calling to create biographies, tightly built and soundly crafted, able to fulfill their important missions of carrying the stories of man down through generations of time.

CHAPTER THREE

BIOGRAPHY FOR "EVERYMAN":
Writing Your Advertising Brochure To Promote That Concept

Those people who left only monuments behind as a record of their existence have vanished with time, whereas those who left ideas have survived. A society without ideas has no history.

— Max Dimont

PLACING THE RESPONSIBILITY ON YOUR CLIENT'S SHOULDERS

In the paragraphs that follow, we will be discussing the rationale—the urgent reasons—for commissioning a personal biography or a corporate history. The reasons for undertaking this worthwhile effort are most easily presented by means of a short, well-written brochure and in conversations you have with those persons whom you hope to transform from prospects into clients.

The importance of this chapter can scarcely be overemphasized, because the success or failure of our enterprise will be determined by how skillfully we motivate our prospects to buy the services we offer. If we are to prevail, we must *sell*! Some writers, accustomed to working alone in confrontation with nothing more threatening than a blank sheet of paper, may feel at first uncomfortable at the prospect of coming face-to-face with a real, live human being who can say either "yes" or "no" to the ideas we present. Experience will build confidence quickly, however, and if we are to establish ourselves as self-employed and self-sustaining writers, we must be able to promote the ideas about which we feel so strongly. It doesn't take much of a nudge, however, to turn a prospect into an eager client. We have all the advantages! After all, we will be giving our prospects the opportunity to exercise one of mankind's most powerful instincts—the desire to leave some kind of a mark upon the world we inhabit—and that impetus will get us over the rough spots.

If we, as writers, are to be successful in encouraging our prospective clients to pay us good money to help them record their life stories, we must get them to ACT! And we must instill in them not only a sense of their own responsibility, but of the urgency with which they should get on with the project. Because most of our clients will be in their sixties, seventies, and eighties, we should remind them gently but insistently that *time is the enemy*.

After first getting our prospect's attention by the presentation of an attractive brochure whose ideas are compelling, we will then proceed to shift from the general to the specific. If it is a good idea for *all* older people to record *their* life stories for the benefit of their heirs, it is a good idea for our prospect to record *his* life story. We must make certain that he acknowledges his responsibility to provide a biographical legacy so that he may "do right" by his heirs.

Now, most of us dislike being put on the spot, but in the business of converting your prospect into a client (by motivating him to do something he should have thought of himself), it is necessary to make him realize that no one other than himself can get the job done. No on else can provide all the information. He can't delegate this responsibility, ask his brother or sister to undertake the task, or entrust his secretary or his junior partner to handle it. It is up to him. Only *he* is in the position to interpret the world from *his* unique viewpoint—to see it through his eyes. And only he can recount the history of the family as he remembers it, and provide the personal and innermost details of a life known (completely) only to himself. If you do your job thoroughly, your prospect will quickly realize that he cannot pass the buck.

He may squirm uncomfortably or even bridle a bit when you fix this responsibility on him, but when faced with the incontrovertible fact that no one knows his story like himself, he will usually become willing to undertake the task of setting down the story of his life (with your considerable help), and to enter into a creative partnership with you.

How to get your prospective client into this receptive state of mind?

That is where the *motivation* comes in. Not one step in this process is automatic, and nothing may be taken for granted. You, in the dual roles of writer and promoter, must engineer each phase knowingly and with a great sense of purpose. Your job, at this point in the proceedings, is to make your prospect aware of his responsibilities, then offer your services in carrying them out. These messages will be conveyed to him through your personal letters, your brochure, and during your selling interview. In the promotion and selling of your service, you present your prospect with a difficult problem—then accommodate him by showing him how to solve it.

Being made to feel a sense of *obligation* to write a biography is not without precedent. A client of mine, active in the hierarchy of the Church of Jesus Christ of Latter-Day Saints (Mormon), told me that it was a matter of church policy for every young man in his middle teens to begin keeping a personal journal—writing his autobiography, if you will—for the benefit of the church and for the enrichment of family members who would follow.

In the early 1970s, Alex Haley, acting under a personal compulsion, produced a monumental book, *Roots*, which chronicled his family's beginnings in Africa. *Roots* went on to describe the family's bondage into slavery, and the fate of later generations as they emerged from the darkness of servitude into modern mainstream America. This great saga of just one black family captured the interest of millions of American readers. Later, when *Roots* was made into one of the pioneer docudramas for television, additional millions of viewers were caught up in the history of this family.

We may remind our prospects how a whole nation sat glued to its television sets during the week when the *Roots* miniseries was being run. It may be helpful to remind ourselves that after all, *Roots* was, purely and simply, biography. And the book and TV series captivated us all. We were fascinated by the personal stories of the major characters and not only the major turning points in their lives, but the minutiae as well. Even though they were *complete strangers* to us! When you are speaking to your prospective clients, you may suggest that if all America could be caught up in the saga of Haley's family, surely the great events as well as the mundane details of our *own* lives will be of even greater fascination to flesh-of-our-flesh, blood-of-our-blood; our own grandchildren and great-grandchildren.

BIOGRAPHY AS LEGACY—SOMETHING OF SPECIAL VALUE

Many of us—perhaps *most* of us—deplore that (almost to the exclusion of everything else) our civilization seems to have been caught up in the pursuit of material wealth and the collecting of *things*. The accumulation of dollars and things seems to have gained respectability as an end in itself. In this mad scramble for possessions and money, many of the old values—family unity, corporate and personal loyalty, unassailable integrity, the ability to share of ourselves—appear to have been lost.

We do little, however, to *restore* the old values, feeling, perhaps, that in attempting to cement family unity we fly in the face of "modern" trends; that in maintaining old loyalties we demonstrate only complacency rather than the virtue of steadfastness; that in sharing of ourselves we may somehow reveal too much and become uncomfortably vulnerable. For whatever reasons, our culture seems to value us more for our possession of *things* than for adherence to *principles*—and this particular imprint of "modern society" is a sorry commentary on our social evolution. It is a mistake to abandon the old and tested fundamentals; to forsake the upright tenets we learned from our parents and grandparents in the nuclear families of yore; to disdain the articles of faith upon which our ancestors founded their beliefs. And it is a greater mistake not to hand down what remains of these philosophies and admonitions to our children, their children, and their children's children.

As we speak to our prospective clients, we must look to the legacies we leave to our progeny and *their* children. And we must remind them that by "going along" with current trends of what appears to be rampant materialism, we lend only greater dignity to *things* and wealth when those are *all* we leave to our heirs. There is nothing wrong with *things* and *dollars*, mind you, but in and of themselves they represent an incomplete legacy. They are not enough.

It is paradoxical that we leave almost nothing of the value systems we have employed which have allowed us to become successful people. When we leave no biographical or personal history, no record of the hardships we suffered, the lessons we learned at so great a cost go by the board. The mistakes and triumphs encountered, the thoughts we had—even the moral codes to which we subscribed—go with us to the grave. It is almost as if we were *hiding* the fact that somehow, through trial-and-error, experience, luck, and good counsel, we had evolved a philosophy of life which had proved to be workable.

Why should this be so? Why should we think that a proper legacy be constituted only of objects and wealth? I think of objects and wealth as just "stuff" and the money with which to buy *more* "stuff." Brings to mind a comedy routine performed by entertainer, George Carlin, in which he describes security as a state of being surrounded by all your own "stuff." The word, "stuff," used often enough, begins to transmogrify—begins to lose its original meaning and to take on a life all its own. That is the way it seems in real life—the more "stuff" we have, the more dependent we are upon that "stuff," and the more time and energy is consumed in moving that "stuff," protecting and insuring that "stuff," cleaning, polishing and maintaining that "stuff," and for that matter—being *controlled* by that "stuff."

What ever happened to ideas?

Everyone wants to *feel* needed, and you will want to make your prospect feel the importance of the biographical and philosophical legacy which is his to leave. He must be reminded of the worth and of the impact of his *ideas*!

Is Grandfather to be remembered only for the business block downtown, the big house on the hill, and the monthly check from the trust account? Is Grandmother to be represented to her heirs only as the former owner of the fine blue-white diamond and that lovely piece of Chippendale? Or shall Grandmother and Grandfather also be remembered as warm, vital human beings, who scraped their knees as kids, went to school, fell in love, worked hard, and spent their lives evaluating ideas, thinking, forming opinions, laughing, crying, making mistakes, realizing triumphs, reaching conclusions and interacting with the issues and people of their times?

We must ask our client if he is satisfied to allow the accumulated knowledge and the lessons of a lifetime to be wasted.

We must ask him if it is his wish that sixty, seventy, or eighty years of learning, experience and thought be forgotten—disregarded as though his questing mentality had never existed. We must ask him if he is content with contemplating the prospect of such a loss. And we must remind him that if he leaves no record of where he has been, of what he has learned, of what he has encountered, it will be almost as though he had not lived at all.

Our present limited system (of bequeathing only money and property) all but dictates that this be so. As things stand, we will be remembered only by what we accumulated, not as the people we were. Often, our only records of having lived are the objects we leave behind—a headstone seen and recognized by perhaps a half-dozen people in any given year and an oral tradition of storytelling which is valid for only one generation. Our stories are quite simply lost and forgotten when our last close friends and relatives also die.

Ask your prospective client if he wants to entrust the telling of his life story to the frail memories of people as advanced in years as himself. Ask him, too, if he is assured that these elderly "others" will be able to tell his story completely and correctly. Ask him if he is content to devolve upon others the right to interpret his life—and every subtlety, every nuance of it—for him.

Storytelling and the "oral tradition" are fine for as far as they go—but word-of-mouth communications have severe limitations. For one thing, the opportunities for telling our stories are not always easily come by. Any seasoned senior citizen can attest to the frustration inherent in trying to recount childhood experiences and relive the past for the benefit of his grandchildren.

CHILDREN—A LIMITED-ATTENTION-SPAN AUDIENCE

Your prospective client is probably quite familiar with the difficulties often encountered with audiences of children. And if *you* haven't experienced the "agony of defeat" when trying to communicate with one or more wriggling children, just ask any grandmother or grandfather. For years, grandparents have been trying to get their grandchildren to *listen* to them! To pay some heed to what they've been trying to *tell* the little buggers.

Any grandmother or grandfather worthy of the name has encountered this situation. Picture the scene:

"Granny" is settled comfortably by the fire on a blustery Sunday afternoon, and the children are playing quietly nearby. All is domestic tranquility, and the cup of familial blessings runneth over.

"Tell us a story, Grandmother," one of the little ones will say.

"Well," murmurs the delighted grandparent, "what would you like me to tell you about?"

"Tell us about when you were a little girl and the 'olden days,'" comes the inevitable reply.

So, Grandmother puts on her best story-telling manner and launches into some yarn she has just been *dying* to tell the grandkids for ever so long. The story is progressing splendidly, and the children are all ears, when...

- one of the kids mindlessly pulls the cat's tail, and the living room becomes a battleground, with children, squalling cat and bric-a-brac seeming to fly in all directions;
- one of the children has to go to the bathroom, and suddenly, all of them get the same idea and each wants to be 'first';
- the telephone rings and all rush to the front hall at the same time;
- the mother of this clan suddenly announces dinner, and the kids all run screaming to the dining room, leaving grandmother to collect her scattered thoughts and make her way to the table as best she can; or
- all of the above.

Without being cute about it, all of us over the age of fifty can easily identify with the above situations. Most of us have embarked upon what we hoped would be a mutually rewarding conversation with young children, only to discover that the slightest interruption will serve as an excuse to terminate the story-telling. If we haven't known it already, we quickly find that the attention span of youngsters (geared, perhaps, to the 23-minute TV sitcom) is far shorter than our own. It isn't that the kids aren't interested in what the oldsters have to say—it's just that they don't stay interested *long*!

There is a certain wry irony at work here, as well. Our children *are* interested in the relationships and histories of their ancestors and forebears, but often this interest does not become manifest until our children *themselves* are in their late fifties and early sixties. By then, it is often too late—the mother, father, aunt or uncle who represented the richest lode of family stories may have suffered a stroke, become invalided or died—and the source of information no longer available to those who would "tap" it most avidly. This far-from-rare situation has given rise to countless expressions of "Oh, if I'd only listened..." or "If only I had asked Granny Sue (or Uncle George or Aunt Min) all these questions before she became too forgetful and ill to remember."

Historically, we have made do with recounting our accounts of family history, relationships, and life experiences through the so-called "oral tradition." And before the advent of the inexpensive and dependable tape recorder, this was about all we could expect from families not trained in the skills of shorthand, note-taking or composition. But with the emergence of the free-lance writer as "biographer-for-hire," and the ready availability of quality tape recorders, transcribers and word processors, we no longer have to be content with second best.

The era of BIOGRAPHY AS LEGACY is at hand. And you, the readers of this volume, will be able to capitalize upon this development by getting in on the ground floor.

In our brochures, our business letters, and in our interviews it will be our mission to convince our prospects of the value of one principal idea: *that to leave only the physical evidence of our having lived is to deprive our grandchildren and great-grandchildren of a vital and integral part of their birthright.* The true heritage of America and of our families cannot be accurately measured and assessed only by the number and variety of the objects we owned.

In the main, we have bequeathed *objects*, and our personal, intellectual and cultural heritage is *not* transmitted or communicated to those who are to continue our families. And the instrument most often used in bygone years to transmit at least the genealogical information about the family has ceased to exist. The family bible, once a dependable and valued chronicle of the clan, is quite a thing of the past. And until the concept of BIOGRAPHY AS LEGACY came along, nothing had been substituted to take its place.

When we think about it (and it is our *function* to see that our prospects *do* think about it!), the fact that most of us leave a graphic record consisting of only a few amateur snapshots, some disjointed fragments of correspondence, and perhaps a half-dozen brittle and yellowing newspaper clippings, should give us pause. Until now—until this new concept of biography as legacy was developed—our graphic legacies have been all but accidental. Whatever was left lying around when Mom or Dad, or Grandpa or Grandma died, was passed along to whoever got there first. Only the *dollars* and the *things*—the *stuff* of legacy—were given any dignity at all. The will and the trust instrument took care of the *what* and *how much* factors of the bequest, and everything else was left to chance.

It is time to lend some balance to the kinds of inheritances we leave. Through the instrument of the personal biography and because of the efforts of a legion of newly emancipated free-lance writers, future generations will also be able to account for the human factors—the *who, when, how* and *why*—of life's equation.

I have named my modest Seattle enterprise "Life Preservers of Seattle." That is what I do. I preserve lives on recording tape and on paper. Through the media of tape recordings, typed transcripts, and published books, lives and the lessons of life are "saved" for the benefit and enrichment of future generations.

It is now *your* turn to apply these philosophies to your own enterprise. Most of the material in this chapter was derived from the promotional brochure I use in my own work. Please take these ideas, rearrange them, add to them, supplement my thinking and come up with your own piece of promotional literature—a brochure bearing your own imprimature—your *own* individual stamp. Properly used, such a mailing piece is certain to generate interest and create a clientele which will support you handsomely.

CHAPTER FOUR

PROSPECTING:
Clients and Where to Find Them

A true delineation of the smallest man is capable of interesting the greatest man.

— Carlyle

WHERE TO START

You have this great idea; you've petted and polished the words of your brochure until they are as effective as you can make them; your business cards and stationery have been printed; the librarians have come to know you as the person who has read scores of biographies and company histories; your friends and relatives have all given their approval and blessed your new writing venture. You've studied, researched, and prepared yourself mentally. In your heart, you know that you are as ready as you ever will be to plunge into your new career of writing biographies and company histories on commission.

Now what?

Do you suddenly find yourself, like the social wallflower, all dressed up and nowhere to go?

Are you like the hopeful hunter—in the deep woods and loaded for bear—but not a bear in sight?

Where are you supposed to come up with the two or three paying clients who will support you for the coming year?

Be comforted. Eligible bachelors for the wallflowers are everywhere, and game for the hunters abounds. We just have to know where to look for them.

PROSPECTS: WHO ARE THEY?

A prospective client for your services can be almost any adult. Your prospect need not be the person about whom you will be writing—your prospect may be the son or daughter, a grandson or granddaughter, business associate or distant relative of the man or woman whose life story (or company history) you will be hired to write. *Your prospect is the person who can say "yes" or "no" to your proposition, will sign your contract and pay your fees.*

While your prospect may be almost any adult, if you are writing the personal biography he or she will *usually* be the subject whose life story you are documenting. In a company history, your prospect will *usually* be the principle decision-maker of the company—the one man or woman who is empowered to say *yes* or *no* to a business proposition—usually the president of the company, the chief executive officer or chairman of the board.

But each of us has a story to tell. To wax philosophic for a moment, we would do well to recall the words of Sir Walter Scott, who said:

There is no heroic poem in the world but is at bottom a biography, the life of a man; also, it may be said, there is no life of a man, faithfully recorded, but is a heroic poem of its sort, rhymed or unrhymed.

In essence, the great Scots poet affirms that each of us has a story worth preserving, and our stories, if faithfully and fully recorded, have the power to motivate, inform and inspire. These stories, anecdotes and incidents are the personalized chips and flinders of history, and are of lasting value.

From this assurance we may safely infer that *there are stories of worth*, just waiting to be recorded, in every household in the land and in the shops and executive suites of every successful business in the world.

Your potential market holds for you an embarrassment of riches—literally an entire planet is freighted with prospective clients for your skills. It should be reassuring to know that wherever you go, on whatever continent or atoll, there are mature people in need of your services.

QUALIFYING YOUR PROSPECTS

O.K. So you can't write 'em all.

Let's thin out the hordes by *qualifying* our prospects by running through a mental check-list. The more "yes" answers we get to our little prospect quiz, the more our prospect qualifies for our services. And to qualify a prospect, we have to know as much as possible about that person or company. It is important for us to know something about the prospect's mental ability (receptivity to ideas), his income, his accessibility to us, and the need he, his family, or his corporation has for our services and products.

There are enough prospects for your work so that you can afford to be selective. You don't *have* to write all the biographies or corporate histories. You can take just the cream of the crop.

Since you are now in the enviable (and probably quite unaccustomed) position of being able to select only those people with whom you would like to work, you may be as rigorous in your requirements for them as you choose.

Some of the criteria used in *qualifying* a client are:

• INTELLIGENCE: Don't cast pearls before swine. Approach only those individuals and corporate officers most likely to appreciate the value of the ideas (and the ultimate product) you have to offer.

Your prospects need not be intellectual giants; neither should they be cretins. However, their mental furniture should at least equip them to recognize a good thing when they see it.

• AFFLUENCE: Go where the money is! You don't have to be an elitist—but if you are to be successful, you must use good business judgment. While you will be offering your prospective clients at least three or four different "packages" (tapes only; tapes and typed transcripts; tapes and edited transcripts; tapes and finished books, etc.), there is no need to confine yourself to prospects of only modest means. (In the early stages of your new career, however, you may find it most comfortable to begin with small companies and people of somewhat less stature than the community leaders.) Each refinement in the work you perform will require that you spend more time and effort in completing the job. Conducting interviews and providing your client with *only* those tapes (no written material at all) requires less work than writing a book. You will, of course command fees commensurate with the work performed. Keep in mind, however, that it is no more difficult to sell a rich client than it is a poor one. For the same amount of selling effort on your part, you may as well wear silk as polyester.

• ACCESSIBILITY: There are few of us who could telephone Ronald Reagan, Lee Iacocca or Jane Fonda and expect to be granted an appointment. It is best not to shoot for the moon the first time off the launching pad. There is no harm in dreaming, but unrealistic expectations usually lead to disappointment and disillusionment. Get a few modest biographies or company histories under your belt before going for the big time. Our prospective clients must be accessible to us, and we must be able to meet them with the confidence which can come only from our conviction that we know what we're doing—that we can handle whatever assignment is given us. The word of caution is, then: Don't get in over your head—particularly, early in the game. There are tens of thousands of "ordinary people" (there are no such, but we insist on so labeling them) who will give you welcome and provide you with a respectable income while you are honing your skills. Start with the "little guys" until you have a secure grasp of all the facets of promoting, selling, interviewing, organizing and writing the biography and company history. Hold off on the celebrities until you are more sure of yourself and the depth of your skills.

• NEED: It is obvious that some in our communities will have more need for our services than others. An elderly, affectionate, family-oriented widow, well-off financially who dotes on her grand-children and great-grandchildren is a natural prospect. She is of the right age; of receptive disposition; in a comfortable economic position with considerable discretionary income, and possessed of younger generations who may be expected to appreciate a biographical legacy and family history. Our widow's need is apparent, and it is altogether likely that she will quickly grasp the importance of what we have to offer. Similarly, the president of a family-owned business or the CEO of a close corporation make likely and well-qualified prospects. Company histories which treat the contributions of several generations of the same family do not differ greatly from personal biographies. And such records, be they tapes or bound books, will chronicle the achievements of a family while recounting the progress of a business enterprise. In such cases, the ultimate product is a family history, a business history, and an accurate reflection of the times in which the events occurred, all rolled up into one. Such a book is not only of great value as a family memoir, but as a business document of wide utility: as executive recruitment material; employee handbook; gift to shareholders, and public-relations tool.

• A TALE WORTH TELLING: Each of us knows someone—perhaps several people—who we are just dying to interview because of the stories we just *know* they have to tell. Every community has these people—the matriarchs and patriarchs who built the mills, started the banks, financed the libraries, founded the art museums, supported the theaters, organized the farmers' co-ops, and served on the committees, the school boards, and the city councils which keep our nation going. Having an interesting story to tell does not, of itself, *qualify* a person as a prospect. However, if the other *qualifiers* are also there—the accessibility, the intelligence and the income—a great yarn to tell makes for an interesting assignment, is important historically, and can even serve as a great selling tool. *You simply cannot let this great story be lost, Mr. Prospect. And you are the only one qualified to tell it. You owe it to yourself, and to others, to make certain that it is recorded accurately. Let's work together to see that we preserve this bit of the past.* Sometimes an outright and barefaced appeal to vanity is justified—even required—in the interests of preserving a story of historical importance.

PROSPECTS AND WHERE TO FIND THEM

Prospective clients are everywhere, and may be as close as the family next door or as distant as a corporation doing business on another continent. Don't forget—you can practice your business anywhere you can operate a tape recorder or use a typewriter. If you want to work out of the little town of LaGrande, Oregon, you may do so. (Successful colleagues—a biographer and photojournalist—operate from their home in LaGrande.) Or, if you want to prospect among the wealthy retirees and winter vacationers in Palm Springs, Mazatlan or Honolulu, you may do so with equal ease. Since you have decided upon one of the world's most "portable" vocations, you may work where you please—as long as you prospect successfully and attract the necessary clientele.

Want more tips on prospecting for clients? Ask any successful life insurance agent where he gets *his* prospects—particularly those for whom he hopes to write comprehensive insurance "programs." These prospects usually are achievers, most often found in the mid- to upper-range of affluence. They are, almost without fail, aware people, conscious of their responsibilities and eager to see them successfully resolved.

These are the same people whose names appear on the rosters of private clubs, political action committees, boards of directors, and on the subscribers lists of museums, theaters, ballet companies, symphonies and other civic organizations. Your prospects are likely to be among the "shakers and movers" of the community, the "doers" who welcome challenges and seek to resolve problems, be they community, business, professional or personal.

To gain access to these people, I would suggest you begin prospecting close to home. Talk with your friends. At PTA, Community Club, social gatherings, business luncheons, casual meetings in watering holes or on the golf course, be prepared to talk shop. The old admonition, "Don't hide your light under a bushel" still carries an important message.

It used to be that "talking shop" connoted the dull conversation carried on by duller people who had no other reservoir of ideas than provided by their work. It has been my experience that talking about biographies and living history has quite the opposite effect from boredom. When friends or groups of acquaintances learn that you are interviewing fascinating people, recording the stories of their lives and chronicling the ups and downs of regional businesses, they usually show great interest, and want to know more about what you are doing. Often, new prospects are the happy "fallout" from these chance (or carefully orchestrated) conversations.

"I didn't know you were into that kind of writing," one will say. "You ought to meet my Uncle Ned. He's a crusty old bastard, but a great old guy. And he has a million stories to tell. You know, when he was little more than a boy, he served several years 'before the mast'—still during the age of sail—and he's been everywhere and done almost everything. For years, we've been trying to get him to write some of this stuff down, but Ned's no writer. He needs someone to help him along. Tell you what. I'll speak to Ned about you, and see if I can't arrange..."

Another will volunteer: "You know who you should talk to? A friend of my father's. Back in the twenties, this friend of Dad's started making small hardware items in his basement shop, then he got some financing somewhere and incorporated this little company. All during the Depression, he really had to scrape for every dollar. It just didn't seem like things would ever get better. But after years of struggle, just barely making a living, along came Amalgamated Atrocities—the big conglomerate—and damned if they didn't buy him out, lock, stock, and barrel! Well, it was a rags to riches story, and the old boy, who was widowed by this time, married his former secretary, see, and they set out to..."

And sadly, there will always be one who says, "Oh, drat and damn! If only you had been around before Grandmother MacLaughlin died! She knew stuff about the family that went clear back to County Inverness! And she had it all in her head—never wrote down a thing—and now that she's gone, we'll never be able to..."

Those are the heartbreakers.

Once you become known as a biographer and writer, stories seem to pop up from nowhere, like mushrooms after a spring rain. Prospects are all but thrown at you by those who want to have a bit of the action—those who want to become associated, vicariously, if need be, with the interesting career you have carved out for yourself. But you surely don't have to depend on chance for your prospects. If you are to be successful, you will constantly be adding names to your list of people you want to contact—your prospective clients. Moreover, you will cultivate the purposeful habit of prospecting automatically. It will become part of your nature to be aware of people, companies, and situations which all but demand that you initiate contact.

Where shall we look?

Lists and newspaper articles immediately come to mind. Sometimes, it seems that the world is made up of lists (and when our 'junk mail' arrives in the morning post, we are certain we are *on* every list that was ever compiled).

Groups with common interests list the names of their members. Clubs and organizations have membership rosters. People get their names in the newspapers for accomplishments or for having reached certain mileposts in their careers or social lives.

- MEMBERSHIP LISTS: Almost every organization has a list of its members. Genealogical societies, investment clubs, country clubs, yacht clubs, tennis clubs, civic groups, service clubs, veterans' organizations, health spas, alumni groups, private clubs, political parties and historical societies all publish lists of their members. Many of these lists are in the public domain and may be obtained from your library, from friends, or from the organizations themselves. Other, more carefully guarded lists, may be available from sympathetic organization members willing to help you make contacts so that you may get on with documenting history.

- CORPORATION LISTS: The business sections of most public libraries carry information about local companies, including lists of the company officers and members of boards of directors. These names also appear in the annual reports of publicly held companies, and these reports are readily available from the company offices, from public libraries, or from investment firms dealing in stocks and other securities. Citizens of your community who serve on boards of directors are chosen for their business acumen, their ability to perceive problems and solve them, and their standing in the community—precisely the qualities you, as a biographer, find desirable in prospective clients.

- CULTURAL AND CIVIC LISTS: When you attend the theater, an opera, a symphony, a ballet, go to a museum, arboretum or aquarium, you are usually provided with a program, a libretto or some kind of printed material which provides information about the event and the sponsoring organization. Somewhere in these printed handouts it is usual to find lists of financial "angels," donors, sustaining members, docents, and names of the officers of auxiliary groups which do volunteer work in support of the main organization. These lists can be gold mines, because they contain the names of culturally aware, financially responsible, energetic and outgoing citizens of the town or city in which you operate—the very kinds of people whom you would like to call *clients*.

• BULLETINS AND NEWSLETTERS: Alumni bodies, hobby organizations, volunteer groups and others banded together to promote special interests, produce newsletters and mailings in marvelous abundance. These, too, often carry the names of group officers and community supporters which may be of interest to you.

• CHAMBER OF COMMERCE PUBLICATIONS: I don't know how it is in your town, but in Seattle, the Chamber publishes several directories which have been of great assistance in selecting businesses and corporations most likely to qualify as prospective clients—companies which could use the services of a competent historian. The same list helped in winnowing out those firms which did *not* fit the profile I had established for business prospects. The *Directory of Corporate Headquarters: Central Puget Sound Region* lists companies by their specialty (construction, manufacturing, transportation, etc.) and provides company name, address, telephone number and executive officer. In addition, this volume provides figures for gross annual sales, number of employees, product or service description as well as the Standard Industrial Classification (S.I.C.) code. A parallel publication, the *Directory of Seattle-King County Manufacturers*, provides a general product index, a product classification listing, and an alphabetical roster of companies. The latter furnishes company name, phone number, complete plant or mailing address, and the name of the principal officer and his/her title. In addition, this directory states the markets served by the company, an approximation of the number of workers employed, the range of annual gross sales, the year of company founding, and the principal products manufactured. From such a rich listing, the writer angling for prospective clients may reach some sound decisions. For example, it would be reasonable to assume that the Schwarz Fabricating Company, whose president is Elmer Schwarz, was founded by some member of the Schwarz family. Moreover, when we note that the date of the company's founding was 1938, we know that a fifty-year-old family-owned company has an extensive history which warrants recording. A lot of things have happened within the company during half a century, and surely, members of the Schwarz family have been involved. We see, too, by the listing in the directory, that the company employs between 100 and 249 workers, and has a gross annual income of between $1 million and $4.9 million. It doesn't take us long to deduce that the

Schwarz company is big enough, wealthy enough, old enough, and possessed of enough family interest to be a candidate for our services.

• NEWSPAPERS AND REGIONAL MAGAZINES: The sections on business, the arts and local/social news can provide almost limitless leads to the writer. Neighborhood newspapers, in particular, produce news articles which all but *demand* prompt action on the part of the biographer. The headline, "Roland W. Browns observe their 60th anniversary" cries out for action, particularly when the body copy of the story mentions several children, a flock of grandchildren, and the fact that Mr. Brown had at one time been a bush pilot in Alaska, and had retired as the president of his own charter air service. "Percy Phundstarter appointed to chairmanship" blares another headline. The newspaper story cites Percy's long history with his company, and that after having served as president and CEO, he is now being boosted "upstairs" to chairman of the board. Such an appointment may mean that Percy's years of real productivity and usefulness are behind him, and he is being given the honor of placing Ch. Bd. after his name to get him out from under foot. For whatever reason, Percy's duties with the company are certain to be sharply reduced, leaving the man with a great deal of time on his hands. Obviously, Percy has been a man of some accomplishment, otherwise the appointment would not have been made. And he is a man of means, because CEOs and Ch. Bd.s usually earn respectable incomes. He is an older man, and it is safe to predict that he has sired children, and is now a grandfather. So, here we have an older, wealthy, man of achievement who is also a grandfather with (suddenly, since he has been boosted upstairs) a great deal of time on his hands. He doesn't quite know what to do with all that spare time, and he also begins to reminisce about the "good old days" when he and the business were young. He has a bushel of stories to tell—but no one to tell them to. Poor Percy needs a biographer—*fast!*

CAPITALIZING UPON YOUR TREASURE TROVE OF NAMES

Prospective clients for your services are, literally, all about you. You have entered into a business in which almost *everyone* over the age of sixty is a prospect. The suggestions provided in this chapter are by no means the only ones by which you may avail yourself of large numbers of people who are in need of your help.

Now that we have said all of the above, I will have to admit that most of my clients have come to me through word-of-mouth and the most casual of conversations with friends.

One hot Saturday morning, my (older) neighbor and I were both out working in our yards.

"Hey, Dick!" Ed yelled across the street. "It's time for a break! C'mon over and I'll drag something cold out of the 'fridge."

I willingly dropped my pruning shears and strolled across the street. Ed quickly popped a couple of Pepsis, and, drinks in hand, we collapsed gratefully into lawn chairs in the shade of his patio. We talked about the things neighbors talk about—the weather, the dratted slugs chomping on our tender leaf lettuce, our yellowing lawns, and the flowers in our gardens.

"What have you been up to lately?" Ed asked. "I know you're not at the TV station any longer. Are you still writing?"

This incident occurred not long after I had determined to strike out on my own as a commissioned biographer and company historian. I hadn't yet landed client number one, and my brochure was still at the printers. Thus it was with some hesitation that I began to outline my plans, and explain to Ed the rationale of the services I planned to offer. At the time, I had spoken only to members of my family about my proposed new business. As I told of my new service, I was hesitant, but then my natural enthusiasm took over as I talked of my budding enterprise, "Life Preservers of Seattle."

As I elaborated, Ed at first showed polite interest, then a little enthusiasm, and finally, an eagerness to hear more about this concept of BIOGRAPHY AS LEGACY. I was astonished to realize that, almost without trying, I had him hooked!

"God!" he said. "I wish you had been around before Dad died. He had a helluva story to tell—and we kids know only a few of the high spots of his life. It's a damned shame somebody hasn't thought of this idea sooner. I think you've got a winner!"

He pondered a moment, then continued. "But I'll tell you what. It's *not* too late for old Simon Claridge, over in West Seattle. Simon was a friend of Pop's, and they both wound up in the electrical business. Ol' Simon came to this country from England just about the time of the first World War, and he was so broke that he had to borrow money for a screwdriver and a pair of pliers before he could go out on his first job. Today, he's a millionaire. He has apartment houses all over town, a condo on Waikiki Beach, and just sold his electrical contracting business for a couple of million.

"You've got to talk to this guy. I'll give him a call on Monday, and tell him to expect to hear from you. Be sure to use my name, because he's kind of a tough old bird to get through to. But I'll tell him to sit still long enough to listen to you—and I'm pretty sure he will."

My first client came to me just that easily. A few days after the conversation with my neighbor, Ed, my brochures were delivered from the printers. I wrote Mr. Claridge a letter, enclosed a brochure, and telephoned him for an appointment a few days later. He granted me an interview, and after we had talked for a few minutes, I began to explain how we would work together. It didn't take long for me to note that all the time I was talking, his head was nodding affirmatively. The man was agreeing with everything I said! Not half an hour later, he signed the contract, wrote me a check for my retainer without a whimper, and we were in business.

They won't all be that easy—but signing my first client was simplicity itself. I presented the idea, explained the steps in the process, and outlined the cost. And my prospect accepted the whole premise. Later, I learned that he had attempted to write the history of his immigration to the United States, his early struggles, and the adversities he overcame before achieving success—but found that the task was beyond him.

The world is full of people like Simon Claridge, just as the world is full of writers. One must help the other. The Simon Claridges of the world may have many skills, but most of them are voiceless until we writers *give* them voice. It is a joyful responsibility we have, helping mankind spin his yarns and sing his songs, always secure in the knowledge that *prospects are everywhere!*

We have but to seek them out!

CHAPTER FIVE

DRAFTING THE INTRODUCTORY LETTER AND USING THE MAILS TO PROMOTE YOUR SERVICES

Research is the opium of the biographers; when the fit is on them, any fact, no matter how small, must be included just because it is available.

— *Time*,Oct.13,1961,on *Sinclair Lewis* by Mark Shorer

WHY A LETTER?

A succinct, well-written letter, accompanied by a copy of your brochure, represents your introduction to your would-be client. This letter is your personal representative—your emissary. It serves to introduce you (and the quality of work you produce) to your prospective client. And, as in any introduction, you will want to make the best impression possible.

When we know that we are to be personally introduced to influential and important people in society or business, we take care to make ourselves presentable. We dress appropriately, and inform ourselves as to the proper spelling or pronunciation of names and the preferred manner of address (Miss, Mrs., Ms., for example) for the persons we are to meet. In short, we do everything we can to comport ourselves in as seemly a manner as possible.

The same courtesies should apply to the manner in which we introduce ourselves to others by means of letters.

We should certainly confirm that current business and professional titles are accurate, and that names are spelled correctly. We attach a certain mystique to our names, and appreciate seeing ours in print or pronounced aloud. There are few affronts which grate so annoyingly as seeing our names misspelled, appended with last year's business titles, or hearing them mispronounced. Get them *right!*

Our business stationery should be of high quality, and our letterhead attractive, yet in subdued good taste. We are dealing with an older clientele of a generation which put great stock in the dignity of its business dealings. While it must remain a matter of personal choice for every writer, I prefer restrained letterheads and business cards which invite attention (rather than demanding it) because of their conservative good taste rather than through their blatancy, bright colors, or clever/cutesy logos and advertising copy.

The gimmicky approach is best reserved for peddlers of patented vegetable peelers-dicers-slicers, or the purveyors of used cars and aluminum siding. Biography is a dignified (although far from straitlaced, as you will learn!) craft best approached with quiet sincerity. If all goes well, and your prospect is transformed into a client who puts you to work, you will be placed in a position of great trust. After all, your end product will be the depiction of your client's life, and no prospect will entrust the representation of his or her life to one who treats that subject brashly or casually. Everything about your approach—business cards, letterheads, brochure, personal appearance and demeanor—should be so engineered as to reflect sincerity and inspire confidence.

But be of good cheer. All of this is not nearly as stodgy or complicated as it might sound. If your initial mailing to your prospect can establish the right tone—strike the right chord with your client—what follows should be quite straightforward. And luckily, the competition your letter will face in your prospect's mailbox is not of high quality.

COMPETITION FOR ATTENTION

The U.S. Postal System is used by the unscrupulous and the opportunistic to engulf us with junk mail. Nearly all of us resent this inundation of advertising matter, and many of us discard much of it unopened. Communications addressed to "occupant" or bulk-mail distributions are given little attention in most households.

But a letter sent by first-class mail still commands respect and arouses our curiosity. Upon the receipt of a first-class letter, addressed to us by name, we automatically conclude that the writer has a high regard for the contents of the envelope. After all, has he not spent a premium on postage to insure that his important message is directed only to us?

Because you, the biographer, have used care and discretion in creating your prospect list, you won't be sending out all that many letters. Even if you sent out ten letters a week for a full year, your postage would amount to little more than $100—certainly little enough outlay to interest the kinds of clients you hope to attract.

Use first-class mail only. Eschew the temptation to use bulk mailings to less-well-qualified prospects, even though the postal rates may be less for large, unselective mailings. You are running a "class act," and the quality of your individual mailings should reflect that fact.

Please bear in mind—you need only two to four well-qualified clients *each year* to produce the kind of income you've always dreamed of earning. Be selective!

LETTER CONTENT TO THE UNKNOWN INDIVIDUAL

You're about to draft a letter to a person you have never met. You garnered his or her name from the newspaper, from a friend, or from the membership list of some club, civic or cultural organization. Where to begin?

Bear in mind that this "cover letter" or "approach letter" is no more than an *accompaniment* to your brochure, which is the instrument designed to convey the concept of biography as legacy. You don't have to promote the validity of your service in the letter—all you want is your prospect's attention. You have to get him *interested* enough to pick up your brochure and *read* it!

The following is a sample letter which has produced a great deal of business for me.

June 8, 1989
Mr. Aloysius J. Mullally
1234 Giltmore Lane
Shelby, Ohio 44875

Dear Mr. Mullally:

A few days ago while talking with one of my clients, your name was mentioned, and it occurred to me that the enclosed information might be of interest to you.

This fresh approach to the biography as an integral part of the legacy has enjoyed a most favorable reception by a number of your Shelby contemporaries, some of whom I am certain you know. I urge you to examine the enclosed folder thoughtfully. The concepts outlined should prove stimulating to you, and I hope they also have strong personal appeal.

It will probably be worthwhile for us to explore these ideas a bit more fully. In any event, I would like to meet you, so I'll telephone you during the week of June 12 to see when it will be convenient for us to get together.

I look forward to meeting you.

Cordially,

Jerome P. Scrivener

(Enc.) Brochure

Please note the first paragraph of the letter. I wrote that "...while talking with one of my clients, your name was mentioned..." This was not an untruth. When I send letters to people unknown to me, I call up one or another of my established clients (who have, by this time, also become friends) to ask if they know any of the people on my current mailing list. Because many of my clients are well-established businessmen in the community, frequently they will be able to provide some personal background on the prospects to whom I am sending "approach" letters.

A CAUTION!

Frequently, a friend or client will suggest that I send a letter and brochure to an acquaintance. Even if my friend permits me to use his or her name in my letter, I am always careful to take my friend "off the hook." I do so by making minor changes in the first paragraph of my letter so that it now reads:

Dear Mr. Mullally:

A few days ago, while talking with Colonel Pembroke, your name came up in conversation. While the Colonel in no way indicated that you would be a prospect for my services, it occurred to me that the enclosed information might be of interest to you.

By stating to Mr. Mullally that his friend, the Colonel had *not* "sicced" a salesman (the biographer, in his role as promoter of his services) on him, any ruffled feelings may be spared. In truth, the good Colonel might have said to me, "Hey! Tell you who you ought to look up. That's Al Mullally—and you can tell him I sent you over!" But friendships can be disturbed by even such seemingly innocent actions. Better to take full responsibility for the contact yourself. And you do so when you write "...it occurred to *me* that the enclosed information might be of interest to you."

LETTER TO A REFERRED LEAD—TAPES AND TYPESCRIPTS ONLY

It is the nature of our work to seek prospective clients in almost every income bracket. Thus it is that I offer three general types of service to both my personal and corporate clients. These are:

1) Tapes only
2) Tapes and lightly edited typescripts
3) Tapes and full biographies or company histories

Often, when evaluating the needs or income of a prospect, it will become apparent that the full book-length treatment is beyond his financial reach or is inappropriate. Either the prospect can't afford it, or the requirement is for something less than a formal book. In such a case, the following approach letter (also to be accompanied by a copy of your brochure) is appropriate and effective.

March 19, 1989

Mrs. Jack E. Hepfer
7894 Idlewilde Lane
Caution, N.D. 56984

Dear Mrs. Hepfer:

Recently I completed a commission for Paula Froude which involved the tape-recording of accounts of her family and the most memorable incidents of her life. When the recordings were completed, a lightly edited typescript was produced from the tapes, and now the children and grandchildren have this valuable memoir to pass on to future generations of the family.

It occurred to me that such an enterprise might also be of interest to you. The recording of your reminiscences is a pleasurable and sociable undertaking, and the effort involved will require little more of you than holding up your end of a conversation.

While the enclosed brochure was written to explain the reasons for having a formal biography written and printed, the rationale for doing the "Life Preserver" tapes and typescripts is identical. The "Life Preserver" tapes and typescripts contain all of the information required for the more formalized printed-and-bound biography, at about one-third the expense. Thus, if you or one of your descendants elects to write a family history at a later date, all of your stories and irreplaceable family information will be intact and available.

It will probably be worthwhile for us to explore these ideas a bit more fully, so I'll telephone you sometime during the week of March 27 to see when it will be most convenient for us to talk for a little while. I will welcome the opportunity to meet you and to show you some of the work I have done.

Cordially,

Clarice C. Writeworthy

(Enc.) Brochure

cc: Paula Froude

This kind of letter is most effective, because it allows you to use the name of a mutual friend (Paula Froude) to your intended prospect, thus opening the door to you. It is our hope, of course, that the prospect says, "Well, any friend of Paula's is a friend of mine," and acts accordingly by putting out the welcome mat when you come to call. It's hard to beat the power of a referred lead.

OTHER THOUGHTS YOU MIGHT INCORPORATE IN YOUR APPROACH LETTERS

• I'm a professional local writer, and I have a concept which I think you will find of value. It has to do with *unfinished business.*

By the time most of us near the age of retirement, we have gathered together the loose ends and have put our affairs in order. We've taken some pride in the fact that there are few items on our life's agenda still marked *"unfinished business."*

• No doubt your will has been reviewed from time to time; your trust agreement at the bank is up to date; and the beneficiaries on your life insurance policies are as they should be. You have planned for the systematic distribution of your wealth and your properties through the recognized and accepted legal instruments. Should you suddenly be taken ill, become debilitated—or even die—family members will not be burdened by worries about your estate. You have taken care of everything.

Or so you sincerely believe.

• As things stand now, the legacy you will leave your grandchildren, great-grandchildren, and those who come after them might be likened to a game of Monopoly abandoned on the card table before the play was finished. The evidence of the game is still there to be seen. But the stacks of money, the markers for apartment houses, securities, and other properties are only static symbols—mute reminders of bygone excitement, frustrations and success. Unfortunately, nothing can be known of the players in this phantom Monopoly game, and none of the thrill of the contest remains. Missing from this spectral game are any hints as to the character of the players.

Missing from your legacy—as in the Monopoly game—is your personality. By the symbols of *your* success, you will leave to your heirs evidence of your having lived and prospered on this earth. Because you left the symbols of success—things and dollars—your heirs will know that you worked diligently and well. But you will have left *nothing* of *yourself.* Like the static and cold markers of that dead Monopoly game—objects, securities, properties and even income—cannot recreate the warm, caring, human being who created them.

• The only force which can bring your legacy to life is that of your own dynamism—your words and your counsel.

• You may have left your descendants the key to the strongbox holding your earthly treasures—but you have denied them access to the storehouse of your memory, your intellect, your knowledge, and your judgment.

Not bequeathing to the scions of your family the essence of sixty or more years of experience can be likened to the farmer who makes a great investment in land; buys equipment, seed and fertilizer; tills the soil; plants the seed; tends the young plants and brings to fruition a full and bounteous yield—then fails to harvest his crop!

And *not* preserving the wealth of six or eight decades of learning, experience and thought is a particularly tragic kind of profligacy.

In failing to record our life's story, it is almost as if we had not lived at all. It's a terrible waste; an irreplaceable loss.

• Of what lasting value is all your marvelous family history, that wisdom and knowledge you have stored in your memory, if that information cannot be shared with future generations? This intelligence has served you well during your lifetime—but there it stops—unless you take steps to preserve your life's work for the benefit of others.

• No one knows your story as *you* know it. No one can tell it as *you* can. Only you can guarantee that this important bit of unfinished business is properly concluded. And should you decide against creating this kind of record, there are no provisions for second thoughts. All the lamentations of "If only Grandfather had written it all down somewhere..." or "Oh, I wish we had encouraged Grandmother to record her memoirs..." will not bring the miracle of a second chance—a reconsidering—after illness, debility or death has slammed the door.

• Memory is a fragile thing, and it must be used in its prime.

• Your life's work is incomplete until you have told your story. And only you are equipped to undertake this task.

AN APPROACH LETTER FOR BUSINESS AND COMPANY HISTORIES

Businesses, corporate enterprises, legal partnerships, consulting firms, veterinary hospitals, publishing houses, paint-and-varnish formulators and retail merchandising chains were all started by *people*. And as biographers, *people* and the stories of people are our consuming and primary interest.

In the personal biography, whether we're providing our clients with recorded tapes only, tapes and typescripts, or finished books, we usually interview only one or two people to gather the information necessary for the project we've undertaken. In working with businesses, you will find that anywhere from one to twenty people may be asked to contribute to the project. We will probe more deeply into the differences between the personal biography and the company history in Chapter Eighteen, but for the present, be assured that they are more similar than dissimilar.

The APPROACH LETTER to the prospective business client is very like the approach letter to the individual prospect. And although the audiences served by "company" books, tapes, or typescripts will be more broad than those of the personal biography, we will still deal with personal history and achievement.

The following letter has served me well in gaining access to corporate decision-makers—the people who can say "yes" or "no" to my proposition.

July16, 1989

Mr. Robert Schram
President
Mustang Distilleries
Wapato, WA 98951

Dear Mr. Schram:

In almost every company there is one executive who is appointed as the unofficial archivist, or keeper of the records. Often it is the corporation secretary or one of the administrative vice presidents who is asked to maintain files containing the minutes of board meetings, old annual reports, and a miscellany of magazine articles, newspaper clippings, promotional pieces and speeches about the company.

These historical fragments are retained, usually with the rather vague idea that perhaps "someday" a corporate history will be written. Knowing that writers must have something to go on (other than financial statements and annual reports) to produce such a work, these bits and pieces of data are squirreled away in anticipation of that far-off day, perhaps on the company's fiftieth anniversary, when a company book will be commissioned.

It is unfortunate that by the time a writer is assigned the task of gathering together all the elements that will go into the making of such a book, much of the early company history may be only a patchwork based largely on conjecture and uncertain recollection. The founders or original partners may have passed away, or be unavailable for interview. Business associates who knew the founders intimately will also be elderly. They will have reached a time in life when the acuity and accuracy of memory is sometimes in doubt. Surviving widows and children of founders, early executives and board members are seldom able to provide the business-oriented information required.

These problems of future accurate documentation may be solved immediately and at modest cost. I would suggest that the founders and key executives of your corporation be interviewed now, while they are still in their prime, their memories sharp and recall precise. The voice tapes and type transcripts resulting from these interviews will provide a permanent and accurate record of the company's early history. Both tapes and typescripts may then be preserved in the corporate archives.

Time is the enemy. To be direct, the possibility of strokes, debilitating illnesses and death cannot be discounted. Each such incident seals forever yet another priceless reservoir of information.

In the memories of your founders and first executives repose much of the information vital to the creation of an exciting, readable and accurate corporate history. Facts and figures about the early days of the business are probably already recorded. But the human stories of struggle, humor and triumph—the very elements which will guarantee that your company book will be read and used—may be lost for all time if measures are not taken to assure their preservation.

Nothing takes the place of foresight.

I feel qualified to make these recommendations because I have been active in writing for more than thirty-five years, and have written numerous newspaper and magazine articles, biographies and corporate histories. Within the last fifteen years, almost everything I have written has derived from personal and telephone interviews. Through constant use, I have developed interviewing skills which allow me to help subjects recall some of the most interesting and pivotal incidents in their lives. The approach is low-key and informal, and the interview subjects are put at their ease.

It will probably be worthwhile for us to explore these ideas a bit more fully. In any event, I would like to meet you, so I'll telephone you during the next week to see when it will be convenient for us to talk for a little while. I will also welcome the opportunity to show you some examples of my work.

Cordially,

Claudius X. Inkslinger

ON TOOTING YOUR OWN HORN

There is a world of difference between being a blowhard or a braggart and stating your professional qualifications in a businesslike manner. In the next-to-the-last paragraph of my "corporate" letter, I have given a brief but accurate summation of the experience which gives my recommendations credibility. When you come to the drafting of your own letter designed for the business community, I urge you to put aside any false modesty which may deter you from pointing to your track record—from boldly stating your experience and accomplishments. After all, only your credentials will determine whether you will be retained to do a job of work—or shown the door.

If you have something to be proud of, speak out!

A WORD ABOUT PHRASEOLOGY

If we are skillful at what we do, nothing is written without purpose. The innocuous-looking three-sentence final paragraph of our letter is *loaded*! Let's examine it more carefully to see the subtleties we have packed into its modest length.

It will probably be worthwhile for us to explore these ideas a bit more fully. We say *probably* because we cannot presume to speak for our prospect. But the sentence is a positive one, designed to elicit from our prospect an equally positive reaction. We hope Mr. Prospect thinks, "Yes, it probably *will* be worthwhile to spend a few minutes with this writer fellow. Let's see what he has to say."

Moreover, the sentence is non-threatening. We don't come out and say that we will arrive in his office armed with a loaded pen and a contract we're just itching for him to sign. No. We are simply going to "explore these ideas" together—an innocuous-enough sounding venture which, unbeknown to him, will lead him right to the dotted line.

In any event, I would like to meet you, so I'll telephone you during the next week to see when it will be convenient for us to talk for a little while.

This sentence is *charged* with meaning. It conveys no fewer than *four* separate and important ideas which we are attempting to implant in our prospect's thinking.

1) "*...I would like to meet you...*" This is a compliment, and as Mr. Prospect mulls over your ideas, he thinks: "He has probably heard about me somewhere."

2) "*...I'll telephone you during the next week...*" This is an out-and-out commitment on your part. You didn't say, "I'll call you when I get around to it," or "You call me if you think I've got a good idea," or "I'll drop around to your office the next time I'm in your neighborhood." No—you've *promised* to call within the next *seven* days.

Bear in mind, too, that if you've excited his (or her) interest, your prospect will be *expecting* your call within the week. (If you call on the eighth day, it's no deal. By calling later than you promised, you've already shot yourself in the foot. You have established yourself in the prospect's mind as one who can't be expected to keep his word.)

3) "*...when it will be convenient...*" *when* is the "operative word," as the newscasters might say. You didn't write "*...if* it will be convenient..." You wrote "...when it will be convenient..." It is not a small matter. Again, you have assumed that you will receive a *positive* response from your prospect. Attitudes are contagious.

Had you written "*if,*" you would have given your prospect the opportunity to think either *yes* or *no*. A meeting *will* or *won't* be convenient. As it is, you have assumed only that at some time in the near future, it *will* be convenient for the two of you to get together. The only determination which has to be reached is the time of the meeting, not whether or not such a meeting will take place at all.

4) "*...for a little while...*" You're telling a busy executive or business owner that you're not going to chew up a huge chunk of his valuable time. Your prospect will appreciate your thoughtfulness and consideration.

The concluding sentence, "I would also welcome the opportunity to show you some examples of my work," is a little bit of a teaser. This sentence is designed to make your prospect curious. It's show-and-tell time, and if you've sparked even a little bit of interest, your prospect is going to want to see what *other* local business execs have been doing. Maybe he's missed the boat, and should get going on *his* company's history. Nobody, particularly in the business world, likes to be the last one to be aware of new trends, and to jump on a popular bandwagon. If Mr. Prospect's friends and contemporaries at the Downtown Rotary Club are chronicling their company histories, well, by golly, maybe it's time *he* did something along those lines as well.

THAT FINAL POLISH

So much depends on the quality of your approach letters that it is a good idea to have a trusted writer or editor friend read the drafts of your two major letters—the one for personal biography prospects, and the one intended for members of the business community. Properly done, your letters (in conjunction with your brochure) can "pre-sell" your prospects so thoroughly that your selling interview may entail only a perfunctory chat before the contract is signed.

Not only grammar, spelling, and syntax should be nit-picked, but the subtleties of tone and motivation as well. *Each word* should be examined to make certain that it is necessary; that it carries its fair weight of ideas; and that it is the *best* possible word to use in the context of your letter.

And who says a single word cannot make all that much difference? In 1972, when Standard Oil of New Jersey changed its name to Exxon, it cost the company umpteen million dollars to remove the old name and replace it with the new. Worldwide, everything had to be changed. Tons of letterheads had to be scrapped and bales of company uniforms reworked to reflect the change in name. The very signs on the gasoline stations and petroleum depots and refineries in the 100 noncommunist countries in which Exxon operates, all had to be changed. It was a monumental effort—and all for the sake of *one word!* But the new name of Exxon was emblazoned around the world to unify the public's thinking about this powerful corporate entity.

Refine and polish your approach letters until they are as near perfect as they can be made to be. Your success will depend upon how well they are received.

CHAPTER SIX

STAGE FRIGHT:
Making That First Telephone Call To Your Prospect

A life that is worth writing at all is worth writing minutely.

— Longfellow

THE PROMISE WE'VE MADE TO OUR PROSPECTS

In our letters to both individuals and the principals of corporations we have made a promise: "...I'll telephone you during the next week..."

This commitment is designed to accomplish two things:

a) it tells our prospect to expect a telephone call from us within a seven-day period, and

b) it demands of us that we get down to business. If we are to be successful in the enterprise we are attempting to create, we must do what we've said we will do responsibly and promptly.

Before we proceed further, we should separate the dilettantes from the working writers, the undisciplined from the disciplined.

In this business we don't wait for "just the right moment," or for inspiration to strike. We can't afford to daydream while waiting for the muse to pluck a chord in our key.

Biography-for-hire has much more to do with alarm clocks, regular working hours, systematic prospecting, routine letter writing and telephoning, setting up appointments and making in-person contacts than it has with inspiration and the lyrical beckonings of the nine maidens of the arts. It is not the *rive gauche* ambience of Paris in the nineteen twenties we will create for ourselves. Rather, if we are successful, our working environment will contain elements of the busy office, the newspaper city room, the library and the printing shop.

TELEPHOBIA—
THE FEAR OF THAT FIRST TELEPHONE CALL

Entering the marketplace as salespersons, representatives promoting our own products and skills, may be difficult for some writers. The very thought of picking up the telephone to call some stranger in the hopes of arranging a selling appointment may be, at the very least, daunting. But this need not be so.

- Why do we feel like fish out of water when we pick up the phone to make that first telephone call to a prospective client? Probably because the phone is a two-way communication channel, and we don't know how the other fellow is going to respond to our ideas. We don't know what he/she is going to say, and we can't predict how we are going to respond to whatever challenges are thrown down before us. We are used to manhandling communication devices (typewriters and such) that don't sass us back. We've always had the upper hand. But with a phone call to an unknown prospective client, we can't be all that sure of what is going to happen. It is the unpredictable that frightens us.

Most of us can afford to stare at our typewriters, legal pads or CRT/VDTs until the *mot juste* comes to us out of the ether, then we craft our careful prose at our own pace. Since typewriters, yellow tablets and video display terminals don't talk back (usually, although some CRTs have been known to get downright snotty when given the wrong commands), we writers haven't been called upon to fashion the quick retort and the automatic response. But when we get on the telephone, the ground rules are different. It's a whole new ball game. There's *somebody else* on the other end of the line, and we have no way of knowing that we're not going to be dealing with a barracuda.

• To bring the dilemma into perspective, we might ask ourselves what we are afraid of. Some of the possible bugbears are:

a) Rejection. Somebody isn't going to like our ideas.

b) Being made to feel foolish. Surely, someone, sometime, is going to ask us a question for which we have no ready answer.

c) Shyness—Becoming tongue-tied. The thought of "blowing our lines" and sounding inept.

• The answer to all of the above fears is simple. In a word, it is preparedness.

Most of have have been rejected in one way or another. Some of us have collected publishers' rejection slips by the sheaf and by the bale. Rejection isn't anything new, and it isn't fatal. We just try to do better and keep coming back for more.

We can keep from looking (or sounding) foolish by *anticipating* most of the questions prospective clients will ask, and preparing ready answers for them. There will be more on this subject later in this chapter.

We can overcome our shyness and avoid slips of the tongue by typing out the words we plan to use during our telephone approach. There's nothing wrong with having a script. Actors, television newscasters and radio announcers use them constantly. With a little practice, your "canned" telephone approach will sound spontaneous, and you will find yourself ad libbing with ease and facility.

• What is the *worst* thing that can happen to you during a telephone approach? All of the above, of course! We can be shy and ineffectual, be thrown off balance by questions we never anticipated, and forget what we were going to say. Or, we'll find that we are talking to some rude and insensitive lout we wouldn't want to write about for any amount of money. We've lost a prospective client, a stamp and a few minutes of our time. But *so what*? The moment we hang up and break the telephone connection, that unhappy experience is *immediately* in the past, and we'll go on to the next call on our list.

It is important to *forget the failed approaches* and go on to the next call. When you remember that you need only two to a half-dozen clients to see you through a profitable year, the number of walks and strike-outs become unimportant. We count only the home runs!

• What is most *likely* to happen when you telephone a prospect for the first time? On the first few calls, you may stutter and stammer a bit while you're working the "bugs" out of your telephone presentation. For this reason, I would suggest delaying contact with your most promising prospects until you have tested your telephone approach on some lesser prospects. You don't want to blow your chance with one of your "biggies."

A typical telephone approach may go something like this:

PROSPECT (Maid): Hello. This is the Prospect residence.

WRITER: Good morning. May I speak to Mrs. Prospect?

PROSPECT: And whom should I say is calling?

WRITER: This is Miss Collins. I wrote to Mrs. Prospect last week.

PROSPECT: I'll call her. Just a moment, please.

PROSPECT (Mrs. Prospect): Hello.

WRITER: Good morning, Mrs. Prospect. This is Judy Collins. I'm a writer and biographer. You'll probably recall that I wrote you a letter last week, and enclosed a little brochure that had to do with the importance of recording our family histories for our children and grandchildren.

PROSPECT: I don't seem to remember...

WRITER: The brochure spoke of the importance of biography as legacy. It made the point that the stories of our lives are inheritances which may become as meaningful as the material things we leave to our heirs.

PROSPECT: Oh, yes. I do remember it now. You have an interesting concept. I have often thought of doing something like that, but I never seem to find the time. You know, with all the...

WRITER: Mrs. Prospect, I would like to be able to talk with you a little more about this idea, and show you some examples of my work. Perhaps we could...

PROSPECT: Oh, I don't know! Who have you done these for? Anyone I might know?

WRITER: (Name-dropping shamelessly) Why, yes. I did a series of recorded tapes for Mrs. Banker, tapes and typewritten transcripts for Mr. and Mrs. Merchant, and a book for Mr. Optician.

[(N.B.) In the event that you are contacting your first prospect, and have no completed biographies to speak about or to show, you may still put your fears aside. There is no need for consternation. The following response proved effective when I was just starting out.]

WRITER: Mrs. Prospect, I am introducing this idea of biography as legacy in our area. The notion that *every* family should have a written or recorded family heritage began with a writer in the State of Washington, and the concept is rapidly catching on. Writers in Washington, Oregon, California, Kentucky and elsewhere are successfully providing these services, and I'm delighted to now be able to offer them here.

PROSPECT: Oh, I don't know. How much does something like this cost? It sounds like a great deal of work, and I...just at this time...I don't...

WRITER: There are so many variables in the services I offer that it is really impossible to quote prices over the telephone. The cost of this kind of project can range from the very modest to the substantial, depending on the time, work, and numbers of tapes or books to be printed.

It would probably be best if we could get together so that I could show you some examples of my work, and see just what your needs are. At that time, I can also show you how we will go about getting this information together for your children and grandchildren. I can assure you that it will be an exciting project, and that it will be *fun*!

PROSPECT: Well, yes... That might be all right. But with my schedule, I don't...

WRITER: Well, Mrs. Prospect, I'm sure we can work something out. Are mornings or afternoons usually better for you? When do you have the most free time?

PROSPECT: Well, afternoons are usually best, because you see, in the mornings I often have to be downtown for appointments with my bankers, and I have my hair done on Tuesdays, and...

WRITER: Afternoon, then. Would Tuesday or Thursday afternoon be best for you?

PROSPECT: Well, Thursday, of course, would be better. Because you know, after having my hair done on Tuesdays, I usually have luncheon with my son—he's a lawyer who has his offices downtown—and sometimes I don't get home until late, because I like to shop, you know, and it's convenient...

WRITER: Thursday afternoon it is, then. Would two o'clock or four o'clock be more convenient?

PROSPECT: Oh, later, I think! I'm always so sleepy right after luncheon! I don't know what it is! I just don't seem to able to keep my eyes open!

WRITER: Four o'clock on Thursday afternoon it is, then. Will Thursday the ninth be all right, or would the sixteenth be better?

PROSPECT: Let me check my calendar. (Pause, riffling of pages) Yes, I don't have anything scheduled for that afternoon. Yes, Thursday the ninth would be all right.

WRITER: Fine! I'll drop you a note confirming our appointment, and I look forward to meeting you on Thursday. And thank you for your interest.

The preceding is typical of scores of telephone calls to which I've been a party. I will ask you to note that the call was informal, of short duration, and successful. Moreover, it accomplished *the only purpose of the telephone call. It secured the in-person selling appointment.*

THE MISSION OF THE APPROACH TELEPHONE CALL

As stated above (and this cannot be emphasized too strongly nor too often), the *only* mission of your telephone call is to set up a situation in which you and your prospective client are face-to-face, talking about the services and products you can offer. You've gone to all the work to secure your prospect's name, you've written a letter and you've made a telephone call. Unless that telephone call results in the granting of an interview, all your work has gone for naught.

The writer/promoter must *inoffensively* but *effectively* take charge of the telephone approach. I hesitate to use the word "manipulated," but you will see in the above example that the writer *maneuvered* the prospect through the use of a series of *alternatives*, none of which may be answered by "yes" or "no," and all of which commit the prospect to binding decisions.

By always giving your prospect a *choice* (between morning and afternoon; Tuesday and Thursday; two o'clock and four) you have avoided any situation which would require a *no* answer. ("May I see you next Tuesday?" "No—I'll be busy all day on Tuesday.") We want to skirt any issue which would introduce a *negative* into our approach. (We also give our prospects the illusion that *they* are the ones in control of the situation. After all, they were the ones who set the time and day of the appointment.) Psychologists and other behavioral scientists can probably discourse for hours on this subject; all we know is that maintaining a *positive* stance during the telephone approach is helpful in achieving our goal—the in-person appointment.

Now that we know the purpose of the telephone approach, we might examine some of the things it is *not*.

- The telephone approach is *not* an opportunity for you to sell your services or your product. A prospective client cannot sign a contract and hand you a retainer check over the telephone.

- The telephone approach is *not* the time to talk prices and estimates. Any realistic estimate will require an in-depth knowledge of your prospect's needs, and this knowledge cannot be obtained during what should be a five-minute phone call.

- The telephone approach is *not* your opportunity to argue the merits of biography as legacy. Other than brief affirmative statements about this concept, you would be advised to avoid using the approach phone call as a platform for your "big guns." Save your most convincing arguments for the in-person interview, where eye contact and body language can be an important adjunct in gauging your prospect's enthusiasm (or lack thereof). Even though your prospect attempts to lead you into complex avenues, try to turn him aside—dissuade him by saying, "These are areas we can cover in detail when we meet. What you are asking just doesn't lend itself to satisfactory resolution over the telephone."

• The telephone approach is *not* the time to discuss *anything* in great detail. Keep it short. Keep it simple. Keep in mind your *only mission—to nail down an appointment for your selling interview!*

KNOWING WHAT YOU ARE GOING TO SAY DURING THE TELEPHONE APPROACH

I have already suggested that a "script" outlining what you are going to say during the telephone approach is a good idea. You don't have to stick precisely to the words you have written. In truth, it is much better if you *don't* cleave to your prepared "speech," word-for-word. If you do, it's likely to sound wooden and false.

But by having some words in front of you as you speak on the telephone, you at least have some sort of road map to restore your sense of direction if you get lost. Your script will allow you to get back on the main highway if your prospect's questions and diversions lead you too far out into the boondocks. It is not wise to let things stray too far afield; we must avoid detours lest we lose track of our original goal.

Following are some notes (typed all in capitals for easy reading while on the phone) I keep in front of me when I am making an approach call to a corporate or business prospect. If you find this idea to be useful, I suggest that you type out words most comfortable to you. After all, the precise words are unimportant—it's the *message* that counts.

APPROACH CALL TO BUSINESS PROSPECTS

Good morning, Mr. ________________. My name is Dick Sawyer. I'm the writer and historian who wrote to you last week about the advisability of getting together the information for your company history.

I would like to be able to talk with you about this idea, and let you see some examples of my work. When we meet I can show you just how we would go about gathering this information. In any event, it will be helpful if we can get together to discuss this idea more fully.

Are Tuesdays or Thursdays (Mondays or Wednesdays) better for you? Mornings or Afternoons? Nine-thirty or Ten-thirty?—Two or Four?

I look forward to meeting with you, and with any others of your staff who you think might contribute to this project.

There! That's simple enough. We've told our prospect who we are; what we propose; why we propose it; and when we can meet with him. The words need be neither elegant nor polished. They must only supply us with a rudimentary track to run on.

COUNTERING OBJECTIONS ON THE PHONE

Certainly, we may expect some objections to come our way when we are making our telephone approaches. In many instances, such objections on the part of our prospect are almost reflexive; automatic. Most often these are but delaying tactics. Someone tries to sell us something, and our sales resistance immediately comes into play. We use this ploy to "stall" the would-be seller until we have had time to evaluate the product or service, our need for that product or service, and the person or company making the sales approach.

Remembering that the *sole purpose* of the approach telephone call is to set up the selling appointment, we strive to postpone our full responses to objections until we are vis-a-vis with our prospective client. At all costs, avoid an argument while on the telephone! Remember that it is much easier for your prospect to say "No" to a disembodied voice over the phone than it is when seated face-to-face with a personable writer.

Your best response to challenge is the promise of a later, more carefully considered answer. As in: "I'm certain that I will be able to answer all your questions about cost when we meet, Mr. Prospect."

Or: "Your questions about printing and binding are good ones, Mrs. Prospect, and as soon as we can get together, I'll show you several samples of the bindings and print options available."

"I'm sure that your worries about the amount of interview time involved are needless, Miss Prospect. When we meet, I feel certain that we'll be able to work out a schedule to your satisfaction."

Turn objections aside until you can answer them *in person!*

Quickly, I will admit that this is not always possible. Often, you will be trapped, and must give some kind of response. And the more apt that response, the more confidence you build in your prospect (and in yourself). If you have ready answers for the objections (questions, really, more than objections) posed to you, your prospect is going to respect you for your preparedness, and recognize that you are "on top" of the situation.

For this reason, again, I suggest a script of sorts. Try to think of every objection possible to your proposition, then, at your leisure, compose your responses, type them out, and have them at your fingertips when you are telephoning.

We'll encounter some of these same objections/responses in Chapter Nine, "Up Front and In Person: How to Sell Your Services," but as a kind of preview of things to come, here are some of the responses to objections which I have found to be effective.

PROSPECT: "I don't think I'd be interested..."

WRITER: "Ah, yes. But will your *grandchildren* be interested? You have family history and stories of your own life that only *you* can recall. You are the only person who can tell *your* story. While you may not be interested, future generations of your family will be vitally interested in what you have to say."

PROSPECT: "I don't think so, at this time..."

WRITER: "But *time* is the enemy! That is the very element we are trying to thwart! Today, you're in good health, your memory is good and your recall clear. But who can guarantee what tomorrow will bring? An illness or even a minor stroke could blot out great chunks of your memory—forever. The time to act is *now!*"

PROSPECT: "It sounds like it's going to cost more than I'm prepared to spend."

WRITER: "When we meet, I will be glad to show you the costs of various options open to you: recorded tapes, tapes and typescripts, or the printed-and-bound biography. I feel certain that we can find at least one option that will meet your budgetary requirements."

PROSPECT: "No one in my family is interested in that kind of stuff. Anyway, who'd want to read about *me* ?"

WRITER: (Lightly) "I believe we call that 'false modesty.' You may think your family is not interested *now*, but how about fifty or sixty years from now, when you are gone, and you've taken all of your memories and stories with you? Just how valuable *are* old family books? Let us just suppose that you have a book, written by your great-great-grandfather. Your house catches fire and you have time to salvage only *one item* from that fire. What do you suppose you would snatch from the shelf on your way out the door?"

PROSPECT: "I'm a busy person, and a project like this is going to take too much of my time."

WRITER: "If not you, who? Who will you elect to tell *your* story? And as far as time is concerned, we're speaking of only two hours a week. And I will be glad to work with you wherever and whenever you find most convenient—at your home, your office, or your club—during the daytime or the evening. Because the project is so important, and because you are the only one able to carry it to completion, I will accommodate you in any way possible. It is an urgent matter which should not be delayed."

PROSPECT: "It's not for me."

WRITER: "Exactly. It's *not* for you! It's for your children, grandchildren, and the great-grandkids you'll never have a chance to meet. It is to *these* generations of your family to whom you owe this gift. A gift, I might suggest, without which your legacy is incomplete."

There will be other objections you will be called upon to meet, because we can't anticipate them all. But for some of the more regularly encountered of these off-putting techniques, we can have responses prepared and at hand so that we are not caught flatfooted and stammering for a reply. But we shouldn't sound too glib in our rebuttals, either.

Somewhere between being caught off guard/defensive, and coming off as overly prepared/"slick," there is a comfortable middle ground. If you have anything of the thespian in you, a little low-key acting in such situations will serve you well. The tone you should strive to strike lies midway between sounding secure in your conviction, and too-pat facileness.

Sometimes a quick rejoinder is very effective. In other instances, it may sound too well rehearsed. If you have the skill, you may "play to" your prospect as an actor "works" his audience. When hearing an objection whose rebuttal you have at the tip of your tongue, you may want to pause for a moment, as though reflecting on your answer. Then present your thoughtful reply. As in anything else, practice tends to make perfect. After your first twenty or thirty telephone approaches, you will gain confidence and be quite comfortable (I assure you!) in telephoning strangers.

More importantly, you will gain new respect for the service you offer. One day (it is almost *sure* to happen), as you are talking with an especially interesting prospect, a new urgency will assert itself, unbidden, as you seek that all-important personal interview. The sudden conviction that unless *you can move this prospect* to grant you that all-important selling interview, and unless you can *motivate* him to get on with this important project, the chances of his ever recording his life story are almost nil. It always comes as a jolt when you *know* that unless *you*, through your powers of persuasion, can move this prospect to begin work on his biographical legacy, the likelihood of his being approached by another biographer, later in his life, is all but nonexistent. There aren't that many of us around. What you are offering him is, in all reality, the (last) *chance of a lifetime*.

When the import of this thought strikes home, the weight it carries, and the responsibility which you have assumed (for the benefit of your prospective client, but unbidden *by* him, and unknown *to* him) you will become many times more effective in your telephone approaches. So *much* depends on how skillfully you present your case.

Once you have put your point across to your prospect, and have gained his acquiescence, you will indeed have become a *life preserver*. When you become accustomed to the importance and probity attendant to your mission, your confidence will increase a thousandfold.

Tennyson had Galahad say, "My strength is as the strength of ten, because my heart is pure."

Banal? Threadbare? Downright corny? Perhaps. But when *you* become aware of the rightness of of your chosen pursuit, that chances are good that you will persuade the recalcitrant prospect with all diligence, feeling, perhaps, that your "...strength is as the strength of ten, because the service I purvey is right, ethical, and clean, and unsullied by tarnished product or tawdry motives. And if *I* don't produce this prospect's biographical legacy, *no one* will!"

ON THE INTRACTABLE, ADAMANT "NO!"

But there will always be those who we *cannot* budge. So, when he says "No!" and means it, thank your one-time prospect courteously and hang up the receiver gently. You can't win 'em all.

You might want to suggest he keep your brochure, and reexamine it sometime when he is in a reflective mood. You also might ask if you may telephone him again in one year's time. Prospects have been known to agree to this readily—and you know all along that they are just trying to get rid of you. I fool 'em! I have a monthly file-card system (a "tickler file" if you will), and I put their cards back one full year. Then I call them when I *said* I would call them. Surprisingly enough, most remember me from the first call, and several of my clients have come to me through this technique. I have found that when some people say "No," they mean "No" only for the moment. At a different time, under different circumstances, prospects once thought to be "dead" can become quite amenable to suggestion.

TAKE "NO" FOR AN ANSWER

If you get one "No" or thirty of them in a row, don't lose heart. Bear in mind *always*, please, that in every household in every block of every village or city, awaits a prospective client for your services.

The people who need your services, can afford them, and can appreciate what you are attempting to do, number in the *tens of millions*! We can never hope to reach them all.

And only two to six signed (book) contracts *each year can earn you from $30,000 to $90,000 annually.*

Develop lots of prospects, mail out lots of letters and brochures, make lots of approach telephone calls—and the sheer *numbers* will assure more clients than you can handle. If you *keep your level of activity high*, it is almost impossible that success will evade you.

CHAPTER SEVEN

DRAWING UP EFFECTIVE CONTRACTS AND PROPOSALS

The great lesson of biography is to show what man can be and do at his best. A noble life put fairly on record acts like an inspiration to others.

— Samuel Smiles

THE CONTRACT

Merriam-Webster's *Ninth New Collegiate Dictionary* defines the word *contract* as follows: 1a: a binding agreement between two or more persons or parties; *esp*: one legally enforceable b: a business arrangement for the supply of certain goods or services at a fixed price...

These are the definitions which most aptly apply to the services we writers and biographers provide.

IS A CONTRACT NECESSARY?

Yes. Contracts are helpful in many ways. Most especially, contracts are useful in clarifying our relationships with our clients. Most of our prospects will have never entered into contractual agreements with writers, and they won't know quite what to expect. A well-written contract will serve to remove a great deal of our clients' understandable doubt and uncertainty. If for no other reason, the assurance provided by a simple contract makes it a valuable instrument in dealing with our prospects.

Properly drawn, the contract will set forth the responsibilities of the client and the writer, and make clear who is going to do what for whom, and how much it is going to cost.

The simple contract is also a useful selling tool, in that it may be used during the in-person interview as an outline or "check list" of the services to be provided by the writer. By going over the contract word for word with the prospect, any potential misunderstandings may be quickly recognized and resolved.

A WORD OF CAUTION

While the sample proposal and contract included in this text have been examined by my Seattle lawyer, this should not be construed as blanket approval for use of these documents in all states and in all writer/client situations.

I urge each of you to prepare drafts of your own proposals and contracts, then consult a lawyer friend or legal counsel as to the applicability and correctness of your documents in the legal jurisdictions (cities, counties, states) in which you live and do business. Above all, don't let your lawyer get carried away with legalese! We must not forget that it is our mission to *communicate*, not *obfuscate*! Keep it simple! Your legal forms should be as straightforward as possible, assiduously avoiding all possible whereases and wherefores, parties of the first part and parties of the second part. These archaic abominations only muddy the waters.

THE CONTRACT AS A HALLMARK OF PROFESSIONALISM

I don't know where people get the idea that writers are all dabblers possessed of great personal fortunes—that we work for the sheer joy of it, and by some arcane magic are expected to sustain ourselves on manna, ambrosia, and morning-glory nectar.

This myth must be dispatched quickly and dispassionately. There will be more on the subject of compensation in the next chapter, but for the present, we need only to establish with our prospects that we maintain a fee schedule in keeping with the professionalism of the work we do.

[I once plunged a sweet, lavender-scented little old lady into a state of complete confusion when I brought up the matter of my fees attendant to writing her family history.

"Oh! Are you going to *charge* me for this?" she asked. Her violet eyes popped wide in honest surprise. "I had thought we would have such great fun working together on my story, then, when the book was published, we would all become quite rich and famous!"

Her very words, so help me Hannah!

As gently as I was able, I disabused this sweet *fin de siècle* confection of the error of her ways, and, after a short period of disillusionment, we got down to business and together created a highly readable manuscript. But we very nearly never got it off the ground!]

The *contract* is a businesslike agreement which puts you on a professional footing with your client. When we begin to think of ourselves as skilled professionals not unlike portrait painters or photographers (or for that matter, physicians, lawyers and dentists), we have made an appropriate adjustment in our *own* thinking.

A SAMPLE CONTRACT

The following is the text of a contract which I have used for more than a decade in my work. It is a one-page document which I have printed on my letterhead stationery.

CONTRACT OF EMPLOYMENT

Date__________

This is a contract of employment made by and between Richard Sawyer, writer, hereinafter called "writer" and ________________________________, hereinafter called "client." Writer hereby agrees to provide the following services for client.

OPTION "A" Prepare and provide interview questions designed to elicit the most meaningful and interesting aspects of the client's life experience; conduct and record regular interviews with the client until client is satisfied that all necessary material has been discussed and gathered; supply client with labeled 90-minute cassette tapes in presentation holder. Tapes will be suitable as a source of typescripts to be made by client.

OPTION "B" All of Option A, plus a *rough* typewritten draft of the contents of the recording tapes, the typescripts to be presented in a leatherette or vinyl binder. The rough typescript may be edited and retyped by the client.

OPTION "C" All of Option A, plus a *clean* typewritten draft of the material contained in the recording tapes. This material will have been reviewed, lightly edited and rewritten where necessary for grammatical and syntactical purposes. Further, the material will have been retyped in a neat format, with appropriate headings inserted at the beginning of each typescript noting contents as an aid in locating information. The finished typescript will be presented in a vinyl or leatherette binder. The finished typescript will be suitable for reproduction if this later becomes desirable.

OPTION "D" All of Option C plus ten hardbound copies of the typescripts. (Minimum order)

OPTION "E" All of Option A, plus reviewing, revising, outlining, reorganizing, complete rewriting and extensive editing of the material, and the publication of a formal biography. Final copy will be typed and made camera-ready for reproduction by the photo-offset lithography method. Five hard-bound books will be presented as part of this option; additional books may be purchased at the time of publication. Minimum estimate for Option E: approximately 18 months elapsed time and $__________ in costs.

FEES

The estimate for this service, under Option ______, is approximately $______________. If costs are to exceed the estimate, client will be notified before this occurs. A retainer equivalent to ten percent of the estimate is due and payable upon signing this contract. A billing for one-third the remainder due will be made after tape No. 5 has been recorded; one-third is due and payable at the completion of the last tape in the series; and the remainder is due and payable at the time of the delivery of the tapes (Option A); the tapes and typewritten rough draft (Option B); the tapes and edited typescript (Option C) or the tapes and the hardbound copies of the typescripts (Option D). Option E contracts will be individually negotiated. Client or client's estate shall be responsible for fees incurred by means of this contract.

Writer__________________________Client__________________________

INTERPRETATION OF THIS CONTRACT

The contract is simplicity itself: it defines the responsibilities of the writer and the client, the basis by which fees are charged, and how compensation is to be made.

Under OPTION A, the writer states that he is going to continue with the interviews until both writer and client agree that they've talked about every subject that should be explored. The only end-product of OPTION A is a collection of recorded cassette tapes.

This is the least costly of all the options, but your client should be cautioned that the recorded tapes are, at best, a stopgap measure. Your client should be urged to carry the process one step further. He should engage either someone in the family or a hired typist to produce from these tapes "hard copy," that is, verbatim typewritten transcripts, so that the fragile tapes will not be the only existing source of the information they contain.

OPTION A is chosen usually because of the client's financial limitations, or because a family book has been *projected*—but no one has got around to gathering the information that should go into the book.

Only under well understood and carefully controlled *special circumstances* should recorded tapes be considered as a satisfactory medium for the "permanent" file. Should your client *not* be considering having typewritten copy produced from the tapes within a year or so, he should be made aware of the risks involved in long-term tape storage.

Recorded voice tapes are susceptible to damage from:

1. Humidity
2. Light
3. Heat
4. Magnetic flux (as from electric motors or misuse of degausers too close to the tape storage area).

Even though recorded tapes are stored in cool, dry, dark and shielded areas, damage can occur. After prolonged storage, "bleed-through" or "print-through" (the magnetic transfer of recorded impulses from one layer of recorded tape to another) can garble entire tapes. Professional archivists such as those in the Archives Division, Office of the Secretary of State, The State of Oregon, have found that for long-term storage, the thicker the recording tape (in mils), the longer the tape may be safely stored before re-recording. These archivists have learned that recorded 1/2-mil tape (often found on C-60 and C-90 cassettes) can be safely stored for no longer than five years, *even though storage conditions are ideal*! At the end of this time, the tapes must be re-recorded to preclude print-through damage. Even though thicker (1 to 1.5 mil) tapes be used, a time will come when they must be re-recorded if they are to retain their usefulness, and serve the purpose for which they were intended.

Parenthetically, I must add that working with a client under the terms of OPTION A is almost like picking gold nuggets from a rushing stream. Accepting our fees for such services is a little like taking "found money."

Much of the joy in working with our clients lies in the delight of uncovering long-lost anecdotal treasures of the past, and bringing again to light almost forgotten incidents of (ofttimes) all-but-unbearable piquancy. The "high" of discovery lies in formulating the interview questions, then in interviewing the client to help him or her recover the riches of the past—both of which we are privileged to do under OPTION A. This part of the work is so much fun it almost seems a shame to take money for it! Yet, we bring our skills into play, so we *earn* the $100-$150 fee we levy for each 1.5-hour tape. Still, it is the sniffing out of a good yarn that makes my blood race, and causes me unalloyed delight when devising questions, asking them during the interviews, and working with OPTION A clients. It's like *living* the role of the detective in a good mystery story! With OPTION A we get all the fun without having to spend weeks in writing the book! We should be glad there isn't a law against getting such a kick out of one's work!

OPTION B is also a personal favorite of mine, and has been very popular with my clients as well. One of its great appeals is its relative low cost. It is certainly less expensive than would be the crafting and printing of a book. Yet OPTION B embodies both the merits of the voice tapes and the security of having provided *hard copy* from which additional copies may be made for distribution to every interested member of a family.

From the standpoint of the writer, OPTION B is also attractive. It doesn't require a great deal of time, nor is the arduous work of organizing and writing a book involved. The amount of income to be derived from an OPTION B assignment is considerable, and the end products are attractive as well as utilitarian.

Let's look at the income potential of OPTION B. Calculating (for each tape) five hours of work in developing the interview questions and conducting the interview itself, plus six or seven hours required for producing the typescript of each tape amounts to eleven or twelve hours of work per tape. According to the hourly rates you set for your services, under OPTION B one tape might produce anywhere from $195 to $300—ten tapes will bring in $1,950 to $3,000. Ten or twelve such short assignments (of ten to fifteen tapes each) every year would certainly be welcome, and just the way to "fill out" your income derived from book contracts.

OPTION C is essentially the same as OPTION B, except that additional time must be spent in lightly editing the first rough typescript from the tape, and in retyping the "cleaned up" version in finish form. I make no effort to rearrange the chronology of the material. To do so would entail almost as much effort as writing a full biography, and would involve many hours of work for which we would have to be compensated. Of course, because all the interview material must be typed *twice*, more hours of work are required on an OPTION C contract than on an OPTION B. Thus, correspondingly higher fees (than for OPTION B) are justified.

OPTION D is precisely what it says. The clean copy from OPTION C is taken to a "quick printing" house and reproduced by (probably) some photo-offset lithography process. I suggest that you have your finished product printed on both sides of the page to reduce bulk.

As for the hardbound copies referred to, I have in mind a product called Velo-Bind, a patented hard-back adhesive vinyl binding system whose covers are available in several colors. Material bound in such a system provides a sturdy finished book very much resembling a high school or college yearbook. The spine is of crimped plastic pin-rivet construction which should outlast even conventional glued-and-stitched bindings. Undoubtedly there are other quick bindings which would serve our purposes well. I mention Velo-Bind only because of past good experience with these products. (If you have difficulty in finding a dealer or a printer near your location who uses these products, dial your toll-free 800-number telephone operator for information.)

OPTION E entails the writing and printing of the full biography or company history, and the section of this chapter on PROPOSALS may be of assistance to you in dealing with your prospects.

ON THE MATTER OF FEES

Under the section on FEES, the contract allows you to spell out in unmistakable language, the terms by which you are to be paid.

In the first sentence of this section are the words: "The estimate for this service, under Option _____, is approximately $_____________.

More will be said about determining and approximating your fees in the following chapter. For the present, however, it will suffice to know that gathering information for *most* personal biographies will require ten to fifteen hour-and-one-half interviews. The same applies to most small corporations.

In such situations, in the $_______ blank, I place *two* numbers—the first applying to a ten-interview situation; the second to fifteen interviews. Going into an unknown situation, we can never predict with complete accuracy how many hours of interviews are going to be required to cover the information available.

In an OPTION B contract, for example, I might place the numbers $3,000-$4,500. My estimate, done before I leave my office, indicates that at $25.00 an hour, and 12 hours of work for each 90-minute tape, the figure is (12 X $25.00), or $300. Ten interviews and resulting typescripts would then cost my client $3,000; fifteen interviews and typescripts $4,500.

Under FEES we also speak of retainers, due and payable upon signing the contract. To determine the amount of the retainer, I take ten percent of the number midway *between* the two figures of my estimate. Thus, if my estimate is between $3,000 and $4,500, the midpoint figure would be $3,750, ten percent of which is $375. That is the amount of my retainer.

In this matter of retainers, you can be flexible. If your prospect reads your contract, then whips out his checkbook and writes you a retainer for ten percent of the lower figure ($3,000/$300) of your estimate, accept the check gracefully and adjust your future billings accordingly. "A bird in the hand..." et cetera! You may have been on the trail of this elusive trophy for weeks, and now is not the time to quibble over seventy-five bucks! Put his check in your pocket, and smile when you leave his office! You can get the rest of your retainer later by adjusting your future billings.

THE FORMAL PROPOSAL AND CONTRACT

The following is a PROPOSAL AND CONTRACT OF EMPLOYMENT which I have used when a client indicates interest in a book—a full biography. The wording of the PROPOSAL is as it is because some families are great "string collectors." If mountains of old letters, newspaper clippings, wedding announcements and genealogical data must be perused before we can get on with our interviewing and writing, we must be compensated for the extra work. (See note 2 of the proposal.)

I have found the PROPOSAL AND CONTRACT OF EMPLOYMENT helpful in situations which promise to become somewhat more complicated than the simple interview/organize/write propositions. Each client is different, and if you encounter one whose special requirements seem to call for specialized business agreements (proposals and contracts), by all means devise your own.

There is nothing sacred about either of the documents I have set forth in this chapter. They are simply tools which help us—and our clients—define the body of work to be done, who is to do what for whom, and for how much money.

Mr. George C. Corcoran February 18, 1989

PROPOSAL AND CONTRACT OF EMPLOYMENT

This is a proposal and contract of employment made by and between Richard Sawyer, Writer, and Mr. George C. Corcoran, Client. Writer agrees to provide the following services associated with the writing, printing, or duplicating of the Corcoran family history.

1. Review, rewrite, outline, organize, edit and retype all interview material in logical sequence;
2. Assemble all other written material, newspaper clippings, photographs and related documents necessary for the proper documentation of the book;
3. Prepare draft of the book, to be written from the first-person point of view;
4. Submit to Client for approval the finished draft of the material to be printed or duplicated; and
5. Make any corrections or changes requested by Client.
6. At the time the manuscript is completed, the decision will be made either to have the book privately printed, or duplicated by the photo offset-lithography method. Comparative costs of the two types of imprinting will be submitted to the Client for approval.

ESTIMATE OF WRITING TIME

Total time involved should not exceed 600 hours—this at five hours a day, five days a week for 24 weeks, or about six months of uninterrupted effort. The time span may be somewhat longer than six months because of Client-originated changes and necessary ongoing commitments by the Writer.

PRINTING AND PHOTOGRAPHIC COSTS

All printing, binding, imprinting and photographic costs will be borne by the Client.

COMPENSATION FOR WRITER

The Writer shall receive $25.00 an hour for his work, plus any travel and lodging expenses which may arise, and be compensated at a rate of 30 cents per mile when automobile travel is necessary. A retainer of $1,200 is suggested; statements of actual hours worked and expenses incurred will be submitted to client every sixty days.

Client or Client's estate shall be responsible for fees incurred under the terms of this contract.

Writer ______________________ Client________________________

Seattle, Washington Date ________________________

ISN'T AN ORAL AGREEMENT GOOD ENOUGH?

No. Not any more.

I didn't used to put much stock in contracts and written agreements. They smacked too much of "big business" and the very complexities which had driven me away from large organizations. I wanted no part of them. After all, wasn't a man's word his bond? That would be good enough for me. Or so I thought.

But experience is a great teacher. It took only one slight misunderstanding with my first client to make me realize the importance of some sort of contract or written agreement by which the scope of the work and the amount and method of my compensation were spelled out. In the era in which we live, to expect an oral agreement in a business transaction to be totally satisfactory to all parties to that agreement is to be at best, naive, and at worst, unprofessional and unbusinesslike.

Write a draft of your proposed contract and ask your lawyer to examine it for possible trouble spots. One caveat: it is the nature of lawyers to complicate rather than to simplify. If your legal counsel suggests changes or additions, ask that your document be kept as brief and simple as possible, while still providing you and your client the protection and assurance to which you are both entitled.

When your contracts and proposals are written to your satisfaction, type a master of each and have a number of copies made. In use, I simply staple two copies of my contract together, with a sheet of carbon paper sandwiched between. That way, when you and your client sign the contract or the proposal, each of you has a copy for your files.

Using clear, simple contracts and proposals makes for tidy business relationships with your clients. By trying to anticipate the areas which are most often misunderstood and misinterpreted, and spelling these out in your contracts, you do all you can to assure fewer loose ends and cause for future disharmony.

And because, in your relationship with your client, you will get as close to him or her as a second skin, harmony *must* be the name of the game! Do all you can to foster it. Your foresight will pay tremendous dividends!

CHAPTER EIGHT

SET YOUR HOURLY RATES:
And Write Your Own Ticket!

Occasionally a single anecdote opens a character: biography has its comparative anatomy, and a saying or a sentiment enables the skillful hand to construct the skeleton.

— Willmott

FOR LOVE AND GLORY

The compensation paid to most free-lance writers has been, traditionally, either a wry little inside joke or a monstrous outrage, depending on how badly the writer's ox has been gored. Every writers' group has its own portfolio of twice-told horror stories: about do-nothing or unscrupulous agents; about editors who lose manuscripts; about magazines that pay only upon publication, keep manuscripts tied up for years, then, when your articles finally see print, send checks for amounts that wouldn't pay the babysitter for one night's work.

We tell ourselves that it is all part of the game, and we go on writing and submitting our work. There is such *magic* in seeing our work in print that we (too many of us, at any rate), will suffer any indignity to see one of our bylined pieces in any kind of a publication at all.

Few of us will forget the first piece we had published, and for which we were paid money. I certainly remember my own. It was a short article, less than 1,000 words, accompanied by five photographs. I had written it for a Seattle newspaper's Sunday magazine section. The piece certainly wasn't *literature*, but I put a lot of work in on it, rewrote it a couple of times, and I stroked and polished it until it squeaked! The article had to do with a local hobbyist-turned-entrepreneur who was raising "King Tut" quail for the gourmet market. Trying to get clear photographs of those quick little birds proved to be a real pain, and I burned a lot of film before I was satisfied with the quality of the prints. But when the "package" was finished, I was pleased with my work. (A firstborn child is always beautiful!)

On the Friday night before the paper's Sunday "bulldog" edition was to be printed, I became fidgety. My wife and I were sitting in the living room. I flipped idly through the pages of a book—I went to the kitchen to warm my coffee—I changed the TV channel—I went to the bathroom—and I lit yet another cigarette. Finally, my helpmeet could stand it no longer.

"What on earth is eating you?" she asked. "You're as nervous as a fundamentalist preacher in the *Playboy* penthouse!"

"It's the article," I confessed. "It's in print by now. The bulldog edition of the paper will have been assembled and ready to go out to the out-of-town subscribers. With my article in it!"

"What about it?" she wanted to know. "The paper's had your article for weeks, and on Sunday morning the paperboy will leave a copy of it on our doorstep."

"But that's two days away," I complained.

"You've waited this long, surely you can wait another thirty-six hours."

It turned out I couldn't.

You would have thought we were planning a bank heist! I put on tennis shoes (for silence), donned a dark jacket, and in no time at all we were speeding through town toward the newspaper's printing plant.

"Slow down!" my bride shrilled. "You're driving like a maniac! You'll get a ticket for sure!"

"I hope they're not all gone by the time we get there," I muttered.

"You're crazy, you know that? And you, supposedly a grown man. Until just a few minutes ago, I thought we had all the kids raised and gone, but I see I still have a juvenile delinquent on my hands."

The loading dock of the newspaper plant was floodlit brilliantly. The place was lighted up like a Hollywood premier or the opening of a new Shell station. It would be chancy, at best. I drove by the plant slowly, and parked in the shadows close to the side of the building. I was thankful for some dense shrubs at the end of the dock which would give me cover as I made my sortie.

"You stay here, and keep the engine running," I hissed at my accomplice.

"You Clyde—me Bonnie?" she snickered.

"Very funny. Besides, you're doing Tarzan and Jane. But—I shall return!" And with that, I was out of the car, scooching along and hugging the shadows beside the building.

I reached the bushes, ducked to a crouch, and stealthily maneuvered my way to the end of the loading dock. As I raised my head I noted three men packing a truck with bundles of papers which came rocketing out of the building on rollered loading ramps. I noted something else as well! There, not two feet in front of my eyes, was a broken bundle of newspapers!

Making certain that the men were not looking in my direction, I popped up like some demented marionette and snagged a copy of the fat Sunday edition. Quickly ducking back into my crouch, I turned and went hot-footing it back to the car. As I slid into the seat I leaned conspiratorially close to my reluctant partner in crime.

"I got it!" I fizzed in her ear.

"Got what?" She jumped, startled.

"The paper, dummy, the *paper*!"

Apparently, the excitement had been too much for her. She had dozed off.

In the dim, orange glow of our old car's dome light, I riffled through the paper and dug out the Sunday magazine section. And there, in all it's glory, was *my* article, and *my* byline! God, but it looked elegant!

Second perhaps only to a Gutenberg first folio and the Book of Kells, those lines of print were the most beautiful in all of creation.

I drove home surrounded by an etherial glow. The tires of our car scarcely seemed to touch the pavement. It was Walter Mitty time, and at the wheel of the car was an honest-to-goodness, first-time *published author*!

On the following Monday, I received my check from the paper for my article and the photographs. They paid me $35.00 for the package.

A LITTLE TIME-AND-MOTION STUDY

It wasn't until long after the publication of my quail article that I thought to consider the investment of time and material one of these short pieces involved. Not until I began to structure a pricing schedule for my biographies and company histories did I calculate the hourly rate earned on the earliest of my published newspaper and magazine articles.

The numbers that came up were appalling!

For the article mentioned earlier, "King Tut Quail—One Man's Hobby," the investments of time and money were as follows:

1. Library research, generating interview questions, interviewing the subject of the article + travel time. . . . . 7 hours
2. Photographing quail at subject's home and at Woodland Park Zoo + travel time . . . . 4 hours
3. Transcribing taped notes, writing, rewriting, editing and final typing of article . . . . 20 hours
4. Film and processing costs $14.40

O.K. So here's a little run-of-the-mill Sunday supplement article, not much different from thousands of others turned out by the free-lance writers of America. In this little article (written in 1968) I had invested 31 hours of my time and $14.40 out-of-pocket money. I have discounted the cost of the recording tape, gasoline money, and wear and tear on camera, car, tape recorder and typewriter.

For this article I was paid	$35.00
Less expenses	$14.40
	$20.60

For 31 hours of work, I netted $20.60—a rate of 67 cents an hour!

Let's say, just for the sake of argument, that I was a terribly slow writer, and should have been able to turn out my piece in only one-fourth the time—five hours instead of twenty hours. Even with this adjustment, reducing the total number of hours worked on the article to sixteen, my rate of pay would have been only $1.29 an hour.

Pretty shabby, for a "professional," wouldn't you say?

Even after years of free-lancing, when the words came more quickly and my skills were more highly polished, the rate of pay for most newspaper and magazine pieces was criminally low. Like many of us, I wrote almost for the sheer joy of writing, and the "high" I experienced every time I saw one of my bylined pieces in a respectable journal or magazine. The pay was almost incidental.

Hey! I may have been earning 97 percent of my living in a stable industry which promised nine-to-five working hours and a regular paycheck, but at heart, I *was a writer*!

But I was deluding myself. The chances are that most free-lancers who read this book are doing the same. If you want to scare yourself out of a year's growth, *accurately* calculate *your* hourly rate of pay for the last half-dozen articles you've written. Include every hour spent in research; every hour at the typewriter or word processor; every minute of interview time. The chances are very good that you will at first be disillusioned—then disturbed—and finally, actively angry at what you find. We don't like to waken to the fact that we've been badly used. Or that we've sold ourselves too cheaply—that we've been cheating ourselves.

THE WAY THE BIG BOYS DO IT

If we are to become professionals, we must adopt the *ways* of professionals. In the past, most of us have been too timid to look upon our work as important; too self-effacing to charge for our time, skills and knowledge as though they amounted to something. And certainly, too gratified to see our work in print to risk rocking the boat.

But, hold on a minute!

If we have no faith in our merits, who will?

Let's look at the *real* world! The moment we step into a taxicab, the meter begins ticking away. Whether the cab is stopped for a red light, waiting for us to conclude an errand or driving us to the airport, that meter is charging us for the cabby's time and our few moment's share in his capital investment—his equipment.

In most law offices, there is a charge (based on time spent) for every telephone call, every scrawled note or memo dictated, and every water-cooler conference having to do with our cases or our affairs. In a tightly run legal office, every moment of every working day is accounted for, and charged to *some*one! And in today's market, many lawyers think nothing of charging between $100 and $650 an hour!

Even my dentist charges by the "unit"—in his case, the "unit" is a fifteen-minute block of time. If I'm in his chair for 35 minutes, I will be charged for 2 1/3 units—his hourly fee calculated to the nearest five minutes. He must pay for office space, costly equipment, the salaries of his skilled helpers—dental assistants, dental hygienists and appointment secretaries—and amortize an expensive education and the years of an extended, low-paying "apprenticeship."

Physicians, bankers, pharmacists, veterinarians, tax consultants, stockbrokers and TV repairmen all charge hefty fees of their knowledge and their experience. As they should. And not one of these people blush when they take my money. And they should *not*. After all, they know things I don't know; they have skills I have not; they have undergone training foreign to me and have become skillful through experience. Moreover, many of them have large investments in special tools, equipment, instruments and machines for which I have no need nor desire to own.

I am quite willing to pay an expert handsomely for specialized work skillfully performed.

And what of writers or photojournalists?

Why, as scribes to the ancients, we started out as slaves (only the slaves in Pharaonic Egypt could write) and few of us have burst our chains. We have remained in subservient positions and have been as beggers, doing the tin-cup routine for centuries, accepting gladly that which has been offered us. In the main, we have been totally at the mercy of employers, clients, agents, editors and publishers.

We accept whatever commercial clients deign to pay us.

We agree to whatever terms our agents negotiate for us.

We do not demur at an editor's insulting payment.

We stand impotent and helpless as publishers strip us of foreign, serial, and book-club rights, misrepresent sales, charge us for returns, and shamelessly keep us waiting for our money.

It is time we writers emancipated ourselves from the bondage of a (largely) skinflint industry.

HOW SHOULD WE VALUE OUR WORK AND OURSELVES?

Free-lance writers serve long apprenticeships. We study and read endlessly, attend writers' conferences, and practice our craft with varying degrees of diligence and success for many years before seeing much in the way of tangible reward. For most of us, it's a long, hard struggle.

When we have run the gauntlet, we emerge with skills not possessed by one in one thousand of our general population. We can write! We have taught ourselves through study and practice to express complex thoughts clearly and accurately on paper. And we know the heady joy of capturing that elusive emotion or serpentine line of reasoning in *words*—magical, blessed, unchanging, WORDS—so that those emotional gems or convoluted thoughts are frozen in a form that others may, forever afterward, read and comprehend.

Only an immense investment in education and practice brought us to this point.

Then there is the matter of specialized equipment.

The working writer of today will have difficulty in "making do" with the simple tools of his predecessors. The fountain pen and yellow legal tablet were not much advanced from the goose-quill nib and the sheet of parchment. But when the American, Christopher L. Sholes, produced the first practical typewriter in 1867, the world of the writer changed forever.

Suddenly, he needed costly equipment to compete. First it was the manual typewriter, then faster and smaller electrics. Dictating and copying equipment came into being; then into vogue. "You can't get along without them," their purveyors brayed. And they were right. Today, we cannot.

Within the last decade, the word processor has all but replaced the electric typewriter for the production writer composing "finish" copy. The word processor does all manner of tricks beyond the capabilities of the electric typewriter. It can spell, punctuate, find synonyms and antonyms, format material, make a snap of editing and rewriting, move blocks of material from one part of an MS to another, and print finished work in a form ready to go to the client, the printer or the editor.

The biographer and company historian will also find that a dependable tape recorder is necessary, and a cassette tape transcriber (a playback machine used by the typist transcribing your taped interviews) a great boon. My office is also equipped with a couple of electric typewriters, a word processor and a copying machine.

Immediately, I will say that MOST of the aforementioned equipment is *not necessary.* You can start out with a good tape recorder and a typewriter. But the other machines will make your work go more quickly and pleasantly.

It is important that we recognize that the writer has not only an appreciable investment in his education and training, but in his equipment as well. No longer can we (if ever we could) get by on an inclination to write, a No. 2 pencil and a stack of foolscap or pad of paper.

We have these formidable investments in education, training, and equipment—yet we sell our services for whatever handouts our clients and editors think our product worth. Historically, writers have been the chroniclers of whole civilizations, the recorders of history—yet we have permitted ourselves to be badly used.

At the beginning of this section, I asked the question: "How should we value our work and ourselves?" The obvious answer is: As the recorders and consciences of tribes and whole cultures, we should value our work very highly indeed. And it is time that we put the shoe on the other foot. Instead of our clients deciding what they will *give us* for our efforts, it is we who must henceforth determine how much *we will charge our clients* for the experience, skills, and capital investments which go into the creation of writers' products.

WHO IS MAKING HOW MUCH AND FOR WHAT?

Let's look at some numbers published in the Sunday, February 12, 1984 edition of The Seattle Times/Seattle Post-Intelligencer. The figures are derived from salary comparisons of various occupations. It is a sort of "Who makes what?" compilation—and you might calculate in what company your free-lance writing income places you. Are you down with the Catholic clergy or right up there with one of the NFL football players?

WHO IS EARNING WHAT?

I think that most of us would consider ourselves lucky to make between $27,684 and $33,384 a year solely by our writing. If we considered the work year to be 52 weeks long, and the work week to be of 40 hours, we can translate those annual figures into hourly ones. The top figure—$33,384 a year (equating to $16.05 an hour) is the pay earned (in 1984) by Seattle's garbage collectors. The lower figure of $27,684 (or $13.31 an hour), is that of morticians. Somewhere between those two numbers lie the incomes of pharmacists, historians, chefs, auto salesmen, machinists, computer programmers, mathematicians, union laborers, auto mechanics, Army captains, reporters on daily newspapers, meteorologists and chemists.

Surely, we, as biographers and company historians, should be on economic parity with the *historians* and *reporters on daily newspapers* listed in the above grouping. Working a 40-hour week (in 1984), the newspaper reporter earned $15.63 an hour and the historian brought down $13.94 an hour. It is of interest to note that *Playboy's* Playmate of the Year earned a cool $100,000 in 1984, or an hourly rate of $48.08 an hour, and that a Catholic priest earned $6,000 a year, or $2.88 an hour. One might easily believe that the priest worked far more than the allotted 2080 hours in a year's time, and that the Playmate worked fewer. Providing what benefits to mankind? We had best only speculate.

Back to the reporters and the historians, whose mean wage was $14.79 an hour. These people worked a regular 40-hour week. In our work as commissioned biographers, however, the number of hours we put in at our jobs will probably be fewer. And because of the specialized skills we must possess—those of researcher, interviewer, typist, writer, editor, layout artist, typesetter, project coordinator and lay psychologist—the rate of pay we set for ourselves can be justifiably higher than that of the 40-hour-a-week employee.

If we set for ourselves the arbitrary hourly rate of $25.00 an hour, the annual income theoretically generated would put us right up there with dentists, space-shuttle pilots and state supreme court justices. But we won't be *working* those 2,080 hours a year—we'll be more likely to be putting in 400 to 600 hours for each book we do. A couple of 600-hour assignments at $25.00

an hour will produce a gross income of $30,000 a year. Three such books will produce $45,000. And we will have worked but 1,800 hours.

A WORD ON ESTABLISHING YOUR FEES

It may well be that for the first book or two, or your first couple of tapes-and-transcripts assignments, you will want to keep your rates low while you are becoming familiar with new facets of your craft. These (initial) lower rates would not be out of place, and would probably make both you and your prospect more comfortable. Then, after you have completed a couple of assignments and your confidence has grown, you can gradually increase your hourly rates to a level more in keeping with your advancing skills.

KEEPING TRACK OF THE TIME

To *know* what you are doing, and to know *how long* each step of your creative process requires, it will be necessary for you to *estimate* the hours required for every step of the work you will agree, by contract, to perform. Do all this "noodling" of the figures before you get into your first selling interview. You will be establishing your own fee schedule, considering all the variables, and making certain that you have all the bases covered. You are now in business for yourself, and unless you know where every dime of your money and every minute of your time is going, you're going to wind up just where you were before—back on someone else's payroll and again working for wages.

WHERE THE TIME GOES

For processing each 1.5-hour duration (45 minutes to the side) cassette tape, the time required to perform the following functions must be estimated. (My own estimates for processing a single 1.5-hour tape follow each entry in parentheses.)

1. Preparing the list of interview questions you plan to ask of your client; typing these questions prior to the actual interview. (2 hours)
2. Travel to and from the interview site, setup time and conducting the interview (3 hours)
3. Rough-typing the transcripts from the tapes as in contract Option B (6-7 hours)

4. Light editing, clean-up and retyping transcripts when producing tapes and transcripts as in contract Option C. (6 hours)
5. Perusing and deriving notes from archival material such as correspondence, newspaper clippings, annual reports, reports to stockholders, and other miscellaneous sources. (Charge your hourly rate)
6. Writing a book from material derived from various sources—your recorded interviews, archival material and correspondence, etc. (Charge your hourly rate for actual hours worked.)
7. Coordinating the processing of photographs, printing, binding, jacket or binding imprinting and packaging of the final product. (Charge your hourly rate for actual hours worked.)

At one time or another, you will find yourself in a situation where it will simply be unconscionable to charge your full rate for all the hours put in on a particular piece of work. You may find that your own ineptitude has got in the way, you have not used your time to best advantage, or that you have fallen prey to the (largely mythical) "writer's block." Whatever the cause, you will find that you have gone "over estimate" and if you adhered strictly to your own rules, you would charge your client more than the job is worth. You know it—and you're pretty sure your client will know it when you present an inflated bill.

Don't be foolish. Adjust your fee. If you know that you are charging too much for the work you've done—make it right. Either lower your rates, or discount the number of hours you have put in on the work. You cannot, in all conscience, take unfair advantage of a good thing.

There is a great deal of mature judgment required in determining how to bill your client. Because, you see, the converse of the above situation may, at another time, be true as well. You will have quoted your usual rates, but somehow, you've whisked through the work like a whirlwind, and the finished product is of exceptional quality. Or you've discovered a rich, outside source of research material, the inclusion of which adds appreciably to the value of your client's book. You've turned out a literary gem, yet you're not going to be paid what it's worth.

It would neither be be out of place nor dishonorable to nudge your fee upward (but still within the estimate) to reflect the excellence of the finished product. If you set out to craft a duck, and you end with a peacock, by all means, charge for the peacock. Otherwise, you are liable to forever diminish the *value* of peacocks!

In any event, I do my utmost never to charge *less than* the lowest of the two figures on my estimate, nor *more than* the higher number. Even if the actual hours worked on a project would justify your billing the client for the top figure of your estimate, a fee slightly lower than your top estimate will make your client feel he has been given a "good deal," and this happy state of affairs will pay off handsomely in customer satisfaction. It is a gesture (customer relations or advertising, call it what you will) that you can well afford. Such a generous act on your part will probably prompt your satisfied client to suggest other prospects to you, and to recommend your services to others as being of high quality and reasonable in cost.

Any sacrifice you make by reducing your fee to keep within your estimate will be slight, and the intangible payoff great. There is no advertising as effective as a satisfied client who spreads the word of your excellent work and reasonable fees! Besides, almost any dollar amount between the high and low figures of your estimate will assure that you, the writer, are adequately compensated for the work you have done. And by staying within your estimate, you will assure yourself of the one thing money can't buy—a pleased client quite convinced that he's had his money's worth. Moreover, that client is prepared to go forth, praising you to his friends, business and professional associates, and to other members of the family.

Can you think of better sources of new business?

A SLIP TWIXT CUP AND LIP

Throughout this book, I have painted a rosy picture of the career-oriented commissioned writer. And I have not been false with my readers—there *is* a rosy future for the serious writer who is thorough in what he or she does.

But there can be pitfalls along the way. You have set yourself up as an entrepreneur, and you reap all the rewards and benefits of being in business for yourself. But—you also take all the "heat" when an error is made. To be successful, the commissioned writer *must* pay attention to detail. You are no less a businessman than the independent mechanic or the local pharmacist. And, like them, you may either fail or succeed. As "The Boss," you must run your operation the way you see fit, and suffer or enjoy the consequences, whatever may befall you.

IN BUSINESS FOR YOURSELF

If my counsel were sought, I would urge you to be honest with your clients and faithful to yourselves. Establish the highest standards you can achieve. *Then*, set a realistic value on your time and your skills, know where your time goes, and keep meticulous track of your hours and expenses. Then bill your clients accordingly. If you do these things and produce quality work, you will establish yourself as a professional in your field, and will have begun a proud enterprise which will support you handsomely all of your working days.

CHAPTER NINE

HOW TO SELL YOUR SERVICES DURING THE PERSONAL INTERVIEW

Biography is to give a man some kind of shape after his death.

— Virginia Woolf

YOUR MENTAL ATTITUDE

You can set yourself up for success—or failure. Much of what befalls you will depend upon your frame of mind.

Back in the thirties there was a radio comedian who epitomized the unsuccessful door-to-door salesman. The opening bit on his show was always the same—the sound-effects man doing a "shave-and-a-haircut—six-bits" knock at the door, and the comedian's voice saying, "There's nobody t'home here, IhopeIhopeIhopeIhope!"

Week after week, during his radio show, this comic set up his "low-pressure salesman" character for failure. The comedian's whole act was based on the premise of the perpetual loser. Predictably, in those sorry times, his audiences thought the act was funny as a crutch. They couldn't get enough of this man's comedy, because everyone knew living counterparts to the actor's "failed-salesman" character. During the Great Depression, it was easy to identify with losers: there were so many of them.

We want to do precisely the opposite. When we go out the door on our way to a selling interview, we want to have readied our "selling" persona for *success*—and preparedness coupled with frame of mind is going to do the trick. If we keep our *mental equipment* in smooth running order, we should anticipate few difficulties.

This is not to say that we won't encounter prospects who won't see the merit of our ideas. We will. There will be *any number* of these. But by knowing the worth of the services we offer, we will be so buttressed by the security of our own convictions that the occasional rejection of our ideas will not deter us.

PROSPECTS DON'T *BITE*!

Sure. To this day, I sometimes get a little bit nervous before an interview. I would be less than truthful if I didn't admit to having that "anchored butterfly" feeling in the pit of my stomach on a few occasions as I was ushered into the president's office of a large company, or was coming up the walk of a stately home. It is only natural that some prospects are more important to us than others, and when one is about to meet for the first time a real "biggie" (or is about to call on the first or second prospect we have approached), it is natural to feel the equivalent of stage fright. Every actor of merit, however, will tell you that a little stage fright is a good thing—it keeps you on your toes and bodes well for a good performance.

I won't suggest that you simply put that fear aside, because that can't be done. It will abate only with experience. What I *will* tell you is that in many years of promoting my services I have yet to have a prospect physically hurt me or irreparably crunch my ego.

Oh, there was one hard-shelled old crustacean I approached on the telephone, and he told me in longshoreman's language that he didn't give a .... for having his biography done—all he cared about was the number of products his business turned out. And I hung up on *him* before he could hang up on *me*! After my blood pressure returned to normal, I enjoyed a wry and private chuckle at the old man's expense, and returned to my basic premise. Prospects may be, from time to time, as surly and as miserable as the rest of us—but ornery or no, *they still don't bite*!

Some of our prospects may be so preoccupied with other affairs that they only half-listen to our presentations. Or some may not be astute enough to see the importance of the proposition we put before them. The merits of our ideas may be challenged, but we are not likely to be personally rebuffed. Prospects will not get physical with us, nor will they deal our psyches any crippling blows. Disappointment should be the most severe damage we will have to repair.

We cannot allow our consternation at the thought of interviewing our prospects to immobilize us so that we do *nothing*! Many writers are great at putting things off, and some have developed procrastination to a state of high art. As heads of our own businesses, we cannot afford to join the foot-draggers!

In your business of promoting, selling, and providing personal biographies and company histories, you are both writer and salesperson. The success of your enterprise depends upon the systematic following of the program you have outlined for yourself. All of your fine intentions and all of your work have been leading you to *one* goal—the interview in which you are prepared to sell *your product* and *yourself*. Without those *successful* interviews, in which you come away with signed contracts and retainer checks in your hands, all your preparatory work will have gone for nothing.

It is well to remember that no harm can come to you during the selling interview: No good can come to you without *lots* of them. No biographer I have trained has ever emerged from a selling interview adrip with gore or sorely wounded in spirit. No bad thing is going to happen to you in there!

Your prospects will become your clients, and your clients will become your friends. And you can have neither clients nor these valuable business and personal friendships if you don't maintain a regular schedule of selling appointments.

Make yourself do what is necessary to assure your success!

YOU GOTTA AC-CEN-TU-ATE THE POSITIVE

Years ago, crooner Bing Crosby had a hit record of a song whose lyrics cautioned: "...You gotta ac-cen-tu-ate the positive; ee-lim-i-nate the negative..." The tone and message of these lyrics might be taken as the motto of any promoter. By accenting all the *positive* aspects of the services and products we provide; recognizing and eliminating all the *negatives* we can anticipate, we will go a long way in creating the cheerful and upbeat atmosphere so necessary to successful selling; so conducive to happy client/provider relationships.

THE POSITIVE POWERS WE CAN INVOKE

We already know that we are the purveyors of quality services, and are promoting worthwhile ideas. This knowledge will infuse us with confidence, and to build on this positive image we provide to our prospects, there are rudimentary and common-sense guidelines we are well advised to follow.

On the matter of PUNCTUALITY, little need be said; but nothing should be forgotten. If you have an appointment for 9:00 a.m., move heaven and earth to make certain that you are at the appointed location at 8:50. It is not necessary for you to announce yourself until the stroke of 9:00, but allow enough time to compensate for the unexpected—difficulty in parking, traffic jams, bridges up, and the like.

Being too early for an appointment is not *quite* as offensive as being late for one, but being tardy for a business appointment is as insulting as a slap in the face to your prospective client. By being late for an appointment, a powerful message is sent from you to your prospect. You have told him, through your actions, that *your* time is more valuable than *his*. Such boorish behavior will not be quickly—if ever—dismissed or forgiven. In some cases, your prospect will have gone on to other things, and your opportunity to present yourself and your ideas will have disappeared forever.

Of course, an appointment broken because you failed to keep it is quite beyond the pale and totally indefensible.

As to DRESS, keep your attire simple and businesslike. I would suggest that men and women alike dress as though they were going to work in a bank or a distinguished business office. For the men I would suggest suits or conservative sports jackets and slacks, white or small-patterned shirts and traditional neckties. For the ladies, tailored dresses, suits, or simple costumes in keeping with the stable and responsible image we are attempting to project.

There are no hard-and-fast rules, of course. If your initial interview is to take place at poolside in Palm Desert or at the nineteenth hole at the Kauai Surf Golf Course, it would be nonsensical to get all duded up in a suit and necktie or our little tailored Evan Picone. While it is altogether suitable for us to dress as conservatively or as casually as circumstances dictate, it is still incumbent upon *us* to properly determine what clothing is suitable for our interview. Keeping always in mind that we are dealing with an older clientele, if in doubt about what clothing to wear, we will do well to err toward the conservative rather than the flamboyant.

SCENTS may well be considered as a part of our social and (perhaps) our business attire. We men apply after-shave preparations and the women anoint themselves with perfumes and colognes. In the past, there used to be a nice line of distinction between "after six" toiletries and those which were deemed appropriate for wear during the daytime. In an earlier time, the arbiters of fashion and decorum declared that only light, herbal or citrus scents were appropriate for daytime use. The heavy, sensuous, musky preparations (the pacesetters said) were best reserved for evening affairs when one's senses might reasonably be expected to be attuned less to the workaday than to the voluptuous.

And they were right. Few things are more offputting than shaking hands with a businessman only to have your own right hand (for the rest of the day) bear the stench of a concoction designed to invoke the aura of a Cossack's sweaty harness leather. Nor is it pleasant to be forced to conduct business in the clouds of heavy perfume favored by some of our distaff colleagues.

A major Northwest financial institution includes this sentence as a part of its employee manual: "Scent and jewelry, *if used*, should be used sparingly and not be distracting." (italics added) Youthful readers of this book may find this attitude to be restrictive and stuffy. To any experienced business person, it makes damned good sense. The point? Any extraneous influences can detract from the business at hand—in our case, the presentation of an idea and the signing of a contract. *Anything* which might distract our prospective client should be eliminated.

We can invoke a positive atmosphere by using discretion in the scents we use during business hours. For that matter, there is nothing in the world wrong with making your business calls complimented by a fragrance no more assertive than the clean odor of Ivory Soap!

The observance of COMPANY MANNERS in business dealings can go a long way toward creating the positive atmosphere for which you strive during your selling interview. Nothing Victorian is suggested here, but a display of simple good manners is certain to promote the positive image you want to implant in the consciousness of your prospect.

- Wait to be seated until your prospect is seated, or invites you to take a chair.
- If you are a smoker, refrain from lighting up until your prospect has done so, or has invited you to do so.
- If it is your custom to enjoy a beer or a glass of wine with your luncheon, refrain from drinking alcohol on those days when you have afternoon selling appointments. You will find that some of your mature clients have strong feelings against the use of alcohol, and to go into a selling appointment with alcohol on your breath will, at best, put a damper on your efforts. Besides, even one beer or a single glass of white wine can "take the edge off" your presentation. During the selling interview, you want to be as mentally alert as it is possible for you to be.

PERSONAL ATTITUDES

This is a touchy area, because we are addressing something not very clearly defined. By attitudes, I allude the the manner in which we use the spoken language, how often slang or profanity intrudes upon our discourse, the way we hold our bodies and express our thoughts by body language, and familiarity with our prospective clients.

Almost always, we will find that our prospects are older than ourselves, and in many cases, possessed of appreciably more formal education and material wealth than ourselves. We may be respectful of the age; the education; the wealth—but not to the point of humbling ourselves. How do we treat these people? We certainly should not be in awe of them; this feeling would surely put us on the defensive, and we have nothing to feel defensive *about*! Treading a fine line, I would suggest treating them with courteous deference—then taking our cues from them.

As we speak to them, at first, our language should be proper, and as close an approximation to the king's English (without being stilted) as it is possible for us to achieve. As in social encounters, two strangers "feel one another out," and before long, conversation becomes more casual, and each becomes at ease with the other. It is the same in a selling interview. The first few moments are often somewhat stiff and formal, then the atmosphere clears, the prospect drops a casual cuss-damn or two, and you will realize that the (imagined) gulf between the two of you has narrowed perceptibly.

Each situation is different, and each must be "played by ear." But experience will teach you certain maxims, chief of which is: "Take the 'lead' from your prospect."

Several times when I was a young man, I was invited to suppers and dinner parties whose dining tables sported more silverware than I knew how to use. Feigning deep conversation with my dinner partner, I would glance surreptitiously across the table, or at my host or hostess, to see how *they* were manipulating the fish knife or other unfamiliar bit of flatware. Taking "my lead" from them, I bluffed my way through any number of occasions which might have proved embarrassing had I mulishly tackled the problem on my own. It was not long before I learned. Those of you unfamiliar with conducting selling interviews may take heart. You, too, will learn. Through experience, you will quickly absorb the information you need to conduct successful selling interviews with your prospective clients. They're easier to get on with than you might think.

WHAT'S IN A NAME?

When should you begin to call a prospect by his or her first name? Certainly, *not* during the selling interview. Sometime after the third or fourth taping session, perhaps; sometimes never. It all depends upon the client, and upon your good sense of proportion and fitness.

Recalling always the ages of our prospects relative to our own, we will do well to remember that they were reared in more conservative times. Familiarity with comparative strangers has been, and is, anathema to many.

If my client is a man, and only a decade or so older than myself, and if he habitually addresses me by my first name, I feel no compunctions (after the first four or five interviews) about becoming equally informal with him. Often, but not always, my clients have invited me to address them by their first names, and thereafter I have done so. We are frequently more comfortable and more relaxed with members of our own sex, and with male clients I have found that informality tends to come quickly and naturally.

In thinking back, however, I can recall only one client with whom I was never on a first-name basis. She was a tiny little Dresden-doll figure of a woman whose every mannerism was so feminine that one tended to treat her as one would a fragile figurine. She was widowed, and lived in an immense, formal house with only a small retinue of servants. Her children were grown and gone, yet her home and grounds were kept in a constant state of readiness, almost as though she were about to be called upon once again to play hostess for the grand dinner parties and lawn fetes of yore. She always appeared for our interviews meticulously coiffed and gowned, and to have inflicted her with unwanted familiarity would have been quite beyond my capacity. To this day, I think of her and refer to her as Cynthia Coleman Bayne-Jones, or Mrs. Bayne-Jones.

PHYSICAL AIDS TO YOUR SELLING PRESENTATION

Most of us will have come to our new profession (that of biographer and company historian) via the routes of free-lance article writing, public relations, advertising or some other avenue which has involved writing. Even if we have seen only a few of our poems published in little magazines, chapbooks or local newspapers, most of us will have established some sort of track record for ourselves as writers.

Others will have written articles, short stories, advertising or promotional pieces, perhaps even books. Whatever our output, if we can show our prospective clients *something* of ours in print, our credibility as writers will be given a healthy boost. One of the first questions often asked by prospects is, "What have you done?" If you can trot out a little "show book" of material you have written, you will have established yourself in the eyes of your prospect.

My own first show book consisted of a few newspaper and magazine articles of mine which had seen print, and some articles from a professional medical bulletin which I had edited and (largely) had written for the University of Washington. These, and some copies of editorials I had produced while with the television station made up the bulk of my book. But it was *enough*! The few short pieces in my show book constituted my credentials, and satisfied my prospects that I was serious about my writing, and was competent.

Of course, after I had written and published a couple of my biographies and company histories, I took copies of *those* books with me, and there was no cause for concern. My prospects glanced through these volumes, nodding their heads as they browsed, and handed the books back to me without question. My professionalism was accepted.

So I suggest that you create for yourself a show book.

A good-quality vinyl three-ring binder will do nicely. I found it helpful to insert the pages of my material in plastic loose-leaf protectors carried in almost every stationery store. I bought these 8.5 X 11-inch protectors punched for the three-ring binder, and simply inserted my articles in them so that they wouldn't become dogeared from handling.

THE TYPICAL SELLING INTERVIEW

You should first disabuse yourselves of the notion that there *is* any such thing as the "typical" selling interview. No two will ever be alike. By the same token, each of them will have similarities—and if you are astute and observant, you can control the way your selling interviews proceed.

You've pulled up in front of a fine old house on a quiet street, and you glance at your prospect card. You still have ten minutes before you are supposed to present yourself. There's time to review the facts.

Your prospect, Mrs. Hazel Carson, is a widow. She's about 82 years old (her friend has told you), and has three grown children—two sons and a daughter—as well as six grandchildren upon whom she dotes. Her husband, Glen, a retired corporation lawyer, died five years ago. After Glen's retirement, the Carsons traveled extensively, often taking one or more of their children (and their families) with them on trips to Hawaii and to Europe. Glen and Hazel had both enjoyed gardening, and today, the carefully tended beds around the house attest to the fact that Hazel is still interested in their once-shared hobby.

You glance at your wristwatch, and it's time. Now or never, you tell yourself as you climb from your car. You close the door gently and stroll up the tree-shaded walkway. At the door you pause, adjust your necktie—and ring the bell. Its tones echo in the recesses of the house, and you hear muffled footsteps approaching. The door opens.

HAZEL: Yes?

WRITER: Good morning. My name is Dick Sawyer. You'll remember that we have an appointment for ten o'clock this morning.

HAZEL: Oh, yes, Mr. Sawyer. Come right on in. I've been expecting you. If you'll follow me (walking toward the den) we can just talk in here. It's quiet, and we won't be disturbed.

Will you have a chair?

WRITER: (Seating himself) Thank you, Mrs. Carson. You surely have a beutiful home here. I was admiring your flowers on the way up the walk.

HAZEL:Oh, yes, Glen and I loved to garden, and I try to keep the place up, but it's not the same since he...

WRITER:All the same, this lovely old home has seen a lot of wonderful living, and it must contain a lot of precious memories for you.

HAZEL:We lived here for nearly forty years, and yes, we've done a lot of living within these walls. We raised three beautiful children, saw them all through school and happily married, and now there are the grandchildren to keep me busy and out of mischief! They're a caution, I can tell you!

WRITER:Have you had an opportunity to read the little brochure I sent to you? The one that dealt with the concept of Biography as Legacy?

HAZEL:Yes I did, and I thought it was very interesting. Do you know that I had a grandfather—he was my grandfather on my mother's side—who came from Illinois to California in a covered wagon when he was just a tiny baby? Just a wee little thing, and that terrible journey and all those wild animals and Indian raids and everything. I don't see how they did it. They must have been made of stronger stuff than we are today.

WRITER:Those are the very kinds of stories we're trying to preserve for your children and grandchildren, Mrs. Carson. Are there any written records of that journey? The one your grandfather's family made by wagon train?

HAZEL:Oh, no, but it's all in my head. My lands, I was told that story so many times that I think I have it engraved on my brain! How they lived on "buff and beans"—that's what they called it. "Buff" was buffalo, of course, and that, and some dried beans they had were what sustained them for the last, long stretch before they reached a source of supplies. And they had to abandon on the trail a big old grandfather clock and the little pump organ they were so proud of. For the last two days on the trail they were without water, and it must have been just terrible! Some of their animals died, and everything!

WRITER:You know, your grandchildren are going to appreciate those same stories when they are *your* age. And they'll have those stories because we're going to record them for all time. This is precisely the point I was making in the brochure I sent to you. Each family has stories which are worth repeating, and worth preserving for those children who come along after us.

HAZEL: That may well be, Mr. Sawyer, but they certainly aren't interested in listening to them now! My, what wiggle-tails they are! Can't get them to sit still long enough to have dinner, let alone long enough to tell them something about their great grandparents. Do you suppose they'll *ever* be interested? I don't know that I should go to all this trouble...

WRITER: Of course, that's the very difficulty we're trying to overcome by creating these biographical legacies for them. It is unfortunate that most of us really *don't* become fascinated by the stories of our ancestors until we, ourselves, are in the later years of *our* lives. Unfortunately, by that time, many of our family members who could have told us the first-hand accounts of the very things we want to know, have become ill or have passed away. We simply must recognize that *time is the enemy*, and do something about recording these wonderful stories before it is too late.

HAZEL: Well, yes, I can certainly appreciate what you're saying. I wish I knew more about my grandparents—on both sides of the family. And I wish my mother and father were still around. They could *really* tell you some stories. But, of course, they've been gone for years, now, and it's no use crying over spilt milk. It's too late for them.

WRITER: But it's certainly not too late for *you*! You're still in good health, and it's obvious that your memory is clear—and that you can tell a fine story, as well. You have a knack for remembering details...

HAZEL: I suppose that it's a good idea to put some of these things down. Especially for the grandchildren. There are six of them, you know.

WRITER: You can create a treasure for them which will never lose its value. And they'll thank you all of their years for your thoughtfulness.

HAZEL: Do you really think so? Well, yes—I suppose they would. But isn't something like this going to cost an awful lot of money? And take a lot of time? I mean, I seem to be busier than I've ever been in my life, and these are supposed to be my *retirement* years! I swear, I just don't know where the hours—and the days—go! It just seems that I would be letting myself in for a lot of work.

WRITER: I can assure you that your contribution won't seem at all like work, Mrs. Carson. I think you will find that the two hours a week we spend together will be some of the most rewarding in your life. From my past associations with persons such as yourself, I feel confident that you will enjoy our sessions together. And, you will come away from them feeling wonderful in knowing that the stories and the information you have given me have been safely recorded, and cannot be lost.

HAZEL: But what about the cost? Two hours a week for how long? I don't want to get into some great big elaborate thing that is going to take all my time and cost a great deal of money.

WRITER: Let's talk about the time involved, first. I have found that it usually takes only ten to fifteen two-hour meetings to record all the material we will require. As far as your contribution to our work is concerned, all you will have to do is hold up your end of the conversation. I assure you, you'll come to look forward to our sessions together. Frankly, they're a lot of fun! The most important step in the procedure is to *begin work* while you're in good health, and feeling fine. Now, there are several options open to you, but I would suggest that we at least provide you and your family with the recorded tapes and a clean, typewritten copy of what we have talked about. That way, at least we will get all the material recorded in permanent form, then, at a later date, if one of your children or grandchildren want to write a book of the material—or if you decide that you want me to write your book for you—the information will all be there for us to work with.

HAZEL: You still haven't told me what all this is going to cost.

WRITER: (Taking out contract, WRITER follows the fee schedule outlined in Chapter Eight of this book. WRITER *always* has his pocket calculator at "the ready.") If we did only the tapes, and provided you with a voice recording of all our interviews, we could do this for between $1,250 and $1,875. This would be a minimum contract. But perhaps the most desirable option would be (pointing to contract) Option C, which would give you both the tapes and a clean, typewritten record of everything on those tapes. Under Option C, the costs would run between $4,500 for ten tapes and their transcripts, and $6,750 if our interviews took us to fifteen tapes. The cassette tapes will be delivered to you in a good-looking album, and the typewritten transcripts will be in a sturdy vinyl ring binder. Together, they make a lovely presentation package for your family.

HAZEL: That still seems like quite a bit of money...

WRITER: When compared to what? We spend money on all kinds of things that give us disappointing returns on our investments. A fine automobile goes to pieces within a few years. Furs and clothing become worn and outdated. Stock investments can go sour. Diamonds and precious metals have always been speculative. But a family biography grows in value each year that it exists—the older it is, the more valuable it becomes. What kind of value would you place on a book *written* by that grandfather of yours who, as in infant, was carried across the plains? Why, such a book would be priceless to those in your family. If you can only cast yourself in the role of ancestor, and realize what value your heirs will place on *your* life story just one hundred years, or a hundred and fifty years from now, I think you will appreciate more fully what we can, together, create for those of the Carson clan who are to follow you.

HAZEL: Well, my grandfather was something else. He lived in exciting times, then things were changing. But *I've* never done anything exciting in my whole life! Who'd want to read about anything I've ever done? Raised some kids, grew some flowers, did a little traveling, and buried a wonderful husband. That's all my life has ever amounted to.

WRITER: You know, had your grandfather been asked if *he* had ever done anything exciting, he would have probably said much the same thing. "No, my life has been very ordinary." But let's look at some of the things that have gone on during your lifetime. You were born when?

HAZEL: Oh, do you have to know? All right, then, I was born in 1900—in St. Louis, Missouri.

WRITER: Just one year before Queen Victoria, of England, died and ended the longest reign in British history. During your lifetime you saw motion pictures come of age, the telephone come into general usage, and when you were only three years old, the age of air travel began with the Wright brothers first flight. Radio was born, literally, on Christmas eve when you were six years old, and television came along only thirty-three years later. You have seen the United States involved in five major conflicts—two world wars, the Spanish-American war, Korea and Vietnam—and have seen man walk on the moon! You were born in the horse-and-buggy era, and have lived all the rest of your life in the era of the automobile—an invention which altered the planet. You've seen literature, music, and the arts expand in ways no one had ever envisioned, and you have thus far survived the age of the atom. You and your family have enjoyed levels of education never dreamed of only a century ago, and have leaped oceans and continents in search of enlightenment and adventure. You may yet see mankind strike for the stars—and you tell me you have lived an *unexciting life*? You have been witness to miracles, Mrs. Carson—and your heirs deserve to know how you responded to these wonders, and how they changed your life.

HAZEL: When you put it that way, I guess I have seen a lot of changes during my lifetime. And maybe the grandchildren *would* get a little something out of it if I was to put it all down.

WRITER: And you don't even have to put it all down, Mrs. Carson. That's what I'm here for. All you will do is talk with me. I promise, it won't be any more difficult than having one of your friends over for a cup of tea. We'll talk, and I'll get it all down on tape, then have the information on the tapes typewritten so that you can make copies of our notes, if you like, for distribution to your children and grandchildren. Once we've taken that first major step in recording your experiences, we can then see if you want to go ahead with writing a book.

HAZEL: You said you were going to record this. Does that mean microphones and all that sort of bother?

WRITER: Not at all. I use a small, self-contained tape recorder, and it will lie on the table as unobtrusive as a box of bonbons. I guarantee that after the first five minutes, you'll forget it is even there. The process is totally painless, I assure you.

HAZEL: You think starting with just the tapes and the typewritten transcripts is best. Is that right?

WRITER: Yes. We have to go through those steps even if we are going to eventually produce a book. Why don't we go that far with the process, then talk about writing the book when we have finished the information-gathering part of the job?

HAZEL: Why, yes, I think that would be all right. You don't think I'm being foolish, do you? And you don't think my family will think me a vain old woman for doing something like this?

WRITER: Not unless a dozen or more prominent Seattle citizens are also foolish in the same way. And your family certainly won't think you vain—they will thank you forever for being so thoughtful of them, and the generations of Carsons to come. You're making them a wonderful gift, and one which could not be given by anyone else. Your story is unique, and no one in the world, other than yourself, is qualified to tell it.

(WRITER signs contract in the space provided, then places an "X" where HAZEL CARSON is to sign. Hands contract and pen to HAZEL.)

HAZEL: (Signing contract) Now, will you want something today?

WRITER: Yes, Mrs. Carson. A retainer of ten-percent of my estimate will put us to work. (Calculating) Let's see—the figure midway between between the low of $4,500 and the high of $6,750 would be $5,625. And ten percent of that amount is $562.50. If you will write me a check in that amount, we can begin work as soon as it is convenient for you.

HAZEL: (Writing check and talking at the same time.) How often do you think we should get together for our little meetings?

WRITER: I have found that once a week for two hours works out best. That way, it doesn't take up too much of your time, and during the week between our talks, you will think of things you wanted to tell me during the earlier interview, and go over in your mind incidents you don't want to forget. You might want to make a few notes to yourself, as well, to remind you of things you will want to talk about. We can't be expected to remember everything, and the little reminders are a help.

HAZEL: I'm beginning to get excited about this! Do you think we can finish by Christmastime? It would be such a wonderful surprise gift for Helen and George and Bob if we could...

WRITER: I'm sure we can finish by the holidays if we get started right away. What is your schedule like? What days are best for you?

HAZEL: Well, I seem to have more free time on Mondays than on any other day of the week. Do you suppose you could come at ten o'clock on Monday mornings?

WRITER: (Consulting appointment book.) That would be just fine, Mrs. Carson. Monday morning at ten o'clock it is, then. (Rising) I look forward to seeing you then—and I know that your family is going to love you for the grand gift you are preparing for them. Nothing in the world could show your love for them more emphatically. (Exit)

ARE THEY ALL THIS EASY?

Almost all! Each selling interview is different, of course, and every prospect has some questions which will differ from those Hazel asked, in the example above. Some prospects will put you off for a week, a month, or several months, pleading that they want to consult with their families. If this is the case, bow out gracefully, but *always* with the understanding that *you* will call the *prospec*t again at a specified time. "I can appreciate your wanting to talk with the family about this," I will say. "Why don't you discuss it with them, then I will call you in about a month's time to see what their reaction has been."

This is a non-threatening, not-overly-aggressive tactic which is effective, yet allows *you*, the writer, to retain the initiative. Do all you can to counter the possible client response: "Well, I'll give you a call when I'm ready to do something."

Most selling interviews *are* easy, because by the time you are in the prospect's presence, he or she has understood what you have in mind, and has *already* opted to buy, if the price isn't too steep. They like the idea; what they want to iron out are the details and the cost.

And, most selling interviews are as much social as they are commercial. The prospect wants to appraise this "writer person" to whom he or she will be entrusting sacred family secrets, and with whom he or she will be spending a great deal of time. The prospect wants to "look you over" just as you want to know who you are going to be working with.

There is essentially no competition in our field—most likely, you will be the only writer in your area who is doing this kind of work, so there won't be any "comparison shopping." It isn't as though you were going up against another salesperson selling a shinier car, a more fireproof roof or a quieter refrigerator.

No, the job is yours if you can but convince your prospect of the *value* inherent in Biography as Legacy, and of your *qualifications* for producing that biography with sympathy, understanding and professionalism.

Your skills are needed in *your* community. And *you* are the only one capable of promoting yourself and this new concept of the biographical legacy. Your mission is an important one: to yourself as an entrepreneurial writer; to your community as beneficiary of your skills.

CHAPTER TEN

PROBING THE PAST:
Drafting the Interviewers Questions

Just how difficult it is to write biography can be reckoned by anybody who sits down and considers just how many people know the real truth about his or her love affairs.

— Rebecca West, "The Art of Skepticism," Vogue, 1952

ARE LISTS OF INTERVIEW QUESTIONS NEEDED?

To enter an interview situation without such a list of questions is to approach your client ill equipped and unprepared. Thoughtfully crafted interview questions are vitally important for a number of reasons:

- They will allow you, the interviewer, to direct and control the interview so that all necessary ground is covered, nothing overlooked.

- Well-thought-out questions provide structure for your interview. Antithetically, an unstructured interview is most often an unproductive interview. An interview without direction is like a railway engine without rails; a ship without a course. Like the engine and the ship, an undirected interview meanders all over the map without ever really getting anywhere. It wastes time and squanders your client's money, a breach of ethics from anyone's point of view.

- Thoughtful interview questions provide desirable points of departure for the interview subject; they also provide a route of return to the main line of questioning. A question may trigger a lengthy discursion into a hitherto unsuspected bonanza of information. When the vein has been mined of all its treasure, the last question asked may be repeated to return your client to the time and place the digression. To bring him back, you may say, "That was a splendid story. Now—we were talking about..." With a prepared list of questions, you may take up where you left off, and a sense of continuity established and maintained.

- The list of questions is as important for the interviewer/writer as it is for the client and the finished product, be it tapes, a book or a compendium of transcribed notes. The list of questions will remind the writer what has gone before, and will permit him to hone his questions ever more carefully so that the deepest recesses of memory may be probed. The interviewer may take two or more hours devising the questions by which to stimulate his client's memory. These questions should quest deeply and thoroughly through each area of inquiry. *Detail* and *minutiae* are very much the stuff of biography, and the splendid, subtle nuances of a life simply do not come to light if the interview questions are superficial and ill-thought-out.

GIGO is computerese for "garbage in; garbage out." The implication is plain: if "garbage" is programmed into the computer, the output will also be "garbage." The quality of the output is directly analogous to the quality of the input. The same is true of the interview situation. If the interviewer's questions are improvised as the recording session progresses, they are very likely to be superficial "garbage." It is predictable that the client's responses will likewise be shallow and of poor quality.

WHERE TO BEGIN?

To beg the question, we begin at the beginning. Because biography is the chronicle of individual lives as they relate to their families and the influences of their times, we begin as far in the past as possible.

Each of our subjects must depend upon two major sources for the information we seek. The primary source is memory; the secondary, documents which are but extensions of memory, and which may be used to verify relationships some little way into the past. Only rarely are we fortunate enough to uncover a book or journal that amplifies our knowledge of our subject's ancestors. If documents exist, we must usually satisfy ourselves with genealogical charts and pedigrees or notations in family bibles which provide little more than names, dates and places of birth, marriages, and the names of any progeny of those early unions.

The "beginning" for most of our clients will coincide with their own earliest recollections of great grandparents, grandparents, and their childhood memories of their own mothers and fathers. We will find few of our interview subjects (clients) who have any personal memories of their great grandparents. Such knowledge as they do possess will usually be in the form of family stories passed down from generation to generation. You would do well, of course, to ask if your client has any memory of any great grandparents, but your serious questioning will usually begin with the two sets, paternal and maternal, of grandparents.

WHAT TO ASK?

Let's address the subject of interview questions for a moment. Aside from initially *placing* your client and your client's ancestors in space and time (where they were born, reared, schooled, employed, married and buried), you must ask yourself what kind of structure you are attempting to *build* with the information you elicit. The biographical writer might be likened to a building contractor plunked down in the middle of a great plain upon which is stacked mountains of building materials. From them, the contractor might build a skyscraper, a sixty-store shopping mall, five hundred four-bedroom split-level houses—or 10,000 privies.

Our task is to recreate a life, or several lives, in such as way that our product (the result of our skills) will be meaningful and important to future generations of readers. Because human beings are complex creatures, their lives made up of myriad influences and facts, we must pick and choose from the daunting amount of material available to us. Like a master chef creating his culinary creations in a kitchen filled with the bounty of the land, we must create the right kind of "mix" so that the dish we eventually serve up to our readers is a savory one, and representative of the best that is in our larder. Like the chef, we don't use *everything* that is at hand—we select what is to go into our masterpiece with care and discrimination.

So the biographical writer must do with his creations. He must, through the questions he asks of his clients, pick and choose to achieve that indefinably fine balance between substance and subtlety; earthiness and essence; hard fact and nuance. It is in the information-gathering interview that we begin to exercise our creative skills.

The sample questions which follow are intended as *guidelines only*! They are *some* of the questions I have used in *some* of my interviews. However, this list of questions can, and should be expanded and improved upon. Few things in this book are intended to be static or set in concrete. They are the basics upon which you can build. Once into your interviews, improvise, extemporize—and ask about every subject which piques your *own* curiosity! Limit yourself only by the dictates of good taste—and even then, be *daring*!

The following sample questions have been derived from lists of interview questions which have have been, for me, effective and productive. They are written as though I were addressing a client during the course of an actual interview. The questions within categories are in no particular order—only grouped together as they relate to the individuals or incidents which are being discussed.

Most of the questions which follow are derived from interviews with woman clients. Although most questions are of the "unisex" persuasion, each questionnaire should be individually tailored to the a specific client.

QUESTIONS ABOUT GRANDPARENTS AND THEIR FOREBEARS.

Grandmothers, Maternal and Paternal

Let's talk first about your maternal grandmother—the grandmother on your mother's side. Did your maternal great grandparents or grandparents come to the United States from a foreign country? When did members of her side of the family first come to the United States? From what country? Have any stories about crossing the ocean trickled down to your generation? Are there relatives on your mother's side of the family still living in a foreign country? What country?

What brought your mother's people to this country? How did they travel to get here? In what part of the United States did they settle? Are there any old family bibles or genealogical records about this side of the family? Where are these located? Have you access to them?

In what year was your maternal grandmother born? Where was she born? What was her full maiden name? Where was she reared? In what regions, states, or cities did she live when she was a young girl? Do you know where she attended grammar school? High school? Did she go to college?

What sort of image comes immediately to mind when you think of your mother's mother? What is your earliest recollection of your maternal grandmother? What sort of relationship did you have with her? Where did she live when *you* were a little girl? How often did you see her? Are there particular incidents which come to mind about things you used to do with her? What is your fondest memory of her? How was she usually dressed?

How would you characterize her? Was she stern? Loving? Jolly? Determined? Grave? Serious? Devout? Scholarly? What kinds of stories did she used to tell you? Did she ever mention famous or eccentric relatives? Did her family ever change its name other than through marriage? What was the original name? What religious faith did your maternal grandmother follow?

Are there any stories of nobility or lost fortunes on her side of the family? Did this grandmother ever relate any stories of ESP (extrasensory perception) the supernatural or the occult which have been passed down through the family? Did she have any favorite home remedies for common ailments? In what areas did she excel?—homemaking, needlework, art, music, cooking, gardening, etc. Did she teach you any skills? Did she ever make a toy or doll for you? Any of your clothing?

What kind of an influence did she have on your life? Did she teach you about morals? The importance of ethics? Education? Religion? In your opinion, what kind of relationship did she have with her husband—your maternal grandfather? Was she a dependent or an independent woman? Did she ever work outside the home, or make financial contributions to the family income?

Do you recall her passing? When did she die, and of what cause? What kind of funeral service was held for her? Where is she interred?

(NB: When you have finished asking these questions about the *maternal* grandmother, start right back in at the beginning, and ask the same questions about the *paternal* grandmother. Although this might appear to be an awkward approach—asking the same questions you posed only a little while before—the two grandmothers about whom the questions are being asked differ in so many regards that the client is scarcely aware that the same set of questions is being used.)

Grandfathers, Maternal and Paternal

Now let's talk about your *grandfather* on your *mother's* side of the family—your maternal grandfather. What was this grandfather's full name? Where, and in what year was he born? When did members of his family first come to the United States? From what country? In what region or state did they settle? What attracted them to that area of the country? How did they travel?

What sort of grammar-school and high-school education did this grandfather receive? Was he able to go to college? What sort of work did he do to support his family? Do you know any of the jobs he held, or the kinds of employment he followed?

Where and under what circumstances did he meet your mother's mother? Do you know any of the details of their courtship? When and where were they married? Church service? What denomination would that have been? Including your mother (father), how many children did this family have?

What sort of relationship did you have with this grandfather? Did you do special things together? Was he a good storyteller? What kinds of stories did he tell you? Bedtime stories; ghost stories; legends; stories about the family and the early years of his life? Did he ever make a toy for you? Teach you any skills—fishing, gardening, whittling, hunting, horsemanship, how to use tools?

How was this grandfather usually dressed? Where did he make his home when you first knew him? What is your first recollection of this grandfather? Are there any subtle things you remember about this grandfather—smells and textures, for example? How would you describe him—stern, happy-go-lucky, quiet, boisterous, serious, scholarly? What were his hobbies? How did he like to spend quiet evenings? What were his favorite pursuits on the weekends? Did he have any idiosyncracies? Was he a hearty eater, or picky at the table? Did he smoke? If so, what form of tobacco did he use? Drink? What was his favorite libation?

Was he a man of strong community interests and civic activities? Did he ever serve in the military? During what period of time? What was his rank at time of discharge? Was he a churchgoing man? What denomination? Were you also reared in this denomination? Was this grandfather a Mason, or a member of any other fraternal organization? How was he regarded by his family? By his neighbors? Was he a good friend? How would you demonstrate the quality of his friendship? Did he or his forebears ever change their family name? What was the original? Of what derivation or country of origin is that early name?

Did this grandfather have any strong influence on your life? What was that influence? Was he the "boss" in his family, or were decisions arrived at jointly by him and his wife? When did your mother's (father's) father die? Where? Of what causes? What kind of service was held for him? Where is he interred?

(NB: Ask the same questions about the *paternal* grandfather.)

MOTHER

Where was your mother born? What was the date? What was her full maiden name? Was she born at home or in a hospital? Did a midwife or a physician attend her mother? Did she tell you stories of her childhood and of her "growing-up" years? Recount some of these as you remember them. Where did she live as a child? How much education did she receive? Are there incidents of her youthful life which you would like to record here?

Where and when did she meet your father? What were the circumstances of this meeting? Were there any unusual incidents in their courtship or any hardships they had to overcome? Did both families approve of the pending union between your mother and father? When were they married? Where? Do you know the manner in which your father proposed to your mother? Did she receive an engagement ring? Describe their wedding rings. Did they have a church ceremony? What church? Did they go on a honeymoon? Where?

Where did they make their first home? Were you told how it was furnished? What kind of work did your father do at the time of his marriage? Did your mother work outside the home? How many children did your mother have? (living or not). Give all full names of your brothers and sisters, and dates of their births (and their deaths as well, if this applies).

What is the first recollection you have of your mother? What was she doing? In what room of the house or where did this take place? How was she dressed? What were the circumstances of this event? Why do you suppose that the memory has remained with you all of these years?

What was the best, the nicest thing your mother did for you before you were seven years old? Why was this "the best?" What was the worst thing she did to you before you were seven? Why was this "the worst?" Did either of these events have a lasting effect on you?

Was your mother a strong family person, or were her interests more oriented to community, intellectual or musical pursuits, church, or other areas outside the family? Would you say she was a dependent or an independent person? Were there any stories of her childhood that so strongly impressed you that they had in influence on your *own* life? What are these stories?

Was your mother a natural teacher? What kinds of lessons or ideas of value did you learn from her? What lesson or lessons did she seem determined to teach you? How did she go about impressing these ideas upon you? Did you learn the lessons easily, or were you stubborn about it? Did she (or your father) instill any fears in you, such as fear of other people or failure to achieve, etc.?

If you had to name a single character trait of your mother's, what would that be? What traits of hers do you recognize in yourself? What strengths, motivations, determinations or ambitions did your mother implant in you? What was her ambition for you? What did she want you to become? Did you make your parents proud? How?

What were the first responsibilities your mother expected you to assume around the home? What other responsibilities did you later take on at home? Were you paid for any of these jobs of work? Was your mother more of a friend or an authority figure? When she disciplined you, what form did this discipline usually take? Who was the chief disciplinarian in your family—your mother or your father? Why do you suppose this was so?

Did your mother have a good sense of humor? Could she "poke fun" at herself? Is there an incident you recall which might illustrate her sense of humor?

Did she have any "home remedies" she used on you when you were a sick child? Did she tell you any unusual stories about her family, or about illustrious or unusual ancestors? What was her nickname for you? What did you call her? What did your father call her?

What was the cause of your mother's death? In what year and on what date did she die? How old was she? Where is she interred?

FATHER

Where and when was your father born? What was his full name? Where did he spend the youthful years of his life? Where did he go to grade school? High school? College? What degree did he take? Did he earn his living in the same field as his college major?

Did he tell you stories about his childhood and youth which should be recorded here? What hobbies or special interests did he have as a boy and a young man? What sorts of work did he do when you were very young? Did he ever serve in the military? During what period? What was his rank at date of discharge? Did he ever tell you of any hardships he suffered while growing up? What sorts of things did you learn from your father?

When you think of your father, what kind of a man do you see? Did he spend a great deal of time with you, or was he preoccupied with earning a living and attending to business? What lessons or philosophies about work and responsibility did you learn from him? How highly did he value industriousness? How strongly did your father feel about your continuing education?

What jobs did your father hold during his lifetime, including the earliest ones of which you were told? What position did he hold at the time of his retirement or death? How would you describe your father—kindly, stern, forbidding, demanding, relaxed, carefree, businesslike, etc. Did he pursue any new interests or hobbies in his later years? Did you enjoy any of these "fun" activities with him?

Did your father talk openly with you about his experiences, successes, failures and frustrations, or were these not a part of family discussions? What were family discussions usually about? Where did they take place? Were you privy to the state of family finances when you were young?

Do you have a favorite anecdote about your father? What was his nickname? How did he earn it? What did his friends call him? What did your mother call him? What did you call him? Did he make friends easily? What kinds of activities did he enjoy with his friends? Did he have pals of many years' standing? Did he belong to any fraternal or special-interest organizations? Did he attend church regularly? What church? Did he use tobacco? Alcohol? What was the first work he asked you to do for him and the family? Were you paid for this work? Did he give you an allowance? How much? Did you ever feel overworked and underpaid?

What qualities, or intangibles did your father "give" you?—love, self-confidence, hardships to overcome, advice, understanding, motivation to do better; to go further. What one lesson did he feel it most important to teach you? How did he go about teaching you this lesson? Did you learn easily? What was the best or kindest thing he did for you before you were seven years old? What was the worst thing? Have these incidents had a lasting effect on you?

What are some of your favorite stories about your father, particularly as he related to friends and family members? What is your first recollection of your father? When did he become a "person" to you? Describe the circumstances of that memory. Are smells and textures a part of that memory? Where did this first recognition take place? Looking back, how would you characterize your father when you were very young?

When and where did your father pass away? What was the cause of his death? How old was he when he died? Did you attend his funeral services? Why/why not? Where is he interred?

A TRANSITION

From asking questions about ancestors, we begin, now, to ask our clients to begin telling their own life stories. Although we attempt to ask all of our questions about a particular time frame (grammar school years; high school years; etc.) in the same grouping, a degree of randomness will creep into our questions as well as the clients' responses.

To a degree, we should welcome this randomness rather than fighting it. One recollection will trigger another, and soon we are witnessing a narrative "chain reaction" which will lend great spontaneity and life to our finished product. We may be peppered with bits and pieces of information, all of which we may sort out at our leisure as we organize our books.

The incidence of randomness is also fostered by the very way in which we write down the questions we intend to ask. Not always will we think of everything we want to ask at the moment we are typing out the questions for the grammar-school period, for example. We may indulge in "flashbacks," and refer briefly to the grammar-school period when the interview has taken us into the high-school years.

These small lapses will creep into our questions, and we should not be concerned about them. While keeping the interview "on track" by asking all or most of the questions relating to a particular period in one discrete segment of the interview is helpful, such compartmentalization is not sacrosanct. If you jump back and forth occasionally, this should not be a cause for concern.

After all, it is the *book* which must be organized chronologically, and not necessarily the *questions*. Bear in mind that as you sift through your rough typewritten notes selecting the material for each chapter, you will review *every incident* covered in your interviews, and there is no chance (other than through carelessness) that you will lose or misplace any information vital to the book. *Where* this information appears in the typescripts of your tapes is of no importance.

Now—on to more sample interview questions.

THE YEARS OF EARLY CHILDHOOD

Where were you born? In what city? What time of day? The date of your birth? Did a doctor attend your mother? Were you born in a hospital, at home, or elsewhere? If at home, what is the address of the house in which you were born? Were there any unusual circumstances attendant to your birth? Where was your father at the time of your birth? What was his reaction to your coming into the world?

Describe, insofar as is possible, the home to which you were first brought. Where was this home? Is it still standing? When was the last time you saw it? Did a grandmother, friend, or other relative assist your mother in caring for you? Did anyone other than your parents play a significant role in your upbringing? What other family members, relatives, employees, etc. shared that first home with you?

Who was your first "favorite person" in your household? Was it your father, mother, brother, sister, grandparent, servant—who? Why do you suppose you formed this early attachment? What was it about this person that was so very special to you? Did this affection last through the years?

What first plaything do you remember as being a "favorite toy"? How old were you and in what house were you living? Do you still have this toy?

Most of our early childhood memories are just pleasant impressions and vague recollections. But almost all of us can remember something about the first time we did something of our own volition—the first time we began to become individuals subject to our own self-determination. What incident comes to mind which marked your turning point? Where did this take place?

Describe the area or the town in which you lived in your early childhood. How were you entertained, or how did you amuse yourself before you began your years of schooling? Did you have any pets? Which was your favorite? Why? What activities did your family undertake together? Who tucked you into bed at night? Was it a custom for you to say bedtime prayers? Do you remember the prayer? Can you still recite it? Did you take a favorite toy to bed with you? Did it have a name? Do you know what became of this toy? Did anyone else share your bedroom with you?

Describe the kitchen in the home where you spent most of your childhood. What kind of a stove did it have? What did the stove burn? Was the sink porcelain or metal? How large was the room? Of what material was the kitchen floor made? The counter tops? What kind of table was in the kitchen? Was the kitchen table used more as a work area or for serving meals? Did the older children do homework at this table? What other activities took place there? (*In past generations, the kitchen was frequently the "social center" of the home.*)

Do you recall the dishes from which you ate as a child? Are any of them still in existence? What kind of lighting was in the kitchen? What other details do you remember of this room? Did it have a larder, a pass-pantry or back porch leading off the kitchen? Where was the ice box or refrigerator? When did your family first get an electric refrigerator? Do you remember the ice man? How did you signal the ice man to tell him how many pounds of ice were needed? Do you remember the milk man? Vegetable man? Were any other goods delivered regularly to your home? Describe the vehicles in which they were delivered. Do you recall any incidents relating to these men?—filching ice from the back of the ice wagon; rides in their wagons; feeding apples and carrots to their horses.

In your youth, did your family normally eat their meals together, or were the children served separately? Was it a custom to say grace at the table? Who usually said it? Do you remember the words of the grace usually asked? Who usually prepared your meals? Who served them? Where did you eat your meals? What were some of your favorite meals or dishes? Did Sunday meals differ greatly from weekday meals? Do you recall any dietary differences between what you ate regularly as a child and that which you eat as an adult? What was a typical breakfast for you as a child? Lunch? Describe a typical weekday dinner. Were there any distinct ethnic preferences in food preparation in your home?—English, French, German, Middle European, Scandinavian, etc. Did you often have guests for dinner? Who were these guests of the family? What foods were usually served when guests were invited for dinner? Was the meal served differently, or in a different room from the one in which you usually dined? Did you have household help who assisted in the preparation and the service of the meals?

What was the first mealtime incident you can remember? Do you recall any humorous or disastrous incidents that happened at the dinner table or in a restaurant? Can you remember any such incident that surprised, embarrassed or delighted you? Did you go out to dinner frequently as a child? Can you remember dining on steamships or trains? At hotels and resorts? What are some of the more delightful memories you have of the pomp and ceremony of dining incidents in your childhood? Were you often a dinner guest in the homes of friends or relatives? Name some of your hosts and hostesses. How did their dining customs differ from your own?

When you were a child, what was the most important room in the house to you? Why? What was so very special about this room? What did you do in this room? In what city was this home (and room) located?

Describe the outside appearance of your childhood home. Describe the grounds and gardens. Was the yard large? Did you have a vegetable garden as well as flower gardens? Who usually tended them? What other buildings were on the grounds? Inside plumbing or outside? What was the address of this home?

What rooms were on the ground floor of this house? Did it have a basement? What was it used for?—root cellar, furnace, laundry room, etc. What rooms were on the second floor? What or who occupied each of these? How was the home heated? What kind of fuel was used? What kind of roof did the house have? Was there an attic or garret? What was it used for? What did it look like? Did you entertain yourself with any "spooky" stories about this attic or garret?

Describe in detail the first bedroom you had, the bed you slept in, the furnishings and floor coverings of the room as well as any favorite pictures on the wall. Did you share this room with anyone?

Describe in detail the first living room you can recall: lighting; floor covering; walls; furniture; pictures; decorations; bric-a-brac; art objects; fireplace, heater or radiators; plants; windows and doors; bookcases; musical instruments.

Describe in detail the first dining room you can remember: lighting; walls; table; sideboard; china cabinet and contents; floor covering; pictures; centerpieces, etc.

Remember, now, we are still talking about the very early years. Describe the first punishment you can remember as having received. What form did it take? Who administered it? What had you done to deserve it? Why do you suppose that you remember this incident so clearly?

When was the first time you were really scared? What had happened to you? Describe the circumstances. How did the problem resolve itself? In your later years did you ever encounter a nearly identical situation? What was your reaction the second time?

What frightens you now? Did you have this same fear as a child? Why do you suppose you have this fear? How do you handle it? Have you or any of your family suffered from real phobias? Claustrophobia, agoraphobia, fears of heights or any of the other crippling fears? Do you recall any particularly vivid incidents involving your reactions to fear?

When you were a child, did you have any traumatic encounters with roller skates? Scooters? Bicycles? Horses? Playground equipment such as slides, swings and teeter-totters? Sleds? Ice skates? Toboggans? Rowboats? Treehouses? Skis? Coaster wagons?

Who was your first playmate outside the family? Where did you live at the time? What sorts of activities did you and this playmate enjoy together? What became of this friend? Do you still keep in touch?

Was your relationship with your brothers and sisters very close? In what ways were you close? What did you share? Were you closer to one than to the others? Why? Did you "conspire" against your parents or play pranks on them together? Did any of you run away, or consider running away as youngsters? What were the circumstances? What was the outcome? How did your parents react? Are your siblings still alive? If not, when did they die? What were the causes of death? Where are they interred?

Did religious observances make up an important part of your family life? What church did you attend? What has been the importance of, if not organized religion, then, of ethics and a code of behavior in your life? When did you realize that you had certain principles—things that you could do with comfort, and others that you could not? In what words would you tell your grandchildren of the importance of achieving these ethical standards, and the rewards and penalties of "sticking to them"?

As a child, were decisions easy or difficult for you to make? What about less important decisions or choices—were they difficult for you? Why do you suppose that this was so? Is this still true today? Have you ever had to make any significant, personal sacrifices? Describe.

What was the first really dangerous thing that happened to you? Where were you and what was the incident? How did you free yourself or get out of danger? What was the aftermath of this adventure?

Can you recall any of the early picnics or family outings in which you participated? Where did you usually go for picnics when you were a child? What sorts of foods were considered picnic fare? What entertainments, games or diversions did you usually enjoy along with the picnic? What did you use for transportation to the picnic site? Who usually went on these outings with you?

Do you remember the make of automobile your family drove during your childhood? Were there any long or interesting trips you and the family took during those years? Were there any accidents? Humorous incidents involving cars that you recall? When did you learn to drive? Who taught you? Was it easy for you? Was your teacher patient with you?

KNOW WHEN ENOUGH IS ENOUGH

It may be unrewarding to spend too much time on this pre-school era, because you will find that many of your clients simply have little recall of incidents which happened before they entered school. To many that blissful childhood era is little more than a warm blur of comfort, affection and soft remembrances. Not until your clients (as children) enter the "real world" of competition, when they enter the school system, does recall become more crisp and exact.

But ask the questions anyway! You can never tell when some query of yours will trigger a torrent of memory that will add great richness to your product. The floodgates will open, and the stories will rush forth. Provocative questions can summon forth long-forgotten incidents, and the "trip" you take with your client on such occasions can be emotional and often very touching.

Seeing ourselves getting so close to where our clients "live," in the recesses of memory *must* make us cautious; *must* compel us to use care! We are dealing with the fragile essences of people who have come to place great trust in us, and we cannot betray that trust by allowing ourselves to become unfeeling, even for a moment.

If we do our jobs well, we quickly graduate from the client/craftsman relationship to one of friend/friend. If a writer feels reluctance to "become involved" with people, this business is not for him. You will find that you *do* become involved; you *do* care; you *do* want to provide your newfound friend, your client, with a voice which will ring down the corridors of time to generations yet unborn.

That is what it's all about.

CHAPTER ELEVEN

BEGINNING THE LIFELONG QUEST OF LEARNING:
Interview Questions From Childhood to Early Adulthood

The object of education is to prepare the young to educate themselves throughout their lives.

— Robert Maynard Hutchins

INTERVIEW QUESTIONS FROM CHILDHOOD TO EARLY ADULTHOOD

We are about to enter, through our interviews, the richest storehouse of memories cherished by our clients. In this chapter, our questions will be concerned with the years of youth, adolescence and early maturity, and will cover the eras of grade (or grammar) school, high school, college, and the first, tentative experiments at courtship.

There is a certain fragility associated with these years. In our youth and adolescence, most of us (our clients included) were optimistic, innocent, easily impressed and full of hope for the future. The impressions we carry away from this period in our lives are often vivid, striking, and lasting. And the memories we pack around with us from our childhood and teens seem almost encyclopedic. We seem to remember *everything*!

Not long ago, I journeyed back to Ohio to attend a reunion of my high school graduating class. The small town in which I had lived during the decade of the 1940s had changed but little, and as I drove around those familiar tree-shaded streets, wave after wave of almost total recall swept over me. I was amazed that names, incidents, places, and circumstances had remained intact, although unnoticed, in my memory for so many years. Those memories, like familiar tools in a well-used shop, were at my fingertips when I reached for them.

Were you to ask me detailed questions about that town, its people and my life there, I should be able to talk for hours.

In discussing this period of their lives with your clients, they will do the same. They will remember scores of incidents and details with startling clarity. This is a natural faculty among older people, and you, as biographers, should be aware that a bonanza awaits you when you begin this phase of your interviewing. And because the ground is so rich, I counsel exhaustive, detailed questioning.

My own father, in the last decade of his life, often said, "I don't know what's happening to me. I can give you chapter and verse of some silly thing that happened in 1905, but I can't tell you what I had for breakfast this morning!"

As we age, our long-term memory seems to be little affected while our short-term memory suffers frequent lapses.

An elderly client of mine, a refined and reserved lady of gentle breeding, once burst into tears when I posed a perfectly innocuous question about a dance she had attended when she was a schoolgirl. Puzzled, and somewhat abashed, I asked her what I had said that had disturbed her.

"Oh, it's not *you*, Dick," she said, "it's *me*! You have opened doors that have been closed for half a century! When I started to answer you, the memory of that lovely evening and the wonderful time I had came back to me all in a rush. The young men in their tuxes, and we girls in just *acres* of pastel chiffon and organdy! Oh, my! I can't tell you when I've felt such a tide of emotion. You quite transported me. I was in that ballroom once again, and I could almost hear the band and smell the flowers in my corsage! I'm afraid that for a moment, I became quite overcome. Please forgive an old lady for reliving, for a little while, a treasured moment of her past."

I could have cheered! When I realized what had happened, I felt an elation I dared not show. I had accomplished precisely that which I had set out to do. Through my questions, I had encouraged my client to once again walk in the past, *return* to the past, to describe animatedly, vividly and emotionally, exactly what it had been like. And together, we captured that moment for her eventual heirs.

I had done a good job for my client, and with good questions, compassionately put, you will do likewise.

So—to more sample interview questions about the years of youth. *The following list of questions was originally "tailored" to be asked of a female client, but where possible, I have "unisexed" the questions. In practice, of course, you will pose the questions in such a manner as to fit the sex of your client.*

THE GRADE-SCHOOL YEARS

In your early years, did you have any "phantom" playmate whom you invented for yourself? Do you recall any "made-up" stories told to you by parents or relatives? Were any of your kin great storytellers? What kinds of tales did they weave?

In what year did you first start school? Where was this school, and what was its name? How many classes or grades in your first school? What did you study? What courses did you like the most? The least? Did you have any favorite teachers in the first few years of grade school? Did any events connected with the first two or three years of grade school stand out as memorable? How about going barefoot in the spring? What kind of clothes did you wear to school? Where did you take your lunch as a grade-school student? How did you get back and forth from school? How far was it from where you lived? What games did you play at recess? What did you do after school?

How long did you remain at this first grade school that you attended? How did you feel about changing schools? Did you and your family live in the same house all during your grade-school years?

What kind of a student were you in grade school? Attentive? Uninterested? Lazy? Industrious? Grade schools often created circumstances in which it was easy to get into trouble with teachers. What was the orneriest trick you pulled in school during your grade-school years? Were you caught? By whom? What was the outcome? What kinds of punishment were teachers allowed to mete out when you were in grade school? Were you often on the receiving end of this punishment? Were you ever sent to the principal's office? Made to stay after school? Clean the erasers and wash the blackboard? (Was cleaning the erasers considered to be punishment, or reward?) Did you ever have to take a note home to your parents? If so, to which parent did you give it? Why one over the other?

Can you remember any vacations or trips which you took with your family during your grade-school years? How did you keep busy during summer vacations? Who was your best friend during grade school? What kinds of things did you enjoy together? Did you have a place to go swimming? Describe your bathing suit. Were you active in boating, fishing, tennis, or other sports? Were you involved in Girl (Boy) Scouts or other organizations or clubs?

Often, in the grade-school years, children fantasize about their futures—what they would like to become—who they would like to meet—where they would like to go—who (instead of themselves) they would like to *be*. What sorts of fantasies did you have about the future? What were your favorite childhood dreams? Almost all youngsters have idols who are screen stars, sports figures, or artists, performers or public figures. Who was your idol when you were in grade school? What did you do to emulate your idol?

How did your family traditionally celebrate Thanksgiving? What relatives or friends usually shared the bounty of your table? What were the items on the menu? At whose home did you usually spend this holiday? Was it a family day, or did you often share it with friends as well as relatives? Who prepared the meal? Who served it? Where was it eaten? How was the table set? Was wine or champagne usually served with this holiday meal?

Describe a typical Christmas celebration during your grade-school years. Did you always have a tree? Where did you get the tree, and who provided it? How was it decorated? Lighted? Do you have any of the original Christmas-tree decorations which hung on your early trees? Describe these ornaments. Where are they now?

Did you have Christmas stockings? Where were these hung? Did you usually leave some sort of "snack" for Santa Claus? What was this snack? When did you have your presents—Christmas Eve or Christmas Day? What sorts of "stocking presents" did you have? What was the first Christmas present you remember receiving? Of giving to someone else? Were handmade Christmas presents a custom in your family? Did Santa Claus leave presents hidden in special places, such as in the basement or out-of-doors? Did you ever peek at any of your presents before the "magic day"? When did you find out who Santa really was? Who told you the secret? How did you accept that earth-shaking news?

What did you usually have for Christmas dinner? Who prepared it? What was the traditional dessert? Were the house and front door decorated? How? Was a religious service or church attendance part of your observance of Christmas? As a little child, what did you like most about Christmas? Least? Were there any other family Christmas traditions—singing carols, roasting chestnuts, taking baskets to the poor—that you recall? Did you ever participate in school or church Christmas plays? What parts did you play? Did you ever go on a sleighride?

How about New Year's celebrations? In some families, it was celebrated not only on New Year's Eve with a party, but with a feast the next day—often with goose as the featured dish. Did your family have any such customs associated with ringing in the New Year? Did you make New Year's resolutions? What were they? Did you stick to them?

Where did you attend the seventh grade—your introduction to Junior High School, or Middle School, as it is now called? What was the name of the school, and on what street was it located? Do you remember any courses you took as a junior-high student? Which did you like best? Which least? Did you have any favorite teachers in the seventh and eighth grades? Who were they? What subjects did they teach? In junior high were you active in any after-school activities—sports, hobby groups, or special-study groups? Who were your best friends during the seventh and eighth grades? Are you still in touch with them? Were there any incidents which stand out as being special when you were in junior high? Where did you go on vacations during the seventh and eighth grades? What did you do while on vacation?

Did you pull any pranks on your teachers or fellow students while you were in school? When did you have your first crush on a boy (girl)? Can you remember his (her) name? What attracted you to him (her)? At junior high, where did you usually eat your luncheon? With whom did you eat? Did you buy it at school, from a restaurant, or carry it from home? Of what did a typical lunch consist? Did you stop anywhere after school for snacks, ice cream or cool drinks? What were your favorite soda-fountain concoctions or after-school treats? How much did they cost? How did you get back and forth from home to school? How were your weekends spent?

A NOTE TO THE INTERVIEWER

Rather early on in your interviews with your client, you will learn the date of his or her birth. From this date, it is easy to calculate the approximate time your client entered grade school, high school, and college. You will also be able to approximate the dates (years) when your client graduated from high school and college, got married, and entered the work field.

Knowing your client's date of birth, it is easy to go forward from that date five or six years to estimate the time he or she entered grade school. Some twelve years after the date of birth, he or she would be entering seventh grade, and fourteen years after the date of birth would be entering high school.

I have found it helpful to insert national- and world-news (for the year in question) "milestone reminders" in my interview questions. This device not only helps my client remember the specific year in which certain events happened, but provides future readers with historical "pegs" which will allow them to associate history with events in the lives of their ancestors.

For example: For a client born in 1898, I will say: "About the time you entered high school, the White Star Liner *Titanic* struck an iceberg in the North Atlantic and sank. It was at this same time that Congress empowered the government to institute an income tax, and the Panama Canal opened. Do you remember these events? Do you personally identify with them?" Then I will go on with questions about the freshman year in high school.

For the client born in 1902, I simply look in an almanac, encyclopedia, or other reference which provides year-by-year highlights of history. From these sources I will select material reflecting the incidents of the year about which I am inquiring. My client born in 1902 would be entering high school in about 1916, so I draw my historic "pegs" from that year.

"In 1916," I will begin, "John Dewey introduced the concept of progressive education. In that same year, the Mexican hero, Pancho Villa, entered the U. S. and shot up the town of Columbus, New Mexico. General "Black Jack" Pershing was sent into Mexico to find him. These events occurred some few months before you began high school. Do you remember any of these stories?"

Whether or not our interview subject provides us with any positive response to such questions, at least we will have inserted into the tapes, typescript or book, useful historical milestones—"what was happening when." Readers of fifty to one hundred years from now will thank us for thoughtfully providing them with historic "handles" to newsworthy events which took place concurrent with incidents in our client's life.

THE HIGH-SCHOOL YEARS

What did you do the summer before you entered high school? Where did you spend most of that summer? With whom? Did you take any trips or have a special kind of vacation? Did you have a beau (sweetheart) that year? (NB: It is useful with older clients to use the terms of their youth instead of our more modern counterparts, i.e., *beau* for boyfriend.) What sorts of things did you two do together? What were your parents' rules about going out with boys (girls)? Were you allowed to invite them to your house? How were the young men treated by your father when they came to call on you? By your mother? Did your parents approve of your friends? Did they encourage you to continue seeing any one boy (girl) in particular? Where did you usually go on dates? Did you have a curfew (time to return home)?

Did your beau often arrive with gifts of flowers and candy? If you lingered on the front porch past curfew, did you receive any signals from your parents that it was getting late and you should say goodnight? When was the first time a boy (girl) kissed you? Or were you the one to make the first move? Who was he (she)? What was your reaction? Did you continue to date him (her)?

Puberty is often a very special, and sometimes distressing time for girls (boys). Who taught you the mechanics of the human female (male) body, and gave you a basic understanding of sex education? Did you ask the first questions, or were you approached, at the right time and with the proper information, that you needed to know about procreation and the mechanics of the menstrual cycle? Many young people are not given adequate information when they ask questions about the facts of life, and suffer fears which, while humorous in later years, were no laughing matter at the time. One such concern was the fear of becoming pregnant from kissing. What were some of the "ridiculous" fears you and your young friends entertained?

How did the undergarments, sleepwear and bathing suits of young girls differ in your high-school days from what is worn today? What were the clothing fads of that era of your life? What kinds of clothes did you wear to school? Were your clothes more commonly purchased, or sewn at home or by a seamstress? Where did you shop for your clothing?

Where did you start as a freshman in high school? Describe the building, the classroom and give the street address of the school you attended as a freshman. Who was your first home-room teacher? What subject did you like best as a freshman? Which did you like least? As a freshman, did you cultivate any good friend on the faculty? What extracurricular activities (sports, glee club, student government, drama, speech, newspaper, yearbook) did you become involved with? Who was your best girlfriend (buddy) that year? What sorts of things did you do together?

Did you have a boyfriend (girlfriend) whom you regularly dated? How was this accepted by your parents? What did you and your boyfriend (girlfriend) usually do together for entertainment? Were you disciplined in school at any time during that freshman year? What had you done? What form did the discipline take? What was the high point of that freshman year?

(NB: The questions in the following paragraph are appropriate for clients who were students during some of the years of World War I.)

Were there important changes within your household in the years between 1916-1918? World War I was very much in progress at this time, and the U. S. was involved. What effects of the war did you notice in your own household? Were any members of your family asked to serve in the military? Do you remember rationing? Meatless days? Changed names of food: "Kaiser Cabbage" for sauerkraut, for example? Did the war have an effect on your school? In your community? Were you active in any volunteer organizations, such as Red Cross, Salvation Army, or the Canteens? Did you knit items of clothing for soldiers, or roll bandages?

What vacation plans did you have for the summer between your freshman and sophomore years in high school? Where did you go? What experiences did you have? Did you spend much time by yourself? How important was your privacy in those years? Were you able to achieve any degree of privacy in your home? Did you keep a diary? Did your brothers or sisters ever try to "snoop" or find the key to your diary? What became of that diary? Did you consider your room as your personal "sanctuary" or was it in the public domain where others were free to come and go? Was your desire for privacy observed by all members of your family? How did you react toward the "violators"?

The methods of housecleaning were undoubtedly different, then from now. How were rugs and carpets cleaned before the age of the vacuum cleaner? Were the rugs ever taken outside and beaten in the springtime? How were the wooden floors (polished in the main part of the house; scrubbed in the kitchen and pantry) cared for? What agents were used for polishing? For scouring? What was used for scouring stains out of the sinks? What window cleaning methods were used? How was toast made before the advent of the electric toaster? How were heavy batters mixed before electric mixers came into vogue? How did you dry and curl your hair before driers and permanents came into being? How were clothes and heavy sheets and blankets washed, wrung out and dried? Can you remember a time when you home was without electricity? What inconveniences did this cause? What did you do for heat and light?

During long automobile trips, how did you and the family amuse yourselves? What games did you play (white horses, license plates, etc.) to help the time go more quickly? Were there any "coined words" used by your family—nicknames for familiar objects, for example—which you heard no other place? What were some of the nicknames used by and directed to other family members? What were the derivations of these names? Were you named after some other person, or was your name chosen for some special reason? What about the names (how chosen, and nicknames) of your grandparents, parents, brothers, sisters, cousins, uncles and aunts? Other than the home remedies for illnesses of which we spoke earlier, what were your family's favorite cures for insect stings? Headaches? Poison ivy? Scratches and cuts? Burns? Rashes? Fevers? Indigestion? Constipation?

During your sophomore year in school, in what sports or extracurricular activities did you participate? Did your school have a paper? What was it called? Were you ever active on the paper or the yearbook during your sophomore year? At any time during your high-school years? Who was your favorite teacher during your sophomore year? What subject did he/she teach? What was your favorite subject that year? Which course did you like least? What kinds of grades did you get during your early years in high school? Do you recall any particular "high point" during your sophomore year? Were there any special dances? Did you attend, and with whom? What did you wear? Did you receive (give) a corsage? What dance steps were then popular? Do you remember a special song? A favorite dancing partner?

During the summer between your sophomore and junior years in school, where did you spend your summer vacation? Did your family take any trips this year? Where? How did you travel? What kinds of overnight accommodations did you use? Did you camp out, or go to hotels, tourist courts, lodges, private homes?

How did your family traditionally celebrate the Fourth of July when you were in high school? Picnics? Where? Did you go to the parades? How about fireworks? Did you ever shoot a hand-held firecracker yourself? In your family, who held the "punk" and lit most of the fireworks? What nighttime fireworks did you shoot? Did you attend public fireworks displays? What people did you ask to your home, or to whose home did you usually go to celebrate "The Fourth"?

Your junior year in high school put you into the "upperclassman" category. What was your favorite subject as a junior? Which subject did you like the least? Did you have a faculty counselor during these years? What was the counselor's function, and how did he/she assist you? Did you earn any school honors in your junior year? Act in any plays? Have any disagreements with teachers? Were you ever disciplined for any reason in high school? Did you ever get caught "cribbing" in an examination? What lesson did this teach you? What policy would you suggest to your grandchildren about the perils of "cheating" in class—or for that matter, cheating at *any*thing?

Were you quite active socially during your junior year in high school? What boy (girl) did you most frequently date during this year? Was "going steady" the thing to do? Did you have a "steady"? What sorts of things did you most enjoy doing together? Was this a serious relationship or just an infatuation? Were you allowed to date on weeknights? What time did you have to return home? What was the curfew hour on weekend nights? Were you allowed to ride in cars with boys? When going on a date by car, what were some of the places to go? Did you usually "double-date" or were you allowed to go out alone with boys?

Were there any after-school "hangouts" for teenagers which you liked to frequent? Where were these, and what were their names? What were the attractions of these places? What sorts of after-school treats did you most enjoy? How much did they cost? Were there any places your parents forbade you to go? What were these places? Did you sometimes go anyway? Were there "lovers' lanes" or "spooning" places popular among your friends? Where were these, and can you identify them by name?

Who was your best girlfriend (buddy) during your junior year? Do you know where she (he) lives today? Do you ever correspond? What sorts of activities did you enjoy together? What sorts of things did you confide in one another? Did you double-date with her (him)? Did you ever attend "pajama parties" or "slumber parties" with a group of your girlfriends? What was the agenda of a typical party of this kind?

Did you ever smoke a cigarette during your high-school years? Ever? Did you smoke regularly? Was cigarette smoking common among your peers in high school? What were the results of your first smoking experiments? Did your parents detect that you had been smoking? Were you confronted with it? Challenged because of it? Told to quit?

What were the drinking habits among your peers? When did you take your first drink? What was your reaction? How was drinking regarded among other students? What was your parents' position on teenaged drinking? Was alcohol served in your home? At what age could the children expect to be allowed to "have a sip" or be served a drink by your parents? Do you recall any humorous incidents related to your drinking experiments? Sorrowful or tragic incidents involving you or your classmates and alcohol?

Do you believe that sexual activity among high-school students today is more, less, or about the same as when you were in high school? How do you regard the change in lifestyles, sexual mores, clothing, mannerisms, language and music among high-school students today, as contrasted with the practices with which you grew up? At what age do you think girls should be made aware of the physical changes which take place in their bodies, and told how children are conceived? Do you believe that sex education—the mechanics of reproduction and birth control—should be taught in the schools as well as in the home? In what grade is sex education appropriate for girls? For boys? Should the classes be coeducational, or separated by sex? Why? Did "nice" boys cuss in front of girls when you were in high school? Did the girls (boys) in your circle of friends cuss when they were among themselves?

During the summer between your junior and senior years in high school, did you take any trips or have a particularly memorable vacation? Did you have any feeling of undergoing a "rite of passage" as you approached your last year in high school? Were any of your friends contemplating marriage or careers at this early age?

The senior year in high school is usually quite a high point in academic life, with more freedoms, fewer required classes, more activities of new and different varieties. What did you enjoy most about your senior year? What school were you attending? In what sports were you active as a senior? Any other extracurricular activities? Drama? Dance? Speech? Plays? Cheerleading? Journalism? Variety shows? Music? Student government? Sororities? (Fraternities?) What boy (girl) did you date most frequently as a senior? Where did you meet him (her)? Did you continue to date him (her) after graduation? Can you recall your graduation exercises? What sorts of graduation gifts did you receive? After all was said and done, what had high school meant to you? Had you been stimulated to continue your education?

What kinds of books did you read during your teens? Who were your favorite authors? Your favorite actors and actresses? What were a couple of the movies you remember seeing as a school girl? Did you have a favorite male vocalist in a dance band? Favorite dance orchestra and band leader? Favorite popular song? Favorite flower? Favorite color for personal clothing? Describe a favorite outfit. Did you have a favorite poet or poem? Did you ever attend live theater, the symphony, the opera or the ballet as a young girl (boy)?

During high school did you ever have a paying job—work for wages? What was this job? What hours did you work? How did you use the money? How much were you paid? What sorts of home chores were you expected to do during those years? Where did you do your homework when you had assignments for the next day? Who was the first boy (girl), outside the family, to give you a birthday or Christmas present? What was it? Did you also give him (her) a present?

Did your school hold a senior prom? Did you attend? With whom? What kind of a dress (suit) did you wear? Did your date pick you up in a car? What kind? Was it the custom to have a late supper to go "honky-tonking" after the prom? Did some of your friends stay out all night following the prom? Did you? Where did you go, and how did you spend your time? Did you have a special hair-do for the prom? What cautions did your family give you, or what demands did they make of you, concerning your conduct and hours on that long-ago memorable night?

Some youngsters are given the gift of a trip after completing high school. Were you one of these fortunate ones? What did you do the summer following your graduation from high school? What plans were you entertaining for the future? Had you discussed the idea of a career, more schooling, or entering trade or the world of business? Was marriage common among your peers immediately following high school?

During your four years of high school, had any members of your family suffered serious illnesses? Describe. Had you lost any members of your family to death during this time? Who? By what causes? How had your own health been? Were you one of those who seemed to be subject to every cold that came along, or would you describe your health as good? To what do you ascribe your state of health? Were you an early riser, or did you enjoy sleeping late on the weekends? What did you usually have for breakfast on a school morning? Who fixed it for you? Where did you take your lunch when you were in your senior year of high school? Did you carry it or buy it at the school cafeteria, or at a nearby restaurant? What were some of the "forbidden" roadhouses or after-school places and establishments to which young men might take girls on dates? Why were these places considered "off-limits" by strict parents? Did you ever have an amorous encounter in the rumble seat of a car? Where, and with whom, did this take place?

When did you first learn to drive a car? Who taught you? In what kind of car? When did you first get a driver's license? What state? Describe your first driving test. When did you take your first airplane ride? Can you remember the kind of a plane it was? Did you ever fly in a small private plane or an open-cockpit airplane when you were quite young? Did you learn to operate any kind of a boat? Were you a good sailor? A good deck hand, working with the lines, tying up, and the like?

On inventions and services. Where did your first automobile ride take place? Who was driving? What kind of car? Do you remember when your family had its first telephone installed? Describe the phone. Were you allowed to use it, or was it just for use by the adults in the family? Do you remember your first telephone number? Describe the first phonograph in your home. What were your favorite records? When did you get the first radio in your family? What kind was it? Describe it, and how it operated. What year was this? Did your family make a practice of listening to the radio together? Describe some of the first broadcasts you heard. Programs regularly listened to? Did you hear the broadcast of Lindbergh's famous flight to Paris, in 1927? When did you take your first commercial airplane trip? Where were you going? What kind of a plane was it? In what year did this take place? What invention is most memorable to you? Why? Which event/invention changed your teen-aged life the most? Why?

What were some of the farming and ranching techniques you remember from your youth? Do you remember steam tractors, combines and harvesting equipment? Steam threshing machines? (They looked like railroad locomotives.) When was the first time you saw a gasoline-powered farm tractor?

Describe a typical visit to the dentist's office when you were a little girl. Describe the equipment (foot-powered drill?), procedures and the kind of care you received. Did the dentist use novocaine (invented 1910)? Were you ever hospitalized as a child or a young woman (man)? For what cause? Describe the treatment you received and the medical procedures which were performed.

What kinds of mass transit were in operation when you were a girl (boy)? Horse-cars? Electric street cars? Cable cars? Busses? What were the fares? What type of mail service did you have? What was your relationship with the postman? How many deliveries a day? What was the cost of postage stamps? Do you remember sending or receiving your first airmail letter? Cable? Telegram?

Describe the policemen of your youth. Did they walk their beats, ride horses, motorcycles, or use automobiles? Did you or anyone in your family have any encounters with the police when you were young? Do you remember horse-drawn fire engines? Describe the fire trucks and the scene when going to a fire. Did you ever see a spectacular fire when you were a child? Did you ever visit with the firemen in the firehouse, and watch them slide down the brass pole when the alarm rang? Did they have a firehouse dog? Was it a Dalmatian? Did you ever experience any natural disasters—blizzard, hail storm, hurricane, tornado, or flood?

Newspapers! Did you ever hear a newsboy crying, "Extra! Extra! Read all about it!"? How much did a paper cost when you were a youngster? What newspaper did you read? What was the role of the Western Union messenger boy in your community when you were a youth? Do you remember the significance of three stars stamped in red on the outside of the yellow Western Union envelope? (Telegram containing a notice of a death.)

How about street maintenance when you were a child? Was this done with men and shovels, or did the engineering department have heavy equipment to get the job done? Steam rollers? Did you ever watch men building a house? As the men swarmed over the house, could you recognize the crafts of carpenters, masons, hod-carriers, electricians, plumbers, heating-and-ventilating specialists, roofers? After the workmen had gone home for the evening, did you ever clamber through the half-finished house? Did you ever get into trouble for doing so?

GAUDEAMUS, IGITUR, JUVENES DUM SUMUS

In what year did you enter college? To how many colleges had you submitted applications? How did you decide which college to attend? What was the enrollment when you entered college? What was the cost of tuition? Who paid for it? Had you decided upon a major by the time you entered school? What was this major? Your minor? Did this meet with parental approval? Where did you room during your freshman year in college? Where did you take your breakfasts? Luncheons? Dinners?

Did you pledge a sorority (fraternity) in your freshman year? Describe the rush parties and the granting of the pledge pin. What sorority (fraternity) did you choose? Why? From how many did you receive bids? What were your duties as a pledge? Describe some of the stunts used in hazings and in hell-week for the pledges. Who was your sorority (fraternity) "big sister" (big brother)? Are you still in touch with this special person?

Describe the available curriculum as best you can remember it. What studies were emphasized at your college? What studies did you like best during your freshman year? Which least? Did you have a faculty counselor? What was his/her function? Did you derive any great benefit from having this counselor? What extracurricular activities did you engage in during your freshman year? Scholastically, what differences did you find between high school and college? Was the transition difficult for you? Were you homesick? How did you combat this? Did you have any cultural "meccas"—libraries, museums, theaters—to which you had access? Did you avail yourself of them? Which was your favorite? Why? Who did you date most frequently during this year? What fraternity (sorority) did you most favor as far as "dates" were concerned? Why? What reputation did your house have—that is, were your sorority sisters (fraternity brothers) known as "brains," great athletes, social or student-government leaders? Was yours a "status" house, or an all-around house known for its great girls (boys) who embodied a mix of many attributes? Did friends or family often visit you at college? What was the most difficult transition to make between your high-school and college years? What time did you have to be back in your dorm on class nights? Weekends? Did you ever have "late minutes"? Were you ever penalized for coming in late? What were these penalties?

Describe your living quarters as best you can. Where did you do most of your studying? On the average, how many hours a night were spent in study? Was there a great deal of scholastic pressure? Did you find the work difficult? Did you know anyone who "flunked out"? Were classes formal and rigid, or relaxed and conducted more like round-table seminars? Were you usually seated at desks, tables or lab benches? How many students were in a typical class?

Did any of your high-school friends attend the same college? Were you quickly welcomed into the inner social circles, or was it difficult to "break in"? What were the aspirations of most of your classmates? What were your ambitions that freshman year? What were the key social events of the year? To which did you most look forward? Did you attend most of your school's sporting events? Theatrical productions? Concerts? Lecture-series events? Religious services? What plans did you make for Christmas and other holiday vacations? Did you usually go home for Thanksgiving, Christmas and Easter? Were spring-break trips a custom at your school? Was individual dating permitted? Were you permitted to date, unchaperoned? Were social events chaperoned?

Often, the freshman year in college is a time of great change in social or personal growth. Did you make any significant changes your first year in college? How were your grades at the end of that first year in college? What did you do during your vacation between your freshman and sophomore years in college? Did you take a trip or stay at home with your parents? Live with friends? Go to summer school? Who were you dating this summer? Did you entertain any thoughts of marriage at this time? With whom? What were your greatest interests at this time of your life? Had you encountered any particular difficulties during your first year in college? Were you eager to return in the fall for your sophomore year?

During your sophomore year, who was your favorite professor? What subject did he/she teach? What subjects did you like best? Which did you like least? Why? When you had an hour to spare between classes, where did you spend your time? What student "hangouts" did you frequent? What activities were to be enjoyed there? During your college years, the country was "dry." (This question will not apply to every client, but *all* will recall Prohibition.) What experiences do you recall about prohibition, student drinking parties, bootleggers and speakeasies? Did you ever enter a speakeasy? What were the circumstances?

What dances and music were popular when you were a sophomore in college? Were there roadhouses, dance halls, theaters and night spots which your school (or your family) declared "off-limits" for you? Which were these, and where were they located? Why had they been declared "off-limits"? Did you ever go to them in spite of the warnings you had received? Speaking of warnings and parental counsel during your college years, did these take the form of advice and suggestions, or were you flatly told what you could and could not do? As a mature woman (man), how did you handle parental imperiousness when it came up?

Were you in sympathy with any particular causes during this period of your college career? What did you do to help these causes? Were you active in school or national politics? Where did you live during your sophomore year? Who did you date regularly? What ever happened to this man (woman)?

Did your circle of friends change during your sophomore and junior years in college? Who were your closest friends during this period of your life? Did the course of your studies change? Did you ever change majors? How many times did you do this? From what and to what? For what reasons? Did this change bring about an improvement in your grades? In your attitudes? What professors had the most influence on you? What goals did you set for the coming years?

Was there a vacation trip between your sophomore and junior years? How did your activities change with your increasing maturity? What kinds of summer parties did you give or attend? What summer athletics did you pursue? Who were you dating (at home) most frequently between your sophomore and junior years at college? Were you driving a car by this time? What kind? To whom did it belong? Did you ever have any misadventures with a car during these years? Describe.

Your junior year at college. What new interests (scholastic, romantic, career, or extracurricular) had you developed since entering college? What classes did you like best during your junior year? Least? Why did you like your favorite so much? What was your *worst* class that year? Were you ever disciplined in college? For what offense? What form did the discipline take? Do you recall any of the fraternities' "sweetheart serenades"? What kinds of grades were you earning as a junior? Were you active in any extracurricular activities during your junior year? Where did you go and what did you usually do on week-night dates? On the weekends? What were some of the more popular restaurants or night clubs to which you were escorted while on dates? What secluded areas were most popular with students who wanted some privacy with one another when on dates?

As a university senior, what classes were you taking? Did you have any research or honors projects? What were these? Who was your favorite professor during this year? What subject did he/she teach? What was your favorite subject? Of all your college professors, who did you like the best? What subject did he/she teach? Why were you so drawn to this professor? What lasting influence did he/she have on your life?

As an upperclassman, you had certain freedoms and privileges. How did you spend the added free time during the school day when you were a senior?

What extracurricular activities attracted you during this year? Who did you date most frequently this year? Who was your partner at the senior ball? Were you ever serenaded? Had you ever become "pinned"? More than once? What fraternity pins did you wear, at one time or the other? Was "pinning" at that time, tantamount to an engagement to marriage?

Describe your college graduation ceremony. Where was it held? What was your most memorable graduation gift? Were you given a trip or some extra-special commemoration of your graduation from college? After graduation, what were your plans? Did you want to go on to do graduate work, or get a job to use your new skills? Or did you just want to get married and begin a family? In what subject was your degree granted? What was your degree—BS, BA—what? What was the month and year of your graduation?

Did you consider your graduation to be a pivotal experience in your life? How so? What was the greatest good derived from your college experience? Did your college career alter the course of your life? In what way? With which of your college classmates have you kept in touch?

During that first summer after graduation, how did you spend your time? Did you feel that, with your degree, you had achieved a new level of maturity—that you had somehow "arrived"? Did you ever work as an employee, or work for wages? What eventual use did you make of your college degree, other than to benefit in living a full life, and being able to contribute to the happiness of your husband (wife) and the education of your own children?

CHAPTER TWELVE

EMPLOYMENT, COURTSHIP, MARRIAGE AND FAMILY:

The Middle Years

"I'll tell you the real secret of how to stay married. Keep the cave clean. They want the cave clean and spotless. Air-conditioned, if possible. Sharpen his spear, and stick it in his hand when he goes out in the morning to spear that bear; and when the bear chases him, console him when he comes home at night, and tell him what a big man he is, and then hide the spear so he doesn't fall over it and stab himself..."

— Jerome Chodorov and Joseph Fields,
Anniversary Waltz, Random House, 1954

THE MIDDLE YEARS

You will find that from this point on in your labors with your client that time will become compressed—individual memories of events and people will become, at times, almost a blur of recollection.

One of your clients may say: "Gosh, I don't know. I got married, we had a little apartment for a while, then the kids started to come along, and before I knew what had happened, they were grown and gone—and glory be, we were making plans for our retirement! I just don't know where the years went! At first I was just a little child, exploring the world and growing up. Then I was a student, somebody's sweetheart, a wife and mother—and now I find that I'm an old woman, living in her memories. What has happened to my life? Where has it gone?"

Another will observe: "Don't know where it went. Seems like I have been working all my life. I remember things from my childhood very clearly—the fun I used to have with my grandfather; teachers I had in school; playing ball with the kids; fishing in the summertime with my dad and my mother. Didn't have time to turn around until I found myself in the army, and next came the job of finding work after my military service. Then Amy came along, we fell in love and married, then we struggled to make a go of it. We finally realized some measure of success, and we had some good years. But they went by so fast! Now, here I am, reminiscing with you like some doddering old fool ready for the grave. But dammit, I don't *feel* like an old man! At heart, I'm still the boy we were talking about only a few weeks ago."

A not uncommon reaction. Be prepared for it. At this juncture in your work, an abundance of sympathy, patience, and just plain understanding is called for. Your client will quickly detect and resent any superficial sentiments or fulsomeness on the part of the interviewer. To be effective you must enter into a willing empathy with your client, and help him or her bridge this chasm between childhood and old age. Performing this task with grace and tact will permit you to achieve an intimate relationship with your client which will be invaluable when you sit down to recreate a life in words. Understanding and empathy between subject and writer are of the greatest importance in transmitting those subtleties of *feeling* to the future audience for whom you and your client are expending so much effort.

Following are some of the questions I have found apt for "The Middle Years" of life. *These questions, as the preceding ones, have been tailored for a woman client. If your client is a man, some simple restructuring will bring your line of questioning closer to the mark.*

THE POST-COLLEGE YEARS

Leaving the cloisters of college to go "out into the world" can be a daunting experience. Did you feel threatened by your graduation and impending "initiation" into the challenges of adult life? How did you feel about leaving intimate friends you had made in college? What facets of your college life did you miss the most? How did you hope to apply the education you had received? In retrospect, what were your most rewarding experiences or accomplishments of your college years?

Did you seek employment after college? What field did you enter? What was your entering salary? What was your job title, and how long were you employed in this position? How much were you eventually paid? At the time, did your salary seem commensurate with a college education? In retrospect, does this still seem so? Where did you live immediately after your graduation? What social activities did you pursue? What new friends did you make, and with whom did you most often socialize? Were your new-found friends also college educated? During your adult life, have your closest friends usually been college graduates?

COURTSHIP

When did your husband-to-be come into your life? What was his full name? What were his parents' full names? Under what circumstances did you meet? What was your first reaction to this young man? What type of work did his father do? Did his mother work outside the home? In what capacity? What line of work did you future husband follow? Where had he been born and reared? Where had he attended high school? College? In what subject was his degree? Did he make good use of the knowledge he had gained in college? What did you do on your first date? Was this young man acceptable to your family? How did he get on with your mother, father, brothers, sisters? Your grandparents? Where did he make his home at the time you met? Had you known other members of his family? What were the names of his brothers and sisters? Was his a close-knit family? What evidence did you have of this? What was the date of his birth? Where had he been born?

What drew you two together? What was the common bond you enjoyed? What traits did you see in him that you admired? Did you have a picture in your mind of the kind of man you wanted to marry? Did this man resemble that picture? After you had been dating for a while, what sorts of things did you enjoy doing together? Did he have access to a car? What kind? Was this a continuous relationship, or did you separate from time to time before settling down together? At the time you met your future husband, was there another man in your life? How did you resolve this conflict? Did *he* have other romantic interests as well? How were these resolved? At the time you met, did he have any traits that you *did not* admire? What were his hobbies and interests when you met this man? Was he to maintain these interests throughout his life? Did you share in these interests with him? What pleasurable activities did you most enjoy together?

How long did you date before you became engaged? Where were you when he proposed to you, and *how* did he propose? Anything unusual or inventive about the way he asked you to marry him? What was your first reaction to his proposal of marriage? How long was your engagement before you were married? Did you receive an engagement ring? Do you still have your original ring?

MARRIAGE AND HOMEMAKING

Where were you married? Was it a civil or religious ceremony? What denomination? What was the date? Who performed the ceremony? Who was the best man? Maid and/or matron of honor? Who else was in the wedding party? Where did you hold the reception? Describe the event. Describe your wedding gown. Did you have "something old, something new; something borrowed, something blue"? Please identify these objects. Who gave you away? Was there a special song played or sung at your wedding?

Was there anyone who, had it been possible, might have had the wedding cancelled? Why? Where did you go on your honeymoon? How did you travel? How long was your trip? Describe the first evening and night together as man and wife. Who was the most nervous? Were there any humorous incidents you recall about your wedding night? About your wedding trip? Where did you spend your first night together? Did your friends give you any kind of "shiveree"? What did your parents give you as a wedding gift? His parents? Any other memorable gifts?

After your honeymoon, where did you and your husband first begin housekeeping? Were you buying or renting? Describe, room by room, the apartment or house in which you lived. Is the place still standing? What is the address? What kinds of furnishings did you have? How much was your rent or house payment? Can you recall one of the first meals you prepared for your husband? What was it, and how did it turn out?

Did you immediately shop for furniture to set up your home, or were you given a lot of things from the families? What things did you have to "make do" with until they could be replaced with better or more convenient items? What was the first major purchase you made for the home? How were your "homemaking skills" at the time of your marriage? Had you been reared in a home where there was always household help, or had you been expected to share in the cooking and cleaning at home? Where was your husband working at this time? What was his title or job description?

As a bride, how would you have "graded" yourself as a cook? As a homemaker? Describe one of your early culinary disasters, which seem to befall many brides. What household chores did your husband do? How else did he help at home? Did he do any of the cooking? What were his specialties? What was the kitchen like in your first home? What kind of stove? What was the floor covering? Describe the cabinets, counters and lighting. The kitchen table. Did you ever eat any of your meals in the kitchen? Describe the living room and dining room of this first home—floor coverings, furniture, lighting, plants and wall hangings and pictures. Is any of this furniture still in use in your home or in the homes of your children? Did you have a phonograph? What kind? Did you have a piano or other musical instrument?

Where did you celebrate the first Thanksgiving following your marriage? Who prepared the meal? What family members were present? Where did you celebrate the first Christmas after you married? Did you go out for dinner, or did you prepare it at home? Did you inaugurate any Christmas traditions that first Christmas—traditions which have been followed since that time? Do you still have any of the Christmas ornaments which adorned that first Christmas tree? Do you recall a Christmas present your husband gave you that first year together? What did you give him?

Where did you celebrate the first New Year's after your marriage? Was there a party, or did you go to town dining and dancing, as was the custom in the 1920s and '30s? Or did you prefer a quiet celebration at home? Were you, in the years to come, to be known as a hostess and party-giver, or were your gatherings more intimate and family oriented? What traditional foods did you serve at Thanksgiving? At Christmas? New Year's Day? Easter? On holidays, how did you divide your time between your family and your husband's family?

How would you describe your financial situation during the first years of your marriage—"broke," about average with occasional money worries, or affluent and quite well off? What major adjustments did you have to make in your lifestyle when you found yourself living with a man? Marriage and cohabitation almost always bring about causes of minor irritation, humor, and unexpected circumstances which require a change of habit pattern. What were some of these, relating perhaps to the preparations of meals? The caring for clothing? Punctuality? Time of retiring? Reading or eating in bed? Morning traffic in the bathroom? Other personal idiosyncrasies which had not been encountered before your marriage?

What was your first big "fight" about? Was there a victor and a vanquished, or was a compromise reached? Did the same subject arise another time? What, if anything, did you learn about your husband or his habits that you wish you had known *before* you married him? Did you save any little "surprises" for him? In the early days of your marriage, what nicknames did you have for one another? Did you continue to use these same nicknames throughout your marriage? With what were they replaced? Did you see a great deal of your family after you were married? Did you see much of your husband's family?

List, in order, the apartments or homes in which you have lived, their street addresses and the cities in which they were located, and the years in which you lived in these various locations.

What were the names of the companies for which your husband worked during your marriage? What were his positions there? What job titles did he hold? On what boards of directors did he sit? What role did you play in his career? In what business-oriented decisions did you participate?

During the early years of your marriage, were your husband's hours such that you were able to spend most evenings together? Did you spend most of your week-day evenings at home, in the company of family or friends, or did you go out quite often to dinner and to the theater or other entertainment? What sorts of evening entertainment did you enjoy most frequently? Symphony? Ballet? Legitimate theater? Vaudeville? Opera? The movies? Which of these performances pleased you the most? Which did your husband prefer? To what clubs did you belong at that time of your life? To which business, social, athletic or fraternal organizations did your husband belong? To which did you belong together? Were you active in volunteer work? How did you spend your days? Your evenings when your husband was working? Did you ever have pangs of homesickness, yearning for the family of your youth? How did you combat this homesickness?

During the days of Prohibition (1920-1933) many people were making their own beer and wine, and local bootleggers were valuable persons to know.

Almost everybody knew of a "moonshiner" who produced a "real fine product." Did you know of a dependable bootlegger? What bootlegging activities were you aware of at that time? Did you and your husband ever give or attend cocktail parties at which illicit liquor was served ? What were some of the favorite mixed drinks of the time? What was your own personal favorite? During the era of Prohibition, did you or any of your friends ever encounter bad effects from poorly refined beverage alcohol?

During the early years of your marriage, what sorts of things did you and your husband enjoy during the weekends? Did you have a car from the very first? What make was your first car? What model year was it? Did you drive? What were some of the most noteworthy of your summer vacations early in your marriage?—trips you took together and places you visited. Were you more inclined to enjoy visiting resorts and other "good" places with sheltered activities, or did you enjoy camping, fishing, and in general, "roughing it?"

What was the first home you and your husband owned? When did you buy it? In what city? How long did you live there? Do you recall the purchase price? Describe that house from the outside—the building (frame or masonry), the lot, physical surroundings, lawn, flowerbeds, view, trees, and other buildings on the lot. How many bedrooms? How many baths? How was it furnished? Did it have an attic? To what use was it put? Basement? What was in the basement? What kind of heat did you use?

What was your favorite room in this house? Why was it your favorite? What did you usually do there? Did you have help in the house? In the yard? Did you have a sewing room? What hobbies did you pursue while you were in this house? What were your husband's hobbies at this time? Were they such that you could share them with him? Did he have a workshop in the home? What was special about this house and why was it important to you? What important lessons did you learn about *living* in this house? What milestones in your life took place while your were living there? What caused you to move from this house? How did you feel about moving at the time? When did you move? Where did you move? What was the new address?

AND BABY MAKES THREE

Let's talk about your children, now. When was your first child born? Where? Was this your first pregnancy? Were there any complications? Any amusing incidents associated with that pregnancy? How did you feel about becoming pregnant at that time in your life? Who attended you? How long were you confined to the hospital after giving birth? What was the full christened name of each of your children, their dates of birth, and the cities in which they were born? Were any of your children named after some special person, or did their names have some special meaning to you? How did you choose their names?

How did your husband feel about becoming a father? Did he consider fatherhood a burden or a joy? In what ways did he help you after you brought your firstborn home? Did you have nursing or household help in the home? What changes did having a child produce in your manner of living? How was the health of your first child? Of the others? What early feelings did you have about the role of motherhood, and what changes did you note in yourself as a result of becoming a mother?

What sorts of dreams, plans and aspirations did you have for your children? Did you ever have any miscarriages, or give birth to children who lived only a very short time? Did you and your husband have differences of opinion about the "right" way to raise children? Do you think that there *is* a "right" way to raise them? How did you handle the pressure and frustrations of raising children?

ECONOMIC CONDITIONS AND THE CRASH OF 1929

The Depression of the late 1920s and the early '30s left a deep mark on this nation. What are some of your strongest recollections about that Depression? Where were you living at the time? What effect did the Depression have on your community? How did it affect your parents, in-laws, and other members of your family? What did you see happening in your community, because of the Depression, that was somehow "different" and alarming? What observations did your husband and his associates make about the Depression? Many people lost everything they had during these years. What personal effect did it have on the fortunes of your little family? Did you have a strategy to avoid losses? If you suffered losses, what were they? What was the estimated dollar value of that loss?

Did the Depression have any effect on your day-to-day living? What activities did you temporarily curtail or abandon? What changes in diet did you enforce? What other things did you do to avoid having to spend money? Where did you "cut corners"?

Did the Depression have any effect on your husband's business? Was he required to take a cut in salary, or suffer a demotion within his company? How did you pay your bills during the short "bank holiday" in 1933? Did you have some ready cash on hand to meet current expenses? Were you able to make any wise investments because of depressed prices of real estate and securities? From your own observations, describe some of the manifestations of that Great Depression: the social phenomena of hobos, apple sellers, "riding the rails," and "Hoovervilles" which dotted the nation.

During your early married years, were you active in social, community and civic organizations? Which of these were the most personally rewarding to you, and what were some of the roles you played in them? Why do you feel that one organization, more than another, gave you more personal satisfaction? How do you account for those feelings? What particular projects in which you were involved were the most appealing to you? Why? What kinds of recognition did you receive for your contributions?

In the decade of 1930-1940, what were the most rewarding aspects of your life? Where were you living at this time? What exciting things were your children doing at this time in their lives? How did you participate in what they were doing? What were the most interesting aspects of their development to you? What kinds of students were they in school? Until 1940, did any of them have any serious health problems? In this ten-year period, what circumstances, activities or environment gave you the deepest pleasure?

On the contrary, what situations led to the most serious family problems during the decade of the 1930s? Did you lose any close family member between 1930 and 1940? Who died, and what were the circumstances? When did your mother die? What was the cause of her death? Where is she interred? What effect did this have on you at the time? When did your father pass away? Causes? Interred? Effect on you?

What sorts of activities did you enjoy as a family? Did you have special places where you usually visited or vacationed, or did you try to go someplace different each year? Did you and your husband ever just "get away by yourselves," or were the children always a part of vacation and trip plans?

In the 1930s, your children were in school. What school-oriented activities did you enter into with your children? Were they active in extracurricular activities such as sporting events or theatrical presentations which you and your husband could attend? Were you an "active parent" in school affairs? Was your husband? What schools did your children attend? Did you ever receive any notes from teachers or principals inviting you to come to school to discuss any "jams" your children had got into with school authorities? What was your *worst moment* during their grade-school educations? How was this resolved?

During the decade of the 1930s, all of these news stories made headlines. As I enumerate them, please stop me if you remember any of them clearly, or identify with any of them closely.

- Lindbergh baby kidnapped
- 1935, Hitler became German Chancellor
- The bank holiday, 1933
- Gold standard dropped by U.S.
- Dionne quintuplets born 1934
- Hitler rejected Versaille treaty
- Will Rogers and Wiley Post killed, Pt. Barrow, Alaska
- King George V of England died
- Haile Selassie's Ethiopia overrun by Italians
- Spanish revolution
- Hitler occupied the Rhineland
- World's Fair in New York City, 1939
- Germany and Russia swallowed up the ancient nations of Czechoslovakia, Carpatho-Ukraine, Bohemia, Moravia, Estonia, Latvia, and Lithuania.
- Dirigible *Hindenburg* crashed in flames at Lakehurst, New Jersey

WORLD WAR II

Most Americans who were more than ten years old on December 7, 1941, can remember exactly where they were and precisely what they were doing on that fateful Sunday morning when the Japanese bombed Pearl Harbor, Hawaii. Where were you on that Sunday morning? What were you doing? What was your first reaction when you realized that the United States was at war? What were your feelings a few months later when it became clear that the U.S. was to be involved in an all-out war of survival? What were the most important changes in your lifestyle brought about by our entry into WW II? Were you aware of any Civil Defense activities in your community? Blackouts? Pails of water and sand kept by to put out incendiary-bomb fires? Air raid drills?

Blackout curtains? Antiaircraft guns and balloons? Searchlight batteries?

What shortages affected your family most severely? Rationed food items? Rationed gasoline? Tires? Shoes? Clothing? What *direct* contributions did you make to the war effort? Red Cross? Bond Drives? USO work? What members of your family served in the military during World War II? Where were they stationed? Did they see active combat? In what theaters of operation? What ranks did they hold at time of discharge? What members of your family served in volunteer organizations? What organizations were you connected with during WW II? Was anyone close to you killed during this war? Who? Under what circumstances? Where did this occur?

Civilian wartime travel was quite painful. Did gasoline rationing restrict your activities and travel by car? What kind of ration stamp did you have? "A," "B" or "C"? What experiences did you have during the war with railroad and airplane travel? Did you have any trouble with hotel accommodations? Describe your encounters with the hordes of servicemen trying to get from one point to another on civilian transport. Were you able to assist servicemen in your area in any way? Did you ever open your home to them, or invite any of them to dinner?

What kind of car did you drive during the war? Was it difficult keeping it in repair? Were you able to buy a replacement during the wartime years? Describe difficulties you experienced in finding gasoline, tires, and batteries. What was the first new car you bought right after the war? Do you remember the make? What was the cost of this new car in 1946 or 1947?

What were your first thoughts when you learned that the United States had dropped an atomic bomb on Japan? Did the dropping of the second bomb on Nagasaki in any way change your initial feelings or reactions? Did you agree with this "first use" of atomic weapons? Was it necessary? Would a demonstration bombing of an uninhabited island have produced the same effect on the Japanese? Could we have risked such a demonstration, knowing the uncertainty of the experimental bomb's success; knowing that the demonstration might end in failure?

During the decade of the 1940s, what changes in your attitudes and thinking brought you the most personal growth? What things did you do that were most rewarding to you? In what activity did you feel the most fulfilled as a woman and as a contributing human being? What "changes in direction" did you experience in the 1940s? What incidents brought World War II "closest to home" to you? Did any of your friends lose family members during this war? Whose death affected you most deeply? Why? Who were your closest friends during this period of your life? What activities did you enjoy together?

What incidents of the children's high-school years stand out as being most memorable? Where did each of your children attend junior high school (middle school)? When they went to high school, where did they attend? What activities did you all enjoy together when they were going to high school, or did each of the children go his or her own way? Which of your children was the most athletic? The most culturally oriented? The most thoughtful? Curious? Which was the best student? The best musician? The best cook? The best or most active social critic? The most politically oriented? The best outdoor sportsman? Which was the most mischievous? In what extracurricular activities did your children participate? Plays? Band? Orchestra? Sports? Speech? Yearbook? School paper? Student politics?

During their junior-high and high-school years, how active a role did you play in their school affairs? Were you active in PTA and other school/parent groups contributing to the educational system? What sorts of school activities did the children "drag" you to? Or into?

During the late '40s and early 1950s what trips and vacations did you and your husband take? Did you usually include the children? Where were you living during these years? Did any major events change the pattern of your lives in the 1940s and 1950s? What major illnesses or deaths took place within the family during these years?

Let's talk about your children's college careers. In what subject did each major? Did they affiliate with Greek sororities and fraternities on their college campuses? To what fraternities did each belong? What majors did each child select? When did each graduate? With what degrees? If they did not graduate, what courses did their lives follow after they had finished with college? During their college years, were you able to participate in some of their activities such as homecoming, mother/daughter, mother/son banquets and the like? What were the most rewarding aspects *to you* about your children's college years? Any interesting anecdotes about their respective boyfriends/girlfriends?

Were any of your children in military service? For what period of time? Did they serve in any overseas or off-continent assignments? In which branches of the military did they serve? What were their military specialties—that is, what jobs did they hold? What ranks did they hold at the time of their discharge? Did any remain in the reserves?

Which of your children was the first to marry? Did you feel that you were losing a child—or gaining one? When did he/she marry? Where did your child meet his/her future mate? Where were they married? Describe the wedding and reception. Where did they make their first home? When did they start their family? How many children, to date, their names and dates of birth? How did you feel about becoming a grandmother? Do you/did you play a major role in the upbringing of your grandchildren?

THE MATURE YEARS

During the decade of the '50s—from 1950 until 1960—what activities occupied most of your time? In what club, social or community activities were you active? What was the pattern of your social life? Who did you see; what did you do? What major events took place within the family from 1950 until 1960? Were any family members involved in the Korean military conflict? Did they come out of that war unscathed? What changes took place in your husband's career? Were there any major illnesses in the family within this decade? Did you lose any family members to death? Did you take any trips during that period of time? What role did you play as other grandchildren began to come along? How many grandchildren have you? What are their names and dates of birth? Are any of them especially accomplished? In what ways, and in what areas of endeavor? Who were your closest adult friends between 1950 and 1960?

Have you ever taken trips with your children and their families? How did these work out? Where did you go? For how long were you gone? Would you look forward to more such trips? How frequently do you see your children and grandchildren? How often do you talk with them on the telephone? Who usually telephones whom?

From 1960 until 1970, what major changes took place in your life? During this decade, what kinds of activities took up most of your time? Did you drop out of any groups in which you formerly had been active? Why? Did you join any new groups? Did you join any groups which sponsored activities for the retired? How do you feel about such groups? From 1960 until 1970, what hobbies did you pursue? Did you enjoy craftwork? With which of your friends did you spend the most time during the 1960s? Were you active in church?

With whom did you most regularly correspond? Did you note that your list of correspondents was diminishing because of attrition? Were you becoming more aware of your own mortality during this decade? Did you lose any family members during this ten-year period? Who were these relatives, and by what causes did they die? How did you spend your evenings during this period of your life? Playing cards or other games? Watching television? Writing letters? Attending concerts, the theater, or going to movies? What did you enjoy doing just "for fun"?

Did the Vietnam war affect your family? In what ways? Were any family members called to serve? Were they able to adjust satisfactorily to civilian life when they were discharged? How did you feel toward the young men who fled to Canada, or otherwise refused to serve in this war?

What major changes have taken place within your family between 1970 and the present? What great changes have taken place in your children's families? How has your health been during this span of time? What were some of the most happy, sad, or interesting happenings in your own life during these years? Have you taken any trips or vacations, or made new acquaintances which have proved to be rewarding?

CHAPTER THIRTEEN

A TIME FOR REFLECTION AND CONTRIBUTION:
The Years of Retirement

Those who decide to use leisure as a means of mental development, who love good music, good books, good pictures, good plays, good company, good conversation—what are they? They are the happiest people in the world.

— William Lyons Phelps

THE YEARS OF RETIREMENT

In the past, a great deal of gratuitous nonsense was written about leisure and retirement. The very word, "retirement," was seen as being synonymous with "end of the road," a formal precursor to death. Our grandfathers and fathers complained about being "put out to pasture" at the end of productive lives. Many loathed the thought of no longer "working for a living" with a kind of inchoate dread because the very word *retirement* seemed to denote uselessness. In the past, *retirement* was often a pejorative word which loosely defined that period of limbo between the accomplishments of the middle years and the finality of death. The state of being retired, was, to many hitherto productive men and women, society's ultimate condemnation to an idle life; a life of joyless futility. Compulsive workers found great difficulty in handling unstructured time which they might allot to quiet contemplation, reflection, and pursuits of their own choosing. And they were to be pitied.

We can only assume that it was Hemingway's *machismo* that prompted him to write: "Retirement is the ugliest word in the language." He so dreaded the thought (and actuality) of his own lessened productivity that he committed suicide in 1961. Another chap by the name of Geoffrey Fisher observed, "Who knows whether in retirement I shall be tempted to the last infirmity of mundane minds, which is to write a book." We biographers and company historians certainly don't want to have any truck with shortsighted claptrap such as *that*!

No, we would do better to embrace the ancient wisdom of Seneca and one of the Ciceros. Seneca wrote, "The gradually declining years are among the sweetest in a man's life." And Marcus Tullius Cicero said, "If the soul has food for study and learning, nothing is more delightful than an old age of leisure...Leisure consists in all those virtuous activities by which a man grows morally, intellectually, and spiritually. It is that which makes a life worth living."

Now we're talking!

Thankfully, most of today's retirees have awakened to the possibilities inherent in leisure. When the workplace is abandoned, retirees discover the joys of travel, of returning to school (not for the grades earned or degrees bestowed, but just for the sheer joy of learning), of cultivating new hobbies, and of spending more time pursuing lifelong interests.

As biographers and chroniclers of individual lives, we must be aware that retirement does not spell the end of life. And just because our clients have reached the age of sixty-five does not mean that they have one foot in the grave. The questions we ask during this latter section of our interviews must reflect our awareness that the questing spirits of our clients may *not* have been quelled by their departure from the workaday world or (by) the celebration of this or that "milestone" birthday.

A NEAR MISS

Not many years ago, I was concluding my interviews with a prominent Seattle executive and community leader. The biography I was writing for the family was really a joint effort, in which the lives of both husband and wife were to be chronicled. I had recorded some twenty hour-and-a-half cassette tapes, and presumed that we had captured all the essential information necessary for the crafting of a book.

Bill had retired from the merchandising phase of his work at age sixty, although he remained active on several boards of directors and played stellar roles in certain community organizations after his retirement. At the time the interviews were being conducted, Bill, and his delightful wife, Jan, lived quietly in a sylvan setting more than an hour's drive north of Seattle. The core of their home was what had once been their rustic fishing cabin, but the skills of an architect and the expenditure of a considerable sum of money had transformed the "fishing shack" into a spacious and luxurious retirement hideaway. Throughout the house were curios and artifacts from the four corners of the earth. It occurred to me that some of these had probably been picked up during visits to foreign lands, and thinking to put a "capper" on my interviews, formed another question in my mind.

It was definitely an afterthought when I asked, "And what of the years after your retirement, Bill? Did you and Jan do any traveling? Have any adventures worthy of note?"

The husband and wife exchanged glances, smiled, then burst into laughter.

Confused, I looked from one to the other. I was certain that I had made a gaffe, and scrambled to set the situation right.

"I obviously missed something," I chuckled. "Tell me where I missed the turning!"

Still smiling, Bill answered. "You might put it that way. You see, after I retired, Jan and I took some remarkable trips and had some fascinating adventures. I daresay that we have more than enough material for several *more* books. We'll have to see how the biography turns out, then we can talk about future writing projects."

"I presumed that when a person retired, well, that he *retired*!" My response was lame, and I must have looked puzzled, because Jan diplomatically hastened to explain.

"Bill and I laughed because it wasn't until *after* he had retired that we began some of the most exciting years of our lives. You see, in the late 1940s we had done some mammal collecting for the Field Museum of Natural History, in Chicago. But when we retired, more opportunities came our way—opportunities which allowed us to travel, and to contribute to the Museum's ongoing work in studying the worldwide distribution of mammals."

Bill lit a fragrant cigar, then continued where Jan had left off. "It wasn't until after I retired that we became so involved with the Field Museum. Then, as amateur collectors, we sponsored two expeditions to Iran, and collected and recorded data in Afghanistan, Nepal, Peru, and Western Australia. All with a minimum of professional help, you understand. But we always had at least a graduate zoologist, or mammalogist as a member of the team. We weren't just a couple of old crocks mucking about in the hinterlands, making a mess of things."

So. All retirees are not alike; stereotypical images of them can cause the unwary biographer to miss some great stories. Often it is the last stone overturned which reveals the most precious treasure.

Bill Street was right. There *were* more books in his and Jan's treasure-house of knowledge. I wrote one of these books (*Iranian Adventure—The First Street Expedition*) which was published in 1985 by the Field Museum of Natural History, and there may yet be other books which will derive from the same rich source.

If we, as chroniclers and biographers, are tempted to generalize our perceptions of retirees (our prospects and clients), we place at peril the quality of our work. I will let some of the promotional material for *Iranian Adventure* speak for itself. It dramatically illustrates the story I almost missed because of the mistaken assumption that retirement years are wasted years; years of unproductive woolgathering and the indulgence of sedentary pleasures.

PROMOTIONAL MATERIAL, IRANIAN ADVENTURE

"Do you view retirement as a barrier? Or as a wide-open gateway to adventure? Join two American retirees and a youth as they trek 15,000 miles across the deserts and wastelands of Iran—before Khomeini; before the hostages—in search of rare animals (some last reported in 1875) for Chicago's Field Museum of Natural History.

"Problem: Chicago's Field Museum of Natural History urgently needed an extensive update of its collection of mammals from Iran. The Museum had neither the funds nor the personnel to field a prolonged expedition.

"Solution: An American team of man and wife, recently retired, were in search of purposeful and useful adventure—and were willing to pay for it.

"When Problem and Solution are brought together, the resultant 15,000-mile, seven-month trek across the mountains and desert wasteland of Iran combine the ingredients for high drama. The natural perils of the terrain; the arduous, exacting, and sometimes dangerous nature of the work; the not-so-thinly veiled threats from fierce nomadic tribesmen, trigger-happy Russian border guards and uncertain government officials of a nation in turmoil, provide excitement for even the most jaded of armchair adventurers.

"Do you see retirement only as the opportunity to settle into a cozy armchair before the fire in some secluded restful haven? Not if your names are Bill and Jan Street! They willingly left behind the luxuries and comforts to which they had become accustomed—left them behind in their quest for knowledge and rare adventure. And they got more of both than they had bargained for!"

Iranian Adventure turned out to be quite a book, and a welcome second commission from a source I thought I had mined deeply and had exhausted! We learn to take nothing for granted.

THE PHILOSOPHIES OF A LIFETIME

It is in this section of our interviews that we may safely begin to explore some of the innermost thoughts of our clients. If all has worked as it should, by this time, writer and client have become friends as well as colleagues striving together to assemble the components of an important piece of work—the chronicle of a human life.

It is time to ask some exquisitely crafted and intensely personal questions. As probing as these questions may be, we dare not shy away from them. Without the answers to these finely tuned queries, our books and tapes will be but superficial and unsatisfying "treatments" of the lives we purport to represent. Our final products will be hollow, without the stuff of verity for which we so earnestly strive.

THE QUESTIONS

These, then, are examples of the questions I ask in the final phases of my interviews with clients.

In reviewing your life there must have been a number of forks in the road—turnings or alternatives in schooling, personal relationships, choices of employment. Have you ever been haunted by the feeling that perhaps you made an unwise choice, or that your life might have been more rewarding had you elected to move in a direction opposite or different from the one you chose at the time? How would you counsel your grandchildren about following their hearts and intuition vs. following logic, conscience, or "superior" counsel when making these difficult decisions which can influence an entire life?

What kinds of music do you listen to when you are alone? Have you favorite composers or schools of music you prefer above all others? Do you enjoy the legitimate theater? Have you supported the professional theatrical companies in your city, or participated in amateur or semiprofessional theatrical groups? Which would you rather attend—a legitimate play, a musical, an opera, a ballet, or a symphony concert? What makes you prefer one above the other?

What kinds of books do you most enjoy? Fiction or nonfiction? Why do you enjoy one over the other? Who is your favorite author? Your favorite book? Favorite poem? During this time of your life, what magazines do you usually buy on the newstands, or have delivered to your home? Which do you enjoy the most? Do these publications permit you to have a heightened insight into the kind of mature person you have become?

Have you ever, or do you now, make it a habit to set some time aside for quiet thought and contemplation—time when you are completely alone and away from people and the telephone? During these quiet times, what do you think about? Do the pressing issues of humanity, of war or peace, and of spiritual matters enter your thoughts? Have you ever asked yourself, "What is the purpose of life?" Did you come to any conclusion? What ought the goals of mankind to be? What is the cause of most of the world's problems?

Author, Kurt Vonnegut, Jr. once posed the rhetorical question: "What are people for, anyway?" How would you answer this question?

During your lifetime, you have seen great technological progress. As new ideas and goods come into being, others are lost or left behind. Which of those abandoned tools, devices, relics or ideas do you see as great losses to mankind? What do you miss the most? Why?

What is the most important lesson you have learned in a lifetime? What was the most *difficult* lesson for you to learn? How did you learn these great truths? Are you superstitious? About which symbols, talismans, omens or portents are you superstitious? Are you lucky or unlucky? What would lead you to such a conclusion?

Given the opportunity to relive any period in your life, what period would that be? Why? If you could have lived during any historical era, what time frame would you have chosen? Why? Who were the three most influential people in your life? Why them above all others? What were their roles? What did they contribute to your knowledge or well-being?

On the buying and consumption of goods. Do you buy the best you are able, keep things in good repair, and enjoy them until they are all but worn out? Were you reared by the philosophy of "Wear it out, use it up; make it last, or do without?" Do you heed fashion trends that dictate that our persons, our automobiles and our homes must reflect the latest and "best" in clothing, jewelry, transportation and decor? Do you consider yourself a "traditionalist"? How do you feel about advertising campaigns which create artificial "needs"—campaigns whose sole aim is to encourage the public to buy goods and services they could well do without? Do you resist these pressures, or do you usually go along with the latest rage? How have you counseled your children and grandchildren about buying, seeking out good value for money paid, and about the perils of "consumerism"? Do you use credit cards? Do you think everyone should use them? Why or why not? What are your feelings about America's "disposable" and "throw-away" philosophy whose profligacy depletes fast-disappearing world resources—forests, arable lands, minerals, petroleum?

What will the world be like in 500 years? Will our salvation (if mankind is to be saved) derive from economic, political, spiritual or personal change? A wise man once said that most of the world's problems are brought about by bad manners. What is the role of the individual in promoting peace and harmony among nations and peoples? In the centuries to come, do you see the intense nationalism (as represented by the pervading political stances of the 1980s) to be a greater or a lesser force in world affairs?

What is the role of spirituality in your life? By this I do *not* mean attending your church or synagogue. I refer to the spiritual relationship with your surroundings; with other people; with your universe and your deity. What differences do you see between a "religious" person and one who has strong spiritual beliefs? What are your feelings about the organized religions of our time? Do you see them as primarily devoted to the spiritual uplifting of individual congregations, or directed more to growth, expanded memberships and political activism? Do the "modern" stances of religious bodies please you?

Within memory, the United States came through one of the greatest traumas in our nation's history—Watergate, and the resignation of Richard Nixon as a president in disgrace. What conclusions have you drawn from this American tragedy? How could this have happened in this country? What can be done to prevent similar embarrassments from happening?

What are your feelings about the proposed Equal Rights Amendment to the U. S. Constitution? About the "women's liberation" movement of the '70s and '80s? What gains have women made since the days of your youth? Are there roles you believe women should not assume? What women do you most admire? Why? What men do you most admire? Why?

What are your feelings about:

1. Consumer protection advocacy
2. Zero population growth
3. Nuclear power/radioactive waste disposal
4. Alternative fuels for automobiles and industry
5. The proposed constitutional amendment forbidding the U.S. Government from spending more than it takes in
6. The "flat-rate" federal income tax
7. (Any other current world or national issue which you deem of importance in creating a sense of time-and-place for your biography.)

Tell me if you believe the following three principles (upon which our country was founded) are still true, and if they are still functioning in the United States today.

1. Government of the people, by the people and for the people. (Consider the impact of lobbyists, special-interest groups, pressures brought to bear on legislators, and bribes to foreign purchasers by U. S. businessmen.)
2. The free enterprise system in which supply and demand determine both the price of commodities and goods, and the wages paid to workers. (Consider the impact of trade unions, closed shops, wildcat strikes, Fair Trade laws, corporate price fixing, government subsidies and artificial price supports.)

3. Equal justice under the law. (Consider white-collar crime; crime in government; sentences given to affluent lawbreakers with high-priced attorneys as contrasted with those sentences meted out to low-income prisoners who must depend upon public defenders.)

Have you traditionally voted Republican or Democrat? Why have you maintained this allegiance? Have you ever "switched" parties to support a particular candidate? Which candidate was this? Do you feel that the two-party system should be retained, or is it time to examine the advisability of creating a third or even a fourth political party? Would you like to see new political parties to the right or the left of existing parties? How would you feel about adapting certain features of the English parliamentary system of accountability for the chief executive? By this mechanism, it would be possible to call our president before the combined houses to report on his actions, then be subjected to a vote of confidence or no-confidence. During your lifetime, which presidential election was most memorable for you? During your lifetime, who was your favorite president? Why?

What are your feelings about our government's welfare and public assistance programs, now euphemistically called "entitlements"? How do you feel about the food-stamp program? Social Security? Medicare and Medicaid? Aid to dependent children? Equal-opportunity employment?

Do you have confidence in our current president? Why, or why not? What should be our relationship with Communist China? How do you view the arms race and the relationship we have with Russia? Do you approve or disapprove of the "star wars" defense system being proposed by our government? Should we enter into trade agreements and sell wheat and other commodities to the Russian communists?

What degree of confidence do you have in the governor of your state? Why, or why not? Is he or she a member of your chosen political party? On what state issues do you have the strongest opinions? Please expand on this issue. Have you confidence in the mayor of your community? Why or why not? On what community issues do you feel most strongly? Explain.

How important is love in your life? What role does it play? Tell me about your love for children; for your spouse; for family; for friends. What has it meant to you? What do you believe your love has meant to them? It has been said that the more love is given away, the more it increases. Would you comment on this observation?

What are your feelings about the institution of marriage? Of divorce? The practice of unmarried men and women living together? What purpose does marriage serve? What is the key to a successful marriage? Should unhappy marriages be preserved "for the sake of the children"?

What are the rewards, sorrows, and penalties of having children? What is the greatest joy in having children? What are your feelings about abortion?

Of eating and drinking. What is the importance of food to you? Is it more than just sustenance? Is dining an aesthetic experience as well as a necessary one? How about the importance of alcoholic beverages? What role has the consumption of alcohol played in your life? In the lives of those nearest you? What counsel would you give to your grandchildren and great-grandchildren on the blessings—and sorrows—attendant to drinking ethyl alcohol?

What is your philosophy on the joy—or drudgery—of work?

What of the clothing you wear? How important is it for you to be properly attired for every occasion? Where do you buy most of your clothing? Why? If there were no social pressures—no "dress code"—how would you clothe yourself?

What is your philosophy of crime and punishment? Do you believe in capital punishment? If so, for what crimes? Do you believe our present penal system is working? If not, what reforms would you suggest deserve a try? Is our judicial system tough enough on criminals? Does our present judicial system have more compassion for the criminal than for the victim? How did you feel about the 1985 shooting in a New York subway (Note: substitute any major case now making national headlines), in which a crime victim shot four young men who had demanded money of him? What is your position on gun control? Do you believe that registration of guns would lead to taxation of firearm ownership, and eventually to the confiscation of all personal weapons—as it has in certain European countries? In view of the current world situation, would you like to see an unarmed American citizenry?

What observations have you made about the roles of reason vs passion; judgment vs appetite, i.e., doing what our minds tell us is socially acceptable vs doing what our bodies and our emotions want us to do? How would you counsel your descendents of the wisdom of moderation—compromise—particularly as regards sexual matters?

What have you learned about emotional and physical pain? What was the most physically painful moment of your life? When did you feel the greatest emotional pain and turmoil? Is there merit in not complaining when something hurts? Does stoicism have a place in your life, or do you show it when you hurt? Is there profit in pain, or is pain a valueless experience in feeling?

Please speak to your heirs about the importance of continued learning and the lifelong acquisition of knowledge. How may we cultivate and nurture a curiosity which will endure for all of our years? Where have you garnered most of what you know? From people? From experience? From books and study?

What of our public school systems today? We see high school graduates incapable of understanding the questions on job applications, and incapable of filling them out. These same high school graduates are so untutored that, as military inductees they must be taught, through comic-strip pictographs, how to operate the weapons with which they must defend our nation. So that this deplorable situation may be corrected, what demands must be made of our school boards, our teachers, and our students in the public schools? What are the parents' responsibilities in this sorry scenario?

On friendship. Are you a good friend? What is a good friend? Do you have good friends? What is their value to you? Of what value are you to them? What have friendships brought you? Have you sought the advice and solace of your friends in times of trouble? Have you usually taken their counsel? Do they, in turn, ask your advice? Do you go to your friends in times of trouble, or only in times of joy? When sympathy and compassion are offered you, are you able to accept these gestures in good grace?

Time. How important is time? Can one waste time? What activities or pursuits do you consider wastes of time? In your life, has time run you, or have you governed time?

Good and evil. To you, what is good? What is evil? Do all of us contain some good and some evil? What marks the good person? The person of evil? How do you evaluate those persons with whom you come in contact? How can you discern the good; recognize the evil?

What of wealth and riches? Is the accumulation of material wealth a worthy goal in itself, or does the striving for and accumulating of wealth—as an end in itself—seem to be a goal which would not bring completely satisfying returns? If not just for the money, or the things that money will buy, why is the accumulation of wealth seemingly paramount in the minds of so many of us? Once attained, to what uses should wealth be put? In short, what does lots of money "buy" us?

Supernatural phenomena. Have you or any members of your family ever experienced anything of the supernatural or unexplainable? Contacts with "spirits"? Poltergeists? Ghosts? Extrasensory perception? Precognition? Visions? Levitation? Telekinesis? Out-of-body experiences in the near-death syndrome? What untapped or little-used "powers" do humans have which we either do not exercise, or which we do not recognize? What are your feelings about UFOs—unidentified flying objects? Visits to earth by extraterrestrials? Do you believe that life will be found on other planets? What are your feelings about the exploration of space, manned flights to other planets, and the sending of deep-space probes by the U.S. and Russia? Are these ventures worth the expense? Do you believe them to be necessary or unnecessary?

What is your feeling about prayer? Do you pray? Regularly? For what or whom do you pray? Of what value is prayer to you? How do you see the being or the entity to which you pray—is it an anthropomorphic God who looks like a person, or is it an uncorporeal or bodiless spirit to whom you direct your prayers? Have you ever had a spiritual experience—a spiritual awakening or revelation? If so, could you put this experience in words, and describe how it changed the course of your life?

What roles have humor and laughter played in your life? How important are they to you? What do they do for you—and what good is a joke? Have you a sense of humor? Do you enjoy practical jokes when you are the butt of them? When they are played on others? Describe the most effective practical joke in which you have been a participant.

Pleasure. How would you define it? What sorts of things give you pleasure? When you seek pleasure, where do you usually find it? Can you enjoy pleasure alone, or must pleasure always be shared with someone close to you? What hobbies have you pursued at various parts of your lifetime? Which of your hobbies has persisted for the longest time, and which has given you the greatest pleasure?

What was the single, happiest moment in your life?

What was the most sorrowful moment in your life?

What was the greatest single disappointment you ever experienced?

What of death? All of us have thought of it, and either fear it or accept its inevitability philosophically. Do you fear it and avoid talking about it, or do you accept the idea with good grace? How do you regard your own death? How do you feel about death when it claims a dear friend or a member of the family? If it could be granted you, how would you choose to die? Is the death of your earthly body the end of your existence as a spiritual entity? Do you believe there is life after death—that there is a hereafter? Do you believe that you have lived before? Can you describe anything about your previous lives?

Do you believe that you will live again, and if so, how do you envision this afterlife? Do you expect to retain your human shape, or do you see it as a purely spiritual and ethereal existence without bodily substance? Do you believe that your actions in this life determine the quality or conditions of your next life? Do we choose the conditions or paths of our lives, or does fate play a part in our worldly affairs? Are your beliefs solely Christian, or have you "borrowed" certain beliefs from other religions or philosophies?

You have gone to a great deal of effort to provide these tapes/typescripts/books for members of your family who will come after you. As we were working on this project together, what family members entered your mind most frequently? (Get the full names.) What values do you hope they will find in our completed project? One hundred years from now, how do you think the importance of this biographical legacy will "stack up" against the material legacies you left behind? Would you qualify your answer to explain why you believe as you do?

Are there questions you hoped that I would ask, but have not? If so, what areas should be discussed which we have thus far treated superficially or omitted altogether?

You and I have created something of great value. Please think carefully, then give me the names of three of your friends whom you believe would most appreciate the merit in the concept of biography as legacy. It is my plan to contact them to give them the same opportunity as you have enjoyed—the opportunity of "setting straight the record" for their family and friends.

THE LIST IS ENDLESS AND EVER-CHANGING

Chapters ten through thirteen provide only samples of the kind of questions we must ask. And those questions are the framework we as biographers must construct so that we may build for our client a sturdy and lasting literary structure. When the tool-and-diemaker creates his die of sand, he knows that when the part is cast in metal, it will be only as good as the impression he has made in the sand. So it is with the biographer and company historian. The material from which we must write our books will only be rich if our interview questions have been rich and well thought out. And while the questions we may ask our clients are as limitless as the stars in the heavens, they must be thoughtfully crafted.

We've all heard dumb questions asked by unprepared or thoughtless television and radio interviewers, as in the stale old joke:

"And other than that, Mrs. Lincoln, how did you like the play?"

And the TV reporter, live and at-the-scene following a tornado. "What were your feelings, sir, when you came home from work to find your home destroyed, your crops and livestock gone, and your wife and four children missing?"

These are examples of bad, even vicious, interview questions.

It is possible to be thoughtful, yet thorough, in carrying out the questioning of our clients. We may probe but we may not pry. We can be exhaustive but not exhausting. And we must know when it is time to quit the questioning and get on with the crafting of a book.

CHAPTER FOURTEEN

THE INTERVIEW:
Drawing Out the Best in Your Client

I am not a better man, certainly, for having written his life; but I think that I am a wiser one. And I can only hope that my gratitude to him for that will lighten a little the onus of the life with which I have burdened him.

— Mark Shorer, after having written the life of Sinclair Lewis

DRAWING OUT THE BEST IN YOUR CLIENT

Although Chapter Fifteen will be devoted largely to the selection and use of recording and transcribing equipment, it is not unseemly to insert an admonition here. *Check your recording equipment thoroughly before leaving your home or office!* Not to do so is to invite disaster.

I was once scheduled to interview one of Seattle's most high-powered executives. His company had commissioned me to write a corporate history of the firm, and this man's contribution to the book was of considerable importance. The fellow was so busy that I had had to wait for more than a week before his secretary could schedule the two-hour time slot I had requested for the interview.

I was punctual, of course, and had my tape recorder and list of questions at the ready. Right on the dot of the appointed hour, the man's secretary ushered me into his plush thirty-eighth-floor office—a suite which commanded a breathtaking view of Elliott Bay and the Olympic Mountains beyond. There was no doubt that I was standing on some of the most costly real estate in the city, and was in the presence of one of Seattle's most marketable business talents. Most of us could live comfortably for a year or two on what this man earned in one month as a financial consultant. And his time was so valuable that I shuddered to think what his hourly consultation fees might be.

During earlier, planning meetings, this man and I had established a comfortable rapport, and I was by no means overawed by him. But I wasn't foolish enough to be profligate with his time, either. He had little of it to spare, and none of it to waste. We exchanged brief pleasantries, then I got right down to business. I plugged my tape recorder into a wall outlet, slipped a tape into the machine, and settled into a comfortable chair. I opened my notes to my first interview question, then pushed down the two buttons on my tape recorder that put it into the "record" mode—and nothing happened! The buttons refused to stay depressed, as they should.

I fussed and fumed for a moment, trying again and again to get the buttons to stay in the "down" position, but all to no avail. It was totally frustrating. I don't know how many hundreds of times I had duplicated those same motions, and every time before, the dependable little Sony had entered the "record" mode and performed like a perfect champion. (For several years I had carried a spare, or "back-up" tape recorder with me, but because of the utter dependability of the machine I used, I had abandoned that practice some months before.) But on this day, and before this important client, the tape recorder balked—and I panicked.

"I don't know what's the matter with this damned thing, Stu," I said. "It's never done this before."

"Here, let me give it a try," he said. "I've got one just like it at home, and I've never had any trouble with it."

So saying, he arose from the couch and we both crouched over the coffee table, two grown men fussing and fretting over a mute and recalcitrant bit of Japanese electronics that had us both stumped. Had it not been so costly (in terms of man-hours wasted), the situation would have been comical. As it was, it was merely absurd and embarrassing.

After some minutes of fumble-fingered fiddling and subdued curses, Stu's eyes met mine across the malevolent black box.

"I'm licked," he said. "I don't know what the hell's the matter with it."

"And I'm as apologetic as can be," I said. "It was working just fine yesterday, and I haven't had it out of the case since then."

"Well, I can salvage some of the morning, and we'll just have to reschedule the interview. I have to go to Hong Kong next week, but speak to Joann on your way out and ask her when she can schedule us for another get-together again early next month."

As I departed, I shook his hand, and again expressed my disappointment at the vagaries of my equipment. I also muttered something about having to take my recorder into the shop for a complete going-over so that the unfortunate incident would not be repeated. Stu and I parted amicably enough, but something in his eyes told me that any future unpreparedness on my part would not be so lightly forgiven.

When I arrived home, I again removed the tape recorder from its case and plugged it's cord into the outlet. Same story. The "record" and "forward" buttons still would not remain depressed. Almost as a last resort, I removed the tape cassette from the machine and examined it closely. It was a perfectly good cassette, and nothing met the eye—until I looked carefully at the *back edge* of the dratted thing!

And, you know those two little tabs that can be broken off to prevent a tape from being re-recorded? Sure enough, they had been snapped off! Instantly, I felt like a complete sap! Obviously, the tape was one that I had used for other purposes, and at some time or other, I had thought to preserve what was on that tape—and had snapped off the tabs. When I placed bits of masking tape over the two holes (left when the tabs had been snapped off), the machine functioned perfectly.

Three weeks later, when I again scheduled an interview with my busy executive, I told him in all honesty that my recorder was now functioning perfectly. What I *didn't* tell him was that the recorder was also functioning perfectly the last time we had met—but that it was his dolt of a *company historian* who had been functioning at less than peak efficiency!

So! Know that your equipment is working perfectly before you depart for your appointment. Much needless embarrassment can be avoided by a two-minute recorder check just before you are to meet your client.

One other caution. *Do not routinely depend on batteries or rechargeable battery packs to get you through your interviews!* When conventional AC power is available, by all means, plug in and use it. I even carry an extension cord in my tape-recorder case so that I can tie into house current even though the outlet is some distance from where my interviewee chooses to sit. Sawyer's Maxim: *Batteries only fail during critical moments of an interview, or during situations which can never be recaptured.*

WHERE TO HOLD YOUR INTERVIEWS

Psychologically, it is best to hold your interviews in some quiet setting on your client's home turf. Being surrounded by familiar sights, sounds and smells is conducive to productive interviews. The more intimate the setting, the better. If your client is at home with his surroundings, and feels unthreatened, he will be as much at ease as he ever will be in an interview situation.

If you interview your client in a business office, ask if the secretary cannot hold all but the most urgent of telephone calls until the interview has been concluded. Whether at the office, the club, or in a private home it is important that you and your client are on a one-to-one relationship without third-party presence or intrusion. Only rarely have I interviewed a man and wife or business partners at the same time. Although it is sometimes necessary to interview two or more people at the same time, to do so is to invite garbled tapes and unintelligible cross-talk impossible for the typist to transcribe. Avoid if possible!

The quality of the interview setting is important, and often the writer is able to influence where the work takes place. The client will often ask, "Where would you like to sit?" Or, if this opening is not afforded, the writer will do well to take the initiative by saying (upon spotting a likely setting for the interview), "Will it be all right if we work over here?"

During the interview, distance between client and writer is the enemy. You want to be close without being either threatening or overfamiliar. And I don't like massive pieces of furniture, such as desks and dining room tables—between me and my interview subject. Such physical separation somehow fosters feelings of emotional and psychological separation; the very mind-sets we assiduously attempt to overcome.

If desks and tables are part of the interview-site furnishings, it is much better for interviewer and client to sit 90 degrees from one another. If your client "barricades" himself behind his desk, protected by the pen-and-pencil set, the multiple telephones and the other accouterments of power, execute an "end run" and seat yourself at the *end* of the desk rather than directly across from your subject. Being seated directly across from your subject subtly implies an adversarial relationship, and it is possible for your interview to get off on the wrong foot.

Many settings in the home promote feelings of coziness and confidentiality. Some of my most productive interviews have been held in breakfast nooks and the sitting rooms or dens of private homes. The most deadly settings can be large, formal living rooms in which the client seems to be attempting to put some distance between himself and that *bete noire* of the microphone! Such caution and reserve is demonstrated by very few clients, but when it exists, it must be countered and overcome with tact coupled with a touch of savoir faire if the interviews are to proceed satisfactorily.

A *quiet* location for your interviews is a must! Background noise can wreak havoc with the quality of your tapes. I once attempted to interview a man in his office—situated on a balcony overlooking a manufacturing area which contained an array of heavy punch presses! The constant cacophony of "Ker-chunk...shhh! Ker-chunk...shhh!" made conversation all but impossible. The man had worked in that noisy environment for so many years he was oblivious to the racket. We moved to the unoccupied board room for our interviews, and all was well.

In the home setting, telephones, yapping poodles, screaming kids can all offer their share of frustrations when attempting to produce clear, intelligible tape recordings. One dear lady I interviewed owned a couple of obstreperous boxer dogs, and in "shushing" them, her language was more colorful than anything else on the tapes! Another dear soul thought it would be pleasant to hold our interviews on the deck of her lanai, overlooking the placid waters of Lake Washington. Unfortunately, her home was situated near the hydroplane pits and on a flyway favored by the pilots of float planes. Thus it was that, interspersed with perfumed reminiscences and memories of scented evenings of the long-ago, the howls of supercharged sixteen-cylinder Allison aircraft engines and the snarl of Lycoming and Continental light-plane powerplants fouled my tapes. The incongruity was delightful; but when my typist tried to transcribe the tapes, she was ready to go for my throat!

Be aware of extraneous noises; seek a quiet place!

SETTING THE MOOD FOR THE INTERVIEW

Webster's Ninth New Collegiate Dictionary defines *ambience* as a feeling or mood associated with a particular place, person or thing: atmosphere. And the ambience you and your client establish during your hours together will add or detract from the quality of work you produce.

Ambience is a simple word which defines a complex set of circumstances. While the word itself is precise, that which it describes is imprecise, ephemeral, constantly in a state of flux, and difficult to pin down. The best we can do is to be aware of the many components which go into the creation of our interview-situation ambience, and work to promote those elements which we have found to be helpful.

We've already discussed *place*, and the important role it plays in providing an atmosphere conducive to the relaxed interchange of ideas between you and your client. I have found the exchange of a few minutes of small talk to be helpful before getting down to business. Much of this "mood creation" must follow your inborn instincts—a fancy way of saying, "Play it by ear." The discussion of the weather and the state of garden bulbs might be quite appropriate as pre-interview pleasantries exchanged with an elderly woman with time on her hands. The same casual exchange would be decidedly *in*appropriate for the busy executive who apportions the minutes of his business day with the reluctance of a miser doling out gold coins.

The key, I think, is in the naturalness of your scene dressing. A businesslike tone may be established by your client, and if this is so, by all means go along with it with grace and understanding. Conversely, a lighter, social note may be struck between you and your client, and this is, of course, ideal. The interview should be no more stressful than an occasion of interested conversation between old friends as they exchange confidences.

It seems hardly necessary to mention that the interviewer should smoke only if invited to do so, or if the client also periodically lights up during the interview. As to dress, I have found myself to be most comfortable when my garb is not more casual than that of my client. We are, after all, business people, and should appear for our interviews in presentable clothing. There are exceptions. I have interviewed several of my clients in rural or rustic settings, and because casual, outdoor clothes were *de rigueur*, I dressed accordingly. I find it best to let the client establish the pattern of dress, and for the writer to follow suit. What is to be avoided is excessive contrast. If your client habitually greets you in a dressing gown or in khakis and work boots, it is a sort of put-down for you to arrive in a modish three-piece suit or a too precious little-bit-of-froth from a "label" couturier. Let common sense be your guide, but don't underdress your client.

As interview follows interview, and familiarity with your client leads to friendship (as it almost invariably does), the mutual feeling of ease will bloom, and these guidelines will become unnecessary. "Interview days" become social occasions eagerly anticipated by both you and your client. Often, you will find that small social niceties are introduced into the proceedings. Some of my clients have taken the small interruption when the tape cassette must be reversed (after 45 minutes of work) as an appropriate time to trot out the tea and the cookies, or have the secretary serve coffee.

Be assured that after the first two or three interviews with your clients, any tension which might have insinuated itself into the first meeting or two will disappear, and *mood* will take care of itself. You and your client will find yourselves on a joyful treasure hunt, carried out with the utmost of amiability, in which you, together, sort through the riches of a lifetime.

MYTHS EXPLODED; BUGABOOS DEBUNKED

When I first entered the field of biographies and company histories, I was momentarily dismayed at one of the reactions I sometimes received during selling interviews. When prospective clients, particularly elderly women, learned that I used a tape recorder in my work, they showed some signs of alarm.

"Oh, I couldn't talk into one of those things," one whispy little thing fluttered. "I'd just freeze right up and wouldn't be able to say a word!"

An executive told me, "I don't know how well your tape-recording is going to work. Even after all these years in management, I still cannot use a dictating machine with any sense of assurance. I 'Uh' and 'Er' a lot, and frankly become quite ill at ease and tongue-tied. I write in longhand most of my important written communications, then have my secretary type them up for my signature."

To each of these prospects, and to others like them, I made small reassuring noises—all the while feeling a sinking sensation in the pit of my stomach, and having little confidence in what I told them. I didn't know but what there *was* a real "mike-fright" syndrome. I wasn't sure that someone *wouldn't* freeze up solid, unable to speak a word, at the very sight of a tape recorder.

After signing my first client, it was with some misgivings that I set up my recorder for the first interview. Giving some credence to the mike-fright syndrome, I did not use the hand-held microphone which came with my recorder, but depended instead upon the less obvious self-contained microphone built into the case of my machine.

As I surveyed the interview setting, the recorder tucked unobtrusively on the coffee table between a stack of *Smithsonians* and a candy dish, it seemed suitably benign and unthreatening. Yet my client, Peggy, a woman in her late seventies, eyed the offending Sony with obvious alarm. She chirped and chattered as nervously as a gravid sparrow regarding a cobra suddenly thrust into her nest.

"Am I going to have to *talk* into that...that *thing*?" she whimpered.

I assured her that within five minutes she would forget that the tape recorder was even in the room. When I had positioned the recorder, I had taken care to depress the two buttons which put it into the *record* mode. A hand-held remote "on-off" switch (connected by a long cord to the recorder) allowed me to begin recording almost surreptitiously, with no more obvious motion than a slight movement of my thumb. This "on-off" unit, on its six-foot cord, permitted me to start or stop the recording without calling undue attention to the fact.

"Is that thing on yet?" Peggy asked.

"No," I said with complete honesty. "We haven't yet begun to record."

Apparently mollified, she sniffed slightly, and made me the gift of a slight smile.

We talked for a few minutes, then I produced my list of questions. Without being obvious about it, I started the tape recorder and began the interview. As we progressed, Peggy grew more and more voluble, and the information just gushed from her as from a flowing well. Questions triggered answers which in turn set off chain-reaction recollections, and we were moving along swimmingly. Peggy was obviously enjoying the experience, and appeared delighted to have someone actually interested in listening to the stories she had been "saving up" all the years of her life.

We talked—or rather, *she* talked, and I listened—for the better part of forty-five minutes. Just as I was about to stop the machine to turn over the cassette, Peggy paused, then looked at me thoughtfully.

"Well," she said, "I guess you can turn on your recorder, now, and we'll see how I do."

"It's been running all along, Peggy. We got it all!"

Her eyes widened. "You mean...?"

"Yes," I said. "We have forty-five minutes worth of wonderful information that will be in your book. And I think you'll agree that it didn't hurt a bit."

"Didn't feel a thing," she said. Then her face broke into the radiant smile which I would come to know so well, and her eyes crackled with mischief.

"You fooled me, you did! And I have to admit that being interviewed is a damsite more fun than having a root canal." Her unrestrained laugh was my signal that we were off to the races, and would be plagued no more with imaginary mike-fright or recorder reticence.

Put these myths out of your mind. In more than a decade of interviewing people and recording data for personal biographies, magazine and newspaper articles, and corporate histories, I have never found *anyone* who could not or would not work with a tape recorder running. There may be such people, but with a little assurance from the interviewer, most of our prospects and clients will become comfortable in a "mike-on" situation within the very first moments of the initial interview.

Mike-fright and tape-recorder paralysis are but paper tigers easily put to flight.

THE INTERVIEW

As orderly persons, we tend to organize almost everything from grocery lists to the agenda of our busy days. And we usually do first things first, and follow a certain "order of business" so that we accomplish what we have set out to do in a timely fashion.

As biographers and writers we have been taught to prepare ourselves for interviews by writing out lists of questions we plan to ask of our subjects. Thus prepared, we must caution ourselves, however, *not to regard our lists of questions as sacrosanct!* There is nothing sacred about them! And there is no "right" order in which they should be asked. In writing them down, we have followed a simple chronology only because to do so is logical and easy.

We must remember that we have our lists of questions for only three reasons:

1. We don't want to leave anything out;
2. The questions serve as a "road map" clearly defining route and destination, and;
3. The questions provide a "point of return" following our clients' inevitable digression from the script and excursions into unexplored territory.

I caution the neophytic interviewer not to panic when your interview subject abandons your carefully prepared script and goes plunging off into the underbrush by himself. No harm has been done! You may not know where he is going, and you may not always be able to see him—but you can hear him thrashing around out there, and you know that you can always "bring him back home" again. After all, you have a "locater beacon" (your questions), so you always know where to find him and how to get him back on the track if he gets lost out there in the tules.

The truth of the matter is that you *want* your subject to become discursive. Ideally, some of your questions will trigger reminiscences which will in turn spark recollections of yet other yarns, situations and people in your subject's past. Let 'em ramble! Give your subjects their heads! Allow them free rein! After all, the more of this project they take on for themselves, the more spontaneous will be your material. Ultimately, you will be able to produce an eminently readable book which will just *crackle* with life-like dialogue and incident. And all because you learned to be *a good listener!*

When your interview subject has taken one of these little fliers into the great beyond, and seems to have run out of steam, you can bring him back to the present by some device such as: "That was a fascinating bit of information about your Aunt Maudie's little dalliance with the Fuller Brush man. But before that, we were talking about..." And you're back on the track, following your list of prepared questions.

You see, the *order* in which you record the information is unimportant. You're going to have to reorganize all of the data anyway. The important thing is to keep your client interested, involved, and talking volubly. Once you create an atmosphere in which one idea triggers another, and they start igniting one another like successive firecrackers in a string, you know that you have a successful interview going. You're after that chain reaction of ideas.

Many years ago, in an Atomic Energy Commission film which attempted to portray the principle of the nuclear chain reaction, the special-effects people used mousetraps and ping-pong balls to illustrate the idea. The floor of an immense gymnasium was covered with ordinary mousetraps, each "set," and upon which ping-pong balls had been carefully placed. To illustrate the principle of the chain reaction, a *single* ping-pong ball was tossed onto this field of set mousetraps. After the first trap snapped, one saw a few ping-pong balls in the air; then more; and more and more until the air above the gym floor was a white flurry of flying celluloid balls.

And that is what we are trying to do with our provocative interview questions. We want to set off chain reactions in our clients' minds—chain reactions that will result in flurries of wonderful ideas, each close on the heels of another, which will add the leavening, the spice, and the substance to our books.

Perhaps the *worst* tactic an interviewer can evidence is *impatience*! We must resist the temptation to keep our interview subjects on too tight a leash! And even though we are impatient for our subjects to get on with their stories, we must bite our tongues so that we do not jump in too quickly with the next question on our list.

Remember that nature abhors a vacuum. Long silences on radio or television are referred to in the trade as "dead air." And dead air is costly. But in an interview, dead air can work to your benefit. After your client has finished a story, and has seemed to run down, resist the temptation to quickly ask the next question. Instead, *look* at him expectantly, as if you anticipated a fuller response to the previous question. Let him stew in his own juices for a moment, and use eye contact and subtle body language to show that you expect more.

(After one such silent exchange, a client of mine picked up on an entirely different train of thought and continued talking through an entire forty-five-minute taping sequence—without once being prompted by me! It was a remarkable and revealing monologue which produced one of the most exciting chapters in an extraordinary book.)

More often than not, your client will begin to speak once again, often probing more deeply into his memory than he had thought possible, bringing forth facts or opinions which he had once thought only a part of his most private preserve. It is in such instances that barriers between writer and subject tumble, and we are made privy to the inner recesses of our clients' minds. It is here, too, where we must exercise the most prudent judgment, and vindicate ourselves as the professionals we are. Occasionally, our clients will talk more freely than they intended; be more open than they planned; become more vulnerable than they would elect to be. When it comes to writing our books, we must exercise restraint and good taste, usually opting for the more conservative than the flamboyant. Each case is different; each must be judged on its own merits.

THIS IS NOT *60 MINUTES*!

When a skilled dentist begins probing a sensitive area of an exposed tooth, his touch is light and his manner reassuring. He doesn't go stomping in there wielding a tire iron and chiding us insensitively for being intimidated.

We would be well advised to use the same kind of restraint when *we* begin to probe the sensitive areas of our clients' psyches. If we are quick to detect the subtle indications that we may be drilling close to a nerve, we will not run the risk of offending our interview subjects. And, lest we become carried away with the gravity of the work before us, we may want to remind ourselves occasionally that we are not grilling robbery suspects; we are not playing the role of Mike Wallace on *60 Minutes*; we are not Tomás de Torquemada of the Spanish Inquisition.

Rather, we will couch our questions as tactfully as possible, and in such a manner as to inspire trust and confidence. As the writer/client relationship grows and deepens, you will find that you are delving ever more deeply into the hidden recesses of the life you will be recreating. You will enter the *sanctum sanctora*, hitherto opened only to family members, and perhaps the family's physician, lawyer, or clergyman.

As one so honored, it is well to step lightly.

CHAPTER FIFTEEN

THE TOOLS OF THE TRADE:
From Tape To Typescript

Man is a tool-using animal...Without tools he is nothing, with tools, he is all.

— Thomas Carlyle

Every business requires, at the outset, an investment in capital equipment. The entrepreneur must secure those tools necessary to perform the work to which the business is dedicated, and locate a worksite from which to conduct his operations. A retailer must locate and equip a vacant store and invest in an inventory of the goods he will sell. A machinist must find a suitable industrial building, buy lathes and milling machines and grinders, and purchase the metal stock from which he will fabricate his products. A mechanic must locate a garage from which to operate, and invest in costly tools, cranes, and specialized equipment necessary to his trade. In addition, he must stock a broad inventory of spare parts for each of the cars and trucks he proposes to service.

In each of the above cases, the cost of getting into business for oneself—of capitalizing a new enterprise—can be immense. The retailer, the machinist, or the mechanic is faced with pungling up anywhere from $50,000 to the-sky's-the-limit before he earns a dime. And it usually means that the would-be business owner must mortgage his house, borrow from a lending institution, or exhaust his savings and life-insurance equities to come up with the necessary cash.

In comparison, the free-lance biographer and company historian has it easy! He can work out of his home or apartment, and the capital outlay for necessary equipment is small indeed, when put alongside the expenditures necessary to get more conventional businesses off the ground.

Assuming that the biographer *manque* has nothing more than this great idea and the will to succeed, an initial capital outlay of less than $1,000 will be sufficient.

Let's see what we need to set up shop.

THE "WHY" OF USING A TAPE RECORDER

A small, dependable cassette tape recorder is an absolute necessity. Newspaper reporters and magazine writers may be able to get along with shorthand note-taking, but for the kinds of extended interviews conducted by biographers and company historians, the tape recorder is indispensable.

The reason for this is simple. While reporters for newspapers (and for that matter, for radio and television) depend upon the *highlights* of a story—going only for the *essence* of what the interview subject says—biographers seek a deeper, fuller picture of the persons they interview. It may sound unfair to say that media reporters cover their subjects only superficially, but that observation is most often true. They are trying to fill 10 column inches of type or a two-minute TV spot, and that is all they have space or time for. We, on the other hand, are crafting portraits of whole *lives*, and must be far more exhaustive, and exact, in our approach.

The hen-scratch notes of media reporters are good enough for the small amount of material needed to fill the space or the time slot allotted to them. Our mission, however, is quite different, and the only satisfactory method quickly at hand for us depends upon the use of recorded interviews. Total accuracy and comprehensive coverage should be hallmarks of the work of competent biographers/historians. The only way we may assure ourselves—and our clients—that we will produce such work is by capturing not the "essence" of what is said during interviews, but *exactly* what is said, in the subject's own words, and with his inflections and nuances undistorted by our hasty interpretations and suppositions made while we scurry to take notes.

THE TAPE RECORDER

Cassette tape recorders may be bought for as little as $29.95. You can also spend several thousand dollars for a Nagra or a Uher equipped with enough bells and whistles to challenge an audio engineer. I would recommend neither extreme.

Somewhere in the $85.00 to $200.00 range there are a score of rugged, high quality, dependable cassette tape recorders that are eminently suited to our needs. In my own experience, I have been earning my living with tape recorders for more than twenty years—and I have bought just *two* cassette tape recorders! The first was a Sony TC-110; the second a Sony TC-110A, which is still going strong. With a little care in handling and only minimal maintenance, such machines will go on and on, good for thousands of hours of use.

Accessories with the Sonys which I have found to be useful are the hand-held "on-off" switch (mentioned in an earlier chapter), the NiCd (nickel-cadmium) rechargeable battery pack, and an "on-off" foot pedal which allows the tape recorder to be used as a playback machine when transcribing the recorded tapes.

I like the hand-held "on-off" switch because it can be held in the palm of the hand, and the recording stopped or restarted at any time during the interview without having to call attention to the fact that such is being done. If you share my distrust of mechanical devices, you probably do what *I* do.

When I punch the two buttons which put the machine into the "record" mode, I always peek to make certain that the tape transport system is working properly (that the recording tape is moving from one reel to the other). Bad light often requires that I stand, and look directly down on the machine. And if there are numerous interruptions, I don't like to be hopping up and down like a jumping jack each time I start or stop the machine. Such behavior on the part of the interviewer makes the subjects nervous, and besides, I feel like an idiot leaping about like a frog on a string. The easily palmed "on-off" switch does away with all these unseemly gymnastics, and gives the writer a great sense of security and control.

The NiCd battery pack is a godsend. To this date, I've never lost an interview because my batteries have gone dead at just the wrong moment. By letting your rechargeable NiCd batteries charge overnight (just plug your recorder into any wall socket), you will have fully charged the battery pack, and will be assured of six or eight hours of uninterrupted power for your recordings. And while I always use house current when it is available, I never count on it being there when I need it.

I have successfully conducted interviews during power outages, in automobiles, on sailboats far from shore (and AC current!), and while strolling in the woods with my clients. Though rarely needed, the self-contained power supply provides a flexibility which can be a blessing when it is required.

A word about dry-cell batteries. Most portable tape recorders are equipped to operate on these, but I have found them to be undependable—or rather, I have found *myself* to be undependable. Even the long-life alkaline cells can become low on power (without warning), and unless the writer is more conscientious than I about replacing batteries at regular intervals, such failures can cause embarrassing moments. If your batteries quit at a critical moment in the interview, it is awkward to explain to your client that you must pop out to the 7-Eleven to pick up a fresh supply.

The foot control to be used when playing back your tapes as you (or your typist) types the drafts of your interview material is, at best, a stop-gap piece of machinery. Although its use frees both of your hands for the typewriter, the foot control is not altogether satisfactory. Mine operates on a "depress to play—let up to stop" principle. This would be satisfactory except for one flaw. When I remove my foot from the pedal to stop the playback, the momentum of the recorder/player keeps the tape moving for ever so short a time after I have taken my foot from the pedal. The result is the loss of one, two or three words of the transcription every time I stop the playback. Thus, to make certain that

I have lost nothing of importance, I must manually reverse the machine, then play back the material which I "lost" when the tape coasted on after I had removed my foot from the pedal. Not good. It is much better to buy a transcribing unit (to be discussed more fully later in this chapter) especially designed for use by secretaries and stenographers. Even if you must settle for used equipment, such a unit will save you or your typist great chunks and gobbets of raw frustration.

TAPE CASSETTES

The brand is less important than the construction of the cassette in which the tape is packaged. It is of great importance that the cassettes be assembled with tiny screws (usually Phillips-type screws) rather than by heat-welding.

The reasoning behind this judgment is straightforward. Once in a blue moon, for whatever reason, a tape will become hopelessly snarled in the cassette. Fiddling with the two spools does no good, and the only recourse is to disassemble the damned thing and straighten the twisted tape. The frustration is not unlike the fisherman who suffers a severe "backlash" when he casts, and finds his fishing line tangled in knots on his reel. In either case, there is nothing to do put patiently pick the thing out, slowly and carefully.

But the line on the fisherman's reel is exposed; the tape in a cassette is not. How to get to it?

If the cassette has been assembled with screws, it is a simple matter to remove the fasteners with a tiny jewelers' screwdriver, and sort things out. But if the two sides of the cassette have been *heat welded* together, the only way to get at the tape is by smashing the cassette case—in which event the precious recorded tape will be lost anyway.

No, it is best to use a bit of foresight and anticipate problems. By looking ahead to the time when you may have to take apart a recording cassette, you will be well advised to buy the kinds of cassettes which will allow you easy access to your precious and irreplaceable recorded material. They may cost you a few pennies more, but the payoff will come in not having to curse the gods as you glare balefully at yards and yards of ruined tape on your desk—and in not having to squirm as you explain to your client that a particularly successful interview is going to have to be repeated.

In my experience, the C-90 cassette tapes are of the right duration for an interview. With 45 minutes to the side, this provides space for an hour-and-a-half interview, which is quite enough for one sitting. We don't want to tire our clients, and we want to leave them (as a theater audience), wanting more. The C-30 and C-60 tapes are not long enough; the C-120s are prone to tape transport (their movement from one reel to the other in the tape recorder) difficulties because they are made of thinner material than the shorter-running tapes.

I would suggest that the corner drugstore or the "cheapie" radio/ electronics store are not the places to buy your cassettes. Their prices are not the best; their products certainly not the greatest.

Rather, look in the yellow pages for wholesale suppliers of electronic gear: recording tapes, computer diskettes, and the like. Then, buy your high-quality audio cassettes by the case. For many years, I have been buying TDK-brand, "low-noise" cassettes at wholesale. They come packaged in cartons of fifty; are unlabled so that I may affix my own personalized labels (also available from the same suppliers) to them; and I am never caught short by not having an unused cassette as I prepare to leave the house for an interview. The particular quality I have been using is neither TDK's cheapest, nor is it the company's best-quality tape. But the cassettes have the "screw construction" which I demand, and they have performed dependably, case after case. In case lots and at wholesale, at this writing, they cost about $1.19 each—and you can't do better than that even at "Superdrugstore" sale prices. Also, by dealing with a reputable wholesaler, you will be buying from a single source who has direct contact with the manufacturer. If anything should go wrong with your tapes, you have recourse to your wholesaler, who in turn, can go right to the manufacturer. There is additional assurance inherent in constantly working with products of known characteristics and quality.

Find a brand of tape which suits your needs, locate the wholesaler who handles these tapes, and deal directly with him. You are sure to avoid some "industrial strength" headaches in the future.

CASSETTE TAPE TRANSCRIBERS

Transcribing the recorded cassette tapes can be a chore. It is a time-consuming task, and although listening to the material can make the work interesting for a typist, unless good equipment is available, typing the initial draft can be a bit of a drag. The shortcomings of using the tape recorder (in conjunction with a foot control) as a transcribing instrument have already been described. As unsatisfactory as the foot control may be, doing *without* it is even more painful. Without the foot control, each time the tape is started or stopped, the typist must remove his hands from the typewriter keys to the controls of the tape recorder and back again. After a couple of hours of such exercise, the most patient typist begins to feel like an ill-used marionette.

Some years ago, I purchased a Sony BM-45A "Wordscriber" II desk-top transcribing machine. It has performed to my complete satisfaction. Without doubt, this model has been superseded by something even more grand, but the principle remains the same. For ease in transcribing recorded tapes, some specialized piece of equipment is needed.

A good desk-top transcriber will have the following features:

It will accept standard cassettes;

It will have a tape counter to let the typist know "where he or she is" in the document;

It will have an indexing feature which will allow the typist to return to or locate special sections of interest;

It will have a foot-control unit (or a typewriter-control unit) to provide complete playback control;

It will have a speed control to permit the typist to set the tape speed in keeping with a comfortable typing pace;

It will have tone and volume controls, and

It will have an automatic "backup" feature which will allow the typist to set the machine (automatically) to play back one, two, three or more words of the last section of material typed so that no words are missed when typing is resumed.

Many large electronics firms, Sony included, have several divisions. We tend to think of Sony, Canon, Panasonic, GE and other major suppliers as being limited to radios and TV equipment, cameras, or large appliances. Many of these firms also have office equipment divisions. Direct contact with these special branches (rather than with the purveyors of clocks, radios and washing machines) will lead you to the information on office equipment which you seek. And surprisingly, one division of such a large company may know little about the operations of that same company's other divisions. More often than not, each division is a separate entity, doing business quite independently of other branches of the same parent company. Seek out the location of the specialized sellers of equipment in the telephone book, and don't be put off if your hi-fi retailer knows nothing about the office-equipment branches of the companies he represents in the home-entertainment field.

TYPEWRITERS

If the typescripts derived from your recorded interview tapes are to be used only by yourself in the writing of a biography or a corporate history, the quality of the typewriter used to take off the transcriptions is of little consequence. It can be a rattly old Underwood or a clattering antique Woodstock—it makes no difference.

But, if your typewriter is to be used in typing finished copy from which reproductions are to be made for your clients—or if you plan to use your typewriter in making the camera-ready book pages to be reproduced by a printer, the rules of the game change. When the end product of your efforts are to come from your own typewriter, the quality of that end product must be of the highest.

Anything your client is to see (and pay for) which comes from your machine must be unassailable. It is taken for granted that you will pet and polish the words of your final draft with great care, snare any dangling participles, check for agreement in case, number and tense, and work toward syntactical perfection. But the *technical* aspects of your work also deserve your most critical attention. How does your stuff look on the printed page when it comes out of your typewriter or computer printer?

Are the lines of type straight as a die? Is the quality of print good and dark, and of uniform density? Do you see evidence of chipped, broken or crooked typefaces? Does each letter print with the same sharp impression, or are there "light" letters and "dark" letters? Margins and tabular work uniform and aligned? Have you used a "one-time" ribbon which makes the same density of impression with each key stroke, or have you used a reversible ribbon which prints dark at the beginning of a long chapter, and lighter at the end?

If your typewriter or printer is to be depended upon to produce the finished product of your writing efforts, I would counsel any writer/biographer to buy the highest quality office electric typewriter or letter-quality printer (*not* dot-matrix!) he or she can afford. Portables and dot-matrix printers simply won't hack it, nor will manual typewriters or older, abused office electrics. If you can't afford a top-quality office electric typewriter, or a dependable letter-quality computer printer, then, by all means, contract with a public stenographer or an independent typist to produce your final copy. Even so, it is *imperative* that you carefully examine samples of typewritten or printed material produced on the machine to be used in the typing of your finished product.

After all, your client is going to judge you and your work on the quality of this "end product." Not to personally assure yourself that the typewritten or printed work is the best which can be obtained would be as foolish as a portrait photographer failing to ride herd on the lab which processed his film or a jewelry designer who had no interest in the quality of castings made from his exquisite original sculptures.

You, the writer, are also the producer, director, star, designer, editor, grip and "go-fer" in the production of your epics. There is *nothing* which should escape your scrutiny: the esteem in which your clients hold you, and the reputation you carve out for yourself depend upon how closely you attend to business. In our business, there's no such thing as "Let George do it," or "Blame it on Wilbur." If you're going to be the boss, you must take the brickbats along with the bouquets.

WORD PROCESSORS

It's all been said before. The advent of the computer and the word processor has changed forever the world of the production writer. Things will never be the same. A dependable computer and a powerful word-processing software program are the writer's most useful mechanical aids. Once I began to use these marvelous inventions, I wondered how I had survived so long without them!

Their flexibility is like a dream come true. By today's standards, the system I use is an antique. I bought it in September of 1981! My main-frame computer is a dual 8-inch drive S-100 system manufactured by Integran; my breadboard is by Teletek (the functional system based on CP/M); the printer is a C. Itoh, and the softwear word-processing program is MicroPro's WordStar. It's a mishmash of compatible components skillfully assembled and "married" into the unity of a fine tool by an experienced and competent dealer catering to the specialized needs of writers. And I couldn't ask for more!

The word processor allows me to add and delete material with ease; move sentences, paragraphs or whole sections of copy around in a given file; and edit and rewrite more easily than I would have ever thought possible. No longer is there any penalty for changing my mind at any stage of manuscript production. Even after the final copy has been printed, if I see a change which would improve the work, I can go back into the file (stored on the word processor's floppy disks), make the change, and quickly reprint that section which has been altered. All this in a matter of minutes.

Formatting the copy is a dream. I may elect for "ragged-right" margins or justified; choose any line spacing I find appropriate; throw in as much tabular work as is needed; create exactly the top, bottom, and side margins the copy requires. When I'm satisfied with the quality of writing I have produced, I can then invoke my dictionary program (Oasis Systems' *The WORD Plus*) to check my spelling and provide me with a word count. If the work is then ready to go to the printer, I may then call him up on the phone and send my completed MS to him over the telephone lines, via my modem. Through this modern miracle of communications, the printer may elect to either copy my floppy disk on *his* computer, or set type directly through an electronic tie-in with his typesetting equipment.

I don't pretend to understand all of these minor miracles, nor is it necessary for me to do so. But I do know this: the word processor and its associated electronic marvels are accessible to me and to all of us. *Their use has increased my productivity at least fourfold.*

One further note on computers and word processors. I implore you not to be intimidated at the prospect of having to learn a new skill. The instructions which come with these remarkable machines are becoming simpler as time goes by, and I number among my friends many men and women of mature years—some in their late sixties and early seventies—who have "graduated" to using word processors, and they have made the transition from typewriter to computer with relative ease. I won't say that learning the instructions one must "key into" the computer to operate the word-processing program won't take a bit of study and practice. But it is *doable*, and the rewards are almost beyond calculation.

Bear in mind that you don't have to be an electronics wizard to make one of these things work, and you don't have to know the difference between a "bit" and a "byte" to enter the mainstream of writing-by-word-processor. If you can plug in an electric appliance and follow explicit, step-by-step instructions, within a month or two you'll be as comfortable with your word processor as you were with your first typewriter.

INSTRUCTIONS TO YOUR TYPIST

If you are going to entrust someone other than yourself to "take off" or transcribe the interviews on your recorded cassette tapes, your typist must be instructed as to just what you expect in the way of finished product. Format and spacing are, of course, important. But of even greater importance is *content*. Your typist must be told exactly how much leeway will be permitted in what is transcribed.

The point is this: Most typists exhibit a disturbing tendency which must be guarded against. After transcribing a few pages of the give-and-take between yourself and your client, most typists will metamorphose into something rather *more* than typists—they become *editors*! There is no accounting for this transmogrification—I only know that it is so.

When I began my work as a biographer, I naively assumed that my typist was taking off every word of the dialogue between me and my client save, perhaps, the occasional "uh" or "er." Then, one day, I encountered a typewritten passage in the notes which was not quite clear. I sought out the original tape and listened to it so that I might verify the words with which my typist had presented me.

I was appalled at what I heard! Dear Lord! A "...blue, 1932 Buick roadster with a rumble seat..." had been truncated into the simple word "car." An "...ivory satin wedding gown with a veil and train of antique Flemish lace..." had been downgraded to "a wedding dress." A "...charming and marvelously garrulous uncle of mine, Chauncy, by name, always smelled enticingly of peppermints and pipe tobacco—and with him I always associate the texture of rough, highland tweeds..." was reduced to, simply, "Uncle Chauncy."

Well, my typist and I had a little "come-to-God" meeting that very afternoon. I reminded her that to *me* fell the tasks of writing, editing, and deleting any extraneous material, if any. *Her* mission was to provide me with *precise* and *complete* transcriptions of all that had transpired during interviews with my clients. I was not unkind, but I certainly was firm. I explained to her that much of the information she thought to be superfluous constituted the very "color" words and descriptions which would make the past come alive for the readers of the books I was producing. I impressed upon her the importance of detail, nuance, and the seemingly trivial as being subtle reminders of a past which could not be ignored in crafting books designed to accurately *reflect* that past.

My typist's motives were the best; simply misguided. She said that since I was paying her by the page, she thought to reduce my costs by condensing the material as much as possible. Once I explained my needs to her, we never again had another misunderstanding. But—every time I had to employ an alternate typist, I made certain that she understood precisely what was required of her transcriptions. Every word must be faithfully transcribed from tape to typewritten page, and any ellipsing was to fall to me.

From that time forward, I've had few difficulties in getting the kind of "unexpurgated" copy I required from my typists. I say few difficulties, because in the rare instance, I've found my typists to backslide, and again fall into their old ways of leaving out those "unimportant" details. We must remind ourselves, and those whom we employ, that we must take nothing for granted. Rather, we must maintain constant vigilance on every step in the production of our wares so that quality and accuracy are of the highest order.

THE EDITOR'S BLUE PENCIL, AND WHEN TO "CENSOR"

If we write for enough years, invariably there will come a time (or a number of times) when we will pause to ask ourselves if the bald truth is absolutely necessary for the purposes of our documents, or if it might not be politic (for which read: advisable, diplomatic, prudent, etc.) to shade the truth just a bit. We must also take into consideration the laws of slander, libel and defamation of character, and how these laws might impact upon our clients and upon ourselves. Calumny can be a sticky wicket, and when we cast ourselves in the role of spokesmen and chroniclers of our clients, we must be aware of the traps laid by absolute verity.

To *defame* is to disgrace, malign, or to harm the reputation...by libel or slander.

To *libel* is to write or speak a defamatory statement or representation that conveys an unjustly unfavorable impression.

To *slander* is to utter false charges or misrepresentations which defame and damage another's reputation.

In most states, there are stringent laws which hold miscreants strictly accountable for what is spoken in public or written for the record. And even though it was your client (not you, the writer) who recorded defamatory statements on tape, if legal action were to be taken, you, the writer, might well share blame with your client for being instrumental in bringing about publication of false or defamatory material which could damage another's reputation.

Being wary of such traps, I try to remain alert when such material crops up in my tapes.

For example: One of my clients constantly referred to one of the family in-laws as "old bitchy." She never called her anything else! When I came to write those passages in which the long-suffering in-law was mentioned, I "put a statement into the mouth" of my client, and had her say, in a (synthesized) direct quotation, "So-and-so and I were never on the best of terms..." Thus, I was able to convey the truth without allowing my client to utter (in print) a possibly actionable and certainly pejorative statement about the despised in-law.

In another instance, an executive I was interviewing was speaking of labor troubles many years in the past. As he warmed to his subject, his ire rose in direct proportion to the vividness of his memory. As he began speaking of a prominent labor leader of the time, he said, "And do you know, that son of a bitch had everyone in the state afraid of him. And with good reason! If some business owner didn't go along with signing up with the union, why, the proprietor had his business burned out or the owner just disappeared. So-and-so was having his goon squads work over the holdouts and having people murdered right and left—had 'contracts' let on their lives—and of course, eventually, he got his way. But it was murder—pure and simple murder. And all that miserable bastard got was a rap on the knuckles, because you see, the police were in collusion with him—they were in on the take and being paid off..."

Because my client was naming names and giving dates and examples of business proprietors who had been roughed up, burned out or murdered by union thugs, I was dealing with dynamite. If I had become a party to printing such allegations, I would have been derelict in protecting my client, and would have also made myself liable to possible legal action by either the former union boss's family or the labor union implicated. As Shakespeare observed in *King Henry IV*, "The better part of valour is discretion." And in all of our work, we must heed this admonition to be discrete in that which we cause to be written or put abroad for possible public perusal.

As to when any rephrasing of the truth (or outright censoring, if you like) takes place, I would suggest that this be done only when preparing "clean" typescripts for your client or when writing the draft of your book. I do *not* alter the material when I am transcribing the tapes. On these transcripts, which are for my use only, I prefer to have the exact words of the client as they were spoken in our interviews. Only if "clean drafts" of the interviews or written biographies are to be the final product do I attempt to rephrase (or paraphrase) in more diplomatic language those passages which might prove to be embarrassments or legal liabilities. To put it another way, the only time I am especially careful is when I am preparing the product which the client will receive.

And you'd better believe that I am not going to deliver to my client some document that may well blow up in his face if read by the wrong person. One old fellow, in a fit of either excessive candor or outright braggadocio, told me on tape, "...you know, I chippied around on my wife for years, and she never had the slightest inkling that I was keeping a mistress on the side." Whew! No way am I going to introduce such a time-bomb into the archives of an unsuspecting family!

ON THE SUBJECT OF BUSINESS LICENSES

Licensing procedures vary in municipalities, counties and states. It would do no harm to investigate the laws in your areas of operation, and doing so might obviate your own future embarrassment.

I have registered the name of my company, "Life Preservers of Seattle," with the Seattle, Washington, Department of Licenses and Consumer Affairs, and with the State of Washington Department of Revenue. By so doing, I am subject to paying a modest annual "B & O" (business and occupation) tax to the State of Washington, and a yearly fee for my Seattle business license.

I suppose that if I were purely a free-lance writer, doing my own thing and fulfilling the occasional magazine or newspaper assignment, I could "get away" without having to pay B & O taxes and business licenses fees. But because I charge fixed rates for my work (like lawyers, accountants or dentists), and actively solicit business within my community, I feel more comfortable in establishing my business by following conventional and accepted guidelines. I have been asked by some of my corporate clients if I am listed on the tax rolls as a Seattle business, and it is an assurance to them (and a comfort to me) to affirm that I am a bona fide member of the professional/ business community.

The commissioned professional writer (the biographer and company historian) is not working on the fringes of respectability; is not a dilettante puttering and frivoling about in some vague literary pursuit. He or she has every right to lay claim to the same mantle of professionalism which cloaks bankers and business executives, clerics and civil engineers, architects and auditors. And by paying the fees and taxes to which we are properly subject, we affirm that we have joined the legitimate business community as rightful, dues-paying members.

And as Harry Golden observed, "You're Entitled!"

CHAPTER SIXTEEN

ORGANIZING YOUR BOOK:
What Goes Where?

A well-written life is almost as rare as a well-spent one.

— Thomas Carlyle

One of the writer's most daunting tasks is the facing of a mountain of notes, research papers, references and quotations and wondering where on earth to begin. It has been said that there are as many ways to outline a book as there are books.

THE CUT-AND-PASTE APPROACH

Some writers take scissors to paper and cut out individual paragraphs from their typewritten transcripts, snippets from newspapers and scraps of paper upon which they have hand-written notes. These they paste or tape to sheets of standard typing paper to establish the order in which they intend to treat their material. To me, this method is slow, tedious and unrewarding.

THE VERTICAL, OR TOTTERING TOWERS METHOD

Other writers organize their books vertically by stacking together all the material for each chapter. Thus a den or study may come to resemble an abandoned paper mine, with unstable, unsightly tailings pointing skyward from every desk, bench and tabletop. A bumped table, a suddenly opened window or the family cat on the prowl can wreak havoc with such a system. I also find it untidy and subject to unintentional omissions—a vital slip of paper or an important note is easily lost or misplaced.

THE HORIZONTAL FLURRY SYSTEM

In this system, the writer organizes his material by covering every horizontal surface in his work area with papers, then attempts to sort them out by going from left to right, right to left, up to down. This system can provide a great deal of exercise for the writer as he paces from one end of his material to the other, seeking that elusive scrap of paper he remembers writing, but cannot remember filing. This arrangement invites clutter, and creates so much disorder that composition is all but impossible. It, too, is a system susceptible to accidental rearrangement by vagrant drafts, itinerant pets and the depredations of children who visit the office or den, and decide to "help" in the reorganization of all those fascinating bits of paper.

THE FILE-CARD ARRANGEMENT

Other writers prefer to enter their data on file cards, organizing the material for their book or article by the endless shuffling and rearranging of these cards. I find this approach cumbersome, tiresome, and one which entails a great deal of copying and duplication of work already extant in printed or written form.

THE SCAN-YOUR-NOTES-ONCE-AND-BE-DONE-WITH-IT PROCEDURE

In Chapter Thirteen we described the numbering system for the tapes and typescripts. For example, (1-2) 15 indicates tape one, side two, page fifteen; (11-2) 6 denotes tape eleven, side two, page six. It is important that *every page* of the typescript of *each tape* be so numbered. Such a numbering system permits you to pluck out quickly a single page from a mountain of typescript. This same system also allows you the luxury of using a straightforward and simple method of book and chapter outlining.

ASSIGNING YOUR MATERIAL TO BOOK CHAPTERS

Let's look at the typescript of an interview as it's likely to appear on paper. Our interviews with clients are little more than *directed conversation*, and if we are successful in establishing the tone we seek, the interviews generally maintain that informal air. It should be borne in mind that conversations are not as carefully structured as letters or essays. They wander. Although conversations (and interviews) are generally to the point, we find that bits of extraneous information stray in from time to time, and we are often treated to gratuitous asides and shreds of data which do not properly belong in the particular period of time we are discussing.

When we look at a typescript of one of our interviews, then, we should not expect our clients to always respond only to our questions. For example:

INTERVIEW No. 1 WITH G.S., 6/5/85 (1-1) 3

Q. What was the full name of your maternal grandmother?

A. Oh, she was the dearest little thing. I remember her at my high school graduation. Do you know, you would have thought she was the belle of the ball! My boyfriend, Victor—the man I later married—was on the stage right behind me, and I was as nervous as I could be! I had to deliver the salutatorian

— —

(1-1) 4

address, and I had on a new long dress my mother had made for me. (It's still in a trunk upstairs, would you believe? Pink taffeta!) My grandmother had been ill, you know, but she wouldn't have missed seeing me graduate for anything on earth. And she made an entrance into that little auditorium that would have done credit to a duchess! She was just that kind of a woman. So sweet, and so kind. But a temper? You wouldn't have believed how snappish that dainty little woman could become when something displeased her.

Q. And her name?

A. Oh, yes. Amanda. Amanda Brown Llewellyn. It was Welsh, you know. Her family came from Wales, and when she and my grandfather married, she was only fifteen years old. Could you believe it? They lived with us, or we lived with them—I don't exactly know what the financial arrangements were at the time—but it was Grandmother Amanda, not my mother, who always fixed my breakfast for me and saw me off to school when I was going to grammar school in Bozeman. We had this big old high-ceilinged kitchen at the house in Bozeman, and on those cold winter mornings, there was always a film of ice on the water bucket—and *that* was in the house! But Grandmother Amanda was up and stirring before anyone else in the household. She would start a good fire in that great black-and-silver monster of a Monarch wood-burning stove of ours, and I'll never forget the hot porridge she insisted I eat every morning before starting off for school. And school was nearly two miles away.

They heated the school with a wood-burning stove, too, and I remember that every week, one of the boys in the class was named as "wood-box monitor." That meant that he had to see that there was enough wood chopped and brought into the school to keep the classroom warm for the entire day. And that was some job, let me tell you, when the weather was fifteen degrees below zero, and every window and door in that little old wooden schoolhouse leaked like a sieve. I don't think I was ever really warm, while I was at school. And

— —

(1-1) 5

Mother insisted that during the winter we girls wear long-handled underwear underneath layers and layers of petticoats. It's a wonder we could move at all! And Grandmother Amanda used to knit us those wonderfully warm woolen mittens. And you know, like the pictures in the old picture books, sure enough, she tied the mittens together with a long length of matching yarn which ran through the sleeves of our coats so that the mittens were never lost. I hadn't thought of that for years, and now you are opening doors which have been closed for more than fifty years. Amanda died in 1930, so that will tell you how long ago I'm remembering.

What we see in this interview fragment is typical. The interviewer asks a simple, direct question which triggers all manner of memories. More often than not, recollections of a dearly beloved person or a special place will all come out in a rush, and it is up to us as writers to reassemble the material and assign it to its proper place in the book.

If we look at the above interview from the standpoint of *chapters in the book*, we find material which properly belongs in three chapters of the book—chapters which might be titled:

- Our Welsh Beginnings: Those Who Came Before
- Growing Up in Montana: The Grammar-School Years
- The Teen Years—and a Boy Named Victor

The equipment I use in outlining my books (in determining where to place the material in each of the proposed chapters), is disarmingly simple. A lead pencil and ten or fifteen sheets of ordinary tablet paper, one for each chapter of the book, are all that is required.

And, by scanning your typewritten interview transcripts *only once*, you will have assigned *all* your material to the chapters in which it belongs.

Providing they have validity and worthwhile content, every sentence and every paragraph of your transcribed interviews goes *somewhere* in the book you are going to write. And because you are working with biographies and company histories, chronology—the years of our lives—will be your natural outline. Most things in our lives occur on schedule—they happen about when they are *supposed* to happen. That is, we go to grammar or elementary school when we are in our sub-teens; we go to high school when we're teenagers; we go to work, marry, or go to college when we're in our late teens or early twenties.

In most personal biographies, I have found that the material all but "organizes itself" into eight to fourteen chapters. Each deals with an era (a block of time), a discrete idea, a cohesive series of events, a person or a specific geographic location.

HOW TO SENSE WHAT GOES WHERE

These principles are best illustrated, perhaps, by the inclusion here of the Table of Contents of a biography I wrote for one of my clients.

FOREWORD

Examine the sample Q & A interview (with G. S.) above and note the subjects covered by the interviewee. In scanning quickly through the material, we find that G. S. spoke of:

- her grandmother
- her boyfriend, Victor, who later became her husband
- her high-school years, and
- her grammar-school years in Montana

In outlining a book from such material, I feel that I am safe in putting headings at the top of several pieces of tablet paper. These identify the eras of a normal life, and the major areas of interest about which I have questioned my interview subjects. At this stage of the game, I don't concern myself with creating clever chapter titles—my only purpose is to "break out" the material which goes into each chapter. Thus I will have:

- Great Grandparents and Grandparents
- Mother and Father
- The Preschool years
- Grammar-school years
- High-school years
- The College Years
- Work Experience
- Courtship and Marriage
- A Family of Our Own

Thus, when I read these first three paragraphs of my transcribed notes, I will mark my chapter sheets (*one for each chapter*) in the following manner.

THE HIGH-SCHOOL YEARS

(1-1) 3, 4,

GRAMMAR-SCHOOL YEARS

(1-1) 4, 5,

GREAT GRANDPARENTS AND GRANDPARENTS

(1-1) 3, 4, 5,

When I have completed my outlining of the raw material, identified by tape number and side number [i.e. (3-1) for tape #3, side #1], I will have pages of notes that look something like this.

(1-1) 3, 4, 6, 7, 9 (1-2) 4, 5, 6, 8, (3-1) 7, 8, 9, (3-2) 1, 4, 6, (5-1) 5, 7, 8, (7-2) 3, 6, 7, 9, 10 (8-1) 4, 6, 7, 9, 11, 12 (9-1) 6 (9-2) 4, 5, 6, 7, 8, 9, (10-1) 3, 5, 6, 8, 9, (10-2) 4, 5, 6, 9, 10, 11, 12 (11-1) 1, 2, 3, 5, 6, 7, 8, 9, 10 (11-2) 2, 4, 6, 7, 8, 9, 10, 11, 12, 13, 14, 15 (12-1) 5, 6

After I have gone through, *one time only*, my stack of typewritten transcripts from the interviews, I have identified, by the era in which they occurred, all of the events and bits of information which will make up my book. Moreover, I have assigned a *position* for that material in one of the chapters of the book. Of course, I will start *new* chapter pages when I read a transcript in which my client begins talking about a subject which has not been mentioned before, until all eight, ten, or fifteen chapter outlines of my book are "working" at the same time. I will be making entries on all of them as I go through the typed transcripts.

When I am ready to *write* the chapter on THE HIGH-SCHOOL YEARS, I will then go through my stack of transcripts and pull only those packets such as (1-2), (5-1), etc. (stapled together for ease of handling) which have on them *something* having to do with G. S.'s high-school experience. These packets, then, would be (1-1), (1-2), (3-1), (3-2), (5-1), (7-2), (8-1), (9-1), (9-2), (10-1), (11-1), (11-2), and (12-1).

Only when I begin to create the *internal outline* for the HIGH SCHOOL chapter will I examine the material for the second time. At this point, I will have another piece of blank paper on which I will write the *specific subjects* my client is addressing in that chapter. For example, I know that on transcript (1-1) 3 and 4, I will find information about G. S.'s graduation. On the first line of my fresh sheet of paper (the chapter outline) I will then write:

High-school graduation (1-1) 3, 4,

A little further on, I may find information about her likes and dislikes in scholastics—which subjects she did well in, and those in which she had difficulties. There will be information about friends, favorite teachers, proms and parties, sororities, extracurricular activities (sports, band, drama, speech, etc.) and summer vacations.

The *first time* each of these different subjects is encountered, it is the biographer's responsibility to note the change of subject, and write in a new subject heading on his or her chapter outline page. When all of the packets of information [(1-1), (1-2), (3-1), etc.] have been worked through a second time, the chapter outline page should look something like this:

THE HIGH-SCHOOL YEARS

High-school graduation (1-1) 3, 4, 5, 8

Friends (1-2) 4, 5, (3-1) 8, 9, (8-1) 7, 9, 12

Favorite teachers (x-x) etc.

Proms and Parties (x-x) etc.

Sororities (x-x) etc.

Sports (x-x) etc.

Drama (x-x) etc.

Band (x-x) etc.

Vacation, Freshman/Sophomore Summer (x-x) etc.

Vacation, Sophomore/Junior Summer (x-x) etc.

Vacation, Junior/Senior Summer (x-x) etc.

Plans for College (x-x) etc.

When all the sub-headings have been established, and the packets (x-x) pulled and page numbers (1, 2, 3, etc.) noted where the information is to be found, the writer can then look at his internal (chapter) outline and decide where his chapter lead should be.

Where is the most interesting or powerful material? Is it possible to have an anecdotal lead, or open the chapter with some lively dialogue? Once the *lead* sub-heading is determined, the chapter may be outlined by hand-writing numbers in the margin of your chapter outline, indicating the sequence in which the rest of the sub-heads should be treated.

Since the writing about most sub-headings will involve shuffling through only three to five packets of information, the material in each individual sub-heading lends itself to easy organization. Working with such small units of information is not difficult, and by reducing the mass of information to manageable segments, your task is not formidable at all.

As the old song has it,

"Give a man a horse he can ride,
Give a man a boat he can sail;
And his rank and wealth, his strength and health
On sea nor shore shall fail."

We've cut down to size the mountain of information we've developed, and by reducing it to manageable increments, first to chapters, then to chapter subheadings, we've taken all the terror out of the job. There isn't one among us who can't write easily the half-dozen paragraphs required to tell all we need to know about G. S.'s favorite teachers, or the three pages or so we'll devote to proms and parties.

As writers, we draft one small segment after another, stitch them together in logical or chronological sequence—and if we keep a regular schedule of production, it will seem a short time indeed until we are writing that magic word, *finis* to the last page of our work.

CHAPTER 17

WRITING THE FIRST DRAFT

Writing a book is an adventure. To begin with, it is a toy and an amusement. Then it becomes a mistress, then it becomes a master, then it becomes a tyrant. The last phase is that just as you are about to become reconciled to your servitude, you kill the monster and fling him to the public.

— Winston Churchill

WHEN TO BEGIN WRITING

If your client has opted for what, in my contract, is identified as "Option C", the clean, typewritten transcripts of all interviews, you may begin your light editing and finish typing immediately upon completing your first recorded interview. Since there is no material to rearrange, you may begin work right away.

However, if you are to write a book for your client, I would suggest that you wait until your last interview has been completed, and you have at hand all the archival material—the old newspaper clippings, the letters and correspondence and the written ana and ort of a lifetime—before you begin writing your manuscript. When you know that you are to write a book, it is well to have all these materials at your disposal before you even begin to *outline* the thing, or begin to assign certain materials to specific chapters.

Even though you try your best to organize your questions in chronological sequence, the independence of your interview subject will invariably assert itself. Prompted by one provocative question, your client will be off and running, ranging far afield from the specific question you asked. The result will be answers which are not responsive to your questions, and replies which are way out of chronological order. And though you think you have exhausted (way back on Tape #1) all the material on, say, your client's maternal grandmother, it's almost a sure bet that in Tape #15, when you are winding up your interviews, your client will interject some material that begins with: "I remember one time when my mother's mother—that would have been Grandmother Ida..." Or, having dispensed with the grammar-school years on Tapes #3 and #4, your interviewee is certain to reintroduce the subject on Tape #12 or #14!

Had you carefully outlined your transcribed material (the typewritten drafts produced from the tapes) as you went along, and had begun writing your book manuscript, you would then be faced with "going back into" your outline and your draft to insert the fresh material which came along late in your series of interviews. I don't know why these "late" inserts don't seem to work as well as they might, but in my experience, I've always had difficulty in making these last-minute adjustments match the tone and rhythm of the material I assembled from whole cloth. It's rather like trying to paint over a fresh plaster patch made on a painted wall—the tint is never quite the same; the color never quite matches.

I would suggest that you wait until all material is at hand before you begin writing your book. By the time all your material has been assembled, you will have a very good idea of the scope of your project, and will have probably struck upon an approach to your manuscript as well.

WHERE TO START YOUR MANUSCRIPT —THE LEAD

It is not necessary that you begin writing your book with the first bit of material your client/interviewee utters. Quite to the contrary, in fact. In your first chapter, and indeed, in every chapter, there will be an incident; a statement; an observation which all but cries out for primacy. This may involve an outrageous act, a humorous incident or a hilarious bit of repartee—a dialogue. Your client may have revealed new or unusual information; he may have recounted a dangerous or exhilarating experience; he might have introduced a novel or paradoxical idea. For that matter, he may have exhumed a long-buried family skeleton for all the world to see. It is from such unique material that we will construct our leads.

And all these "goodies" are almost certain to be buried deep within your notes. It is your task as a writer to ferret them out and put them where they will do the most good: right at the beginning of your chapters! As in cards, or chess, or Scrabble, for that matter, you don't use your wild cards or your "power plays" when there are lots of other options open to you. You don't waste them. You hold these in reserve until they will promote your cause most effectively.

It must be the same with good leads. You don't allow them to be wasted, surrounded with mountains of detail and dull-but-necessary background information. A good lead is like a diamond in the rough, surrounded by common soil, or a gold nugget, all but obscured by the ordinary gravel in a stream bed. These treasures are *there*, but it takes a practiced eye to see them, just as it takes a discerning writer to recognize a "hot" lead among the more prosaic passages of his transcribed notes.

It is the function of the lead to snare the reader. And even though you are writing for "captive" audiences—ones who will read their family biographies or company histories no matter how dull—it is your responsibility as a craftsman and a writer to make your work as enticing to your audiences as possible.

Good leads are like the canapes or the seafood cocktails which precede the banquet. They are appetizers, and once having snared us, steer us uncomplaining into the main course with appetites whetted and wanting more. This is the function of leads. They command our attention, provide us with enough "hard" information to give a hint as to what is in store for us, then usher us with novelty, grace or wit into the literary feast which awaits us. A couple of examples might be illuminating.

Here is the lead I used in Chapter One of my biography of M. L. Bean, founder of a Seattle mercantile empire.

"Something was wrong. Inside the tent I sat bolt upright in my bedding and listened. Hard.

Then I heard it again. The horses! It was usual for Father's three horses, Pat, Coalie and Snap, to blow softly and nicker companionably when they were hobbled for the night. But now, they snorted in panic. Their nervous whinnying filled the night and sent a chill of fear through me. Though I was yet a boy, having camped many nights in the open with my father had taught me many lessons. And I knew of only two things in this world which could so terrify a horse.

It had to be cougar or bear."

Certainly not the best lead in the world, but it served its purpose. It "grabbed" the reader and made him want to find out what was going to happen next.

In fiction (and don't forget that we biographers will use many fictive techniques), the lead which I recall most fondly is one of John Steinbeck's, which he used to introduce the reader to his book, *Cannery Row*. And please note that Steinbeck is not only giving us information; he sets a tone that promises a book which will be earthy, warmly human, perhaps ribald, and even funny. Here's the way he introduced the proceedings.

"Cannery Row in Monterey in California is a poem, a stink, a grating noise, a quality of light, a tone, a habit, a nostalgia, a dream. Cannery Row is the gathered and scattered, tin and iron and rust and splintered wood, chipped pavement and weedy lots and junk heaps, sardine canneries of corrugated iron, honky tonks, restaurants and whore houses, and little crowded groceries, and laboratories and flophouses. Its inhabitants are, as the man once said, 'whores, pimps, gamblers, and sons of bitches,' by which he meant Everybody. Had the man looked through another peephole he might have said, 'Saints and angels and martyrs and holy men,' and he would have meant the same thing."

After reading that lead paragraph, who would not want to know much more about the fascinating people of "...Cannery Row in Monterey in California...?" I certainly did, and I had to see how the paradox would be resolved between the two disparate viewpoints which illuminated the inhabitants in such contradictory lights. In short, by his powerful lead, John Steinbeck hooked me—which was precisely what he had set out to do when he wrote that enticing come-on.

In your reading, I would suggest that you collect effective leads; copy them down so that you may refer to them later and use them as models. I would also suggest that you analyze each one—take it apart to determine just what makes it tick. Once the anatomy of the powerful lead is known and recognized, making this literary device work for you will come more easily.

PRIMERS FOR BIOGRAPHER; ROLE MODELS TO FOLLOW

Read good biographies to see how they are done. Delve into the books of Catherine Drinker Bowen (*Adventures of a Biographer*; *Biography: The Craft and the Calling*) and other books about biography written by biographers. See how Irving Stone made the lives of the scholarly, the creative, and the adventuresome come alive in books such as *Men to Match My Mountains*; *Lust for Life*; *The Greek Treasure*, and *The Agony and the Ecstasy*. Read the books of Studs Terkel (*The Good War*; *Working*; *Division Street: America*), a man who forged a career of tape-recording interviews with people and converted their "every-day" stories into first-rate literature.

Before you attempt to write a company history, *read* a half-dozen or so of them. I would recommend such books as Harold Mansfield's history of the Boeing Company, *Vision—A Saga of the Sky*; John Brooks' *Telephone*, which chronicles the first hundred years of the telephone and the history of A.T. & T.; and Robert J. Serling's (brother to actor, writer and director, Rod Serling) *The Only Way to Fly*, the history of Western Air Lines. The libraries are full of such books, and I would commend them to you. Even the monthly interviews with famous subjects featured in *Playboy* magazine have something to offer. If nothing else, they illustrate how professional writers conduct their interviews with (sometimes) intimidating subjects. Until you have immersed yourself in the world of biography and company history, read some of the books and analyzed some of the techniques used by successful biographers and company historians, you are scarcely prepared to "go out among 'em" and perform credibly.

While there are no college degrees to be earned in this specialized field, and there are no reasons for you not to begin to earn your living at this craft within a very short span of time, there *are* certain requisites which must be acknowledged. No arduous course of formal study is required. However, the biographer *manque* must become familiar with what has gone before so that he is not trapped into reinventing the wheel. There is no sense in plowing ground which has been plowed and harrowed half-a-century before. If you're going to be inventive, you must do something no one has done before. In the meanwhile, learn all you can by reading what skillful writers have crafted in the past. As in other "earn-while-you-learn" programs, you may be reading company histories, biographies, and books *about* biography while you are beginning the groundwork for your own business.

THE DRAMATIST IN US ALL

Bear in mind always, please, that you are a creative writer, not a technical writer. There is a great deal more to assembling the incidents, traumas, and joys of a lifetime than there is, for example, establishing the sequence in which rivets are placed and upset when fastening a titanium "skin" to the spars of an aircraft wing. I have done both kinds of writing, and there is a world of difference between the two.

In technical writing, one must present only the facts, evenhandedly, clearly, and sequentially. In the writing of biographies and company histories, just as in writing fiction or nonfiction books, the writer has a great deal of latitude. He may introduce humor; evoke pathos and bathos; call upon the emotions and make them do his bidding as though they were dancers in some splendid *corps de ballet* or musicians in some great orchestra over which the artist (you, the writer) holds complete sway.

Your typed transcripts of the interview proceedings are your paint pots and the blank paper or the CRT's television screen your canvas as you, the artist, go to work. Save for the hard-and-fast information you have gathered during your interviews, you have complete control over your material. You have within your power the ability to make it do your bidding; jump through your hoops; perform as you think it ought.

There is much to learn about the craft of writing, and many facets (definable aspects which make up the subject) to recognize and harness. We cannot hope to cover them all here, but the writer should be aware of the inherent power lent to a book or article by the deft manipulation of TONE, STYLE, COLOR AND PACE.

The TONE of the book you will probably take from the personality of your client. If he is ponderous, pedantic, and very grave in most matters, it would be irresponsible to write a frothy, giddy little biography about him.

Contrariwise, if your client is a merry soul and the embodiment of the blithe spirit, a somber work would not accurately reflect the personality you are trying to mirror, and thus be an immense disservice to your subject.

When it comes to the matter of STYLE, I prefer to cleave not to Plato's view, which maintains that writing either has style or lacks it, but to the Aristotelian school which holds that every piece of writing has style of one kind or another. The philosopher, Aristotle, judged style to be neither particularly good nor bad, but merely characteristic of the author. The biographer will develop whatever style is evidenced in his work in part from his material, from the nature and qualities of his client, and from his own proclivities and predilections.

Some of the adjectives used to describe STYLE in *A Handbook of Literary Terms* (Yelland, Jones & Easton, The Writer, Inc., Boston, 1980) are: austere, conversational, distinguished, elegant, formal, lucid, pompous, sardonic, sensitive, terse, urbane, vigorous, and whimsical.

PACE and CADENCE are yet other variables which are ingredients in this biographical *pastiche* or *potpourri* you are concocting. The two rather go together, in that PACE implies fluency and the rate at which you move your story ahead, while CADENCE speaks to the flow of the language—accented and unaccented syllables and words in juxtaposition—which you use in conveying your tale. PACE and CADENCE both contribute to your STYLE.

Then there is the matter of what I choose to call COLOR. Many of the persons you will be called upon to interview will be colorful in their own rights. Some will be downright characters, so eager to get their memories and recollections on paper that in their haste, they abandon all conventions, lash out at old enemies, recall afresh real or imagined slights and wounds of the past, and paint their friends and family tree with a truly garish palate. Let 'em go! And record (and transcribe) every word! Their responses may shock your tender sensibilities or bring tears of laughter to your eyes—but this is precisely what you seek! Candor. The blessed truth (sometimes) stripped of its civilizing veneer. Honesty, sometimes adrip with venom or burning with the cleansing fire, may add a great deal of COLOR to your finished manuscript. And if you can incorporate this honesty without libeling someone or infuriating *too* many within the family, the gamble is more than worth it.

We must not forget that many of the fine ladies we interview (as they sip their tea from delicate Spode cups) had great grandmothers who smoked clay pipes. And some of the CEOs, board-sitting businessmen and carefully attired professionals of whom we ask questions came from long lines of frontiersmen, loggers, seafaring men or saloonkeepers. When we scrape away the patina (sometimes transparently thin) of civilization and acquired culture, we can uncover some very colorful truths indeed—truths which properly belong in any book you write about these people.

Nearly twenty years ago, in 1967, Seattle author and entrepreneur, Bill Speidel, wrote a book entitled *Sons of the Profits* (Nettle Creek Publishing Company, Seattle, WA). Bill opened Chapter III of that book, "The Bastard," with these words:

"Henry Yesler was a bastard...but I hasten to add, not merely because of the accidental circumstance of his birth. Basing it on that alone would be manifestly unfair to a lot of perfectly nice men whose conception had not previously been blessed by either Church or State. Nor was he the kind of adjective that crops up in the casual conversation of, say, a seafaring man or logger.

Unlike the others, Henry not only was born to the title, he worked at earning it day after day and year after year with a greater degree of success over a longer period of time than anybody else.

By the time he departed from our mortal premises, he was the undisputed holder of the crown."

When he penned these words, Bill Speidel was writing about a real man whose relatives still live in these parts. Henry Yesler was one of the pioneers of Seattle; owned a steam-driven sawmill only a block or so from where this city was founded; has streets and housing developments named after him. But he was a character—a COLORFUL character—and because he was so recognized, Speidel could get away with painting him as the unreconstructed, unrepentant scoundrel he was considered to be.

Writing commissioned biographies for others can have its built-in constraints. Because we are being paid by others to write about them and their families, some of us believe that only the laudable and the complimentary should be touched upon in our manuscripts. Without having been asked to do so, we "whitewash" what otherwise might be a colorful (and more honest) version of the "truth." Because we are taking money for what we do, we sometimes feel repressed in what we have been commissioned to write: we quash the blunt and colorful anecdotes; play up the mundane and "pasteurized" version of the past. We bowdlerize our own work, and we ought not to do so.

But the closer we can stick to the vernacular of the time, region, and circumstance, the closer we are apt to come to truthful representation of people and events. If your client is a plainspoken man who describes an errant great uncle as "A crusty old fart with one glass eye who chewed tobacco and drank moonshine whiskey from a Mason jar—and felt absolutely naked without his .32-20 'poachin' gun," for God's sake don't go nasty-nice and describe this uncle as an "elderly flatulent misanthrope who endured an ocular prosthesis, occasionally used tobacco and spirits, and delighted in hunting game for the table."

Write it like it is. But be warned. If your client is timorous, and before your book goes to press, he may ask you to rephrase your copy or remove mention of the incident altogether. Attempt to dissuade him from "laundering" the truth; "sanitizing" the language. If you are successful, and are able to make your client see the humor in such earthy descriptions, hurrah for you! Generations of future readers will thank you for your persistence. Candor and humor—COLOR—are so rare in family books that they are all the more appreciated when they appear. Euphemisms may have their place, but they dull the sure bite of truth.

ON THE MATTER OF DIALOGUE

A long time ago, *The Reader's Digest* (admire the magazine or no) made a discovery: the more quotation marks they inserted into their articles; the more they "broke up" heavy, forbidding blocks of print with conversation, the more avidly readers devoured the material.

Use dialogue whenever you think it will serve your purposes. Don't forget, you are the artist in this little scene, and you can use what colors and brush strokes you deem appropriate to the material, as long as you represent it honestly. No one is going to complain.

"You mean, I can do like Truman Copote, in *In Cold Blood*?"

"Sure. Why not? Hell, he wasn't in that farmhouse when all those awful conversations were going on. But he recreated them, and..."

"And those ellipses you are using—the three dots, indicating that something has been left out. Do you mean that..."

"Sure! Use 'em. And contractions as well. People just *talk* like that. They interrupt one another; they don't finish sentences; they seldom pronounce the full 'ing' endings on words; and they sure as shootin' use contractions and a few little 'cuss-damns' in their speech."

"But..."

"But, nothin'! You're on safe ground as long as you don't make a caricature of speech. And I'd stay away from dialect, if I were you. Ain't but about one in five hundred writers—and I'm talkin' the pros, now—who can bring it off so it doesn't sound phony and forced."

"But what if my client has just told a straight narrative story, with no dialogue in it? Nobody's talkin' to *no*body."

"If you're good enough, and blessed with a little bit of inventiveness, you can create dialogue, or even internal monologue, as you see fit. Certainly, as a writer, you can envision what is going on within a particular scene, and synthesize a conversation if it will be helpful in moving your story along. Once you think you've 'crawled far enough inside' your client's mind to put yourself in the picture he's describing, you can do almost anything you *need* to do to bring off a good scene. All of the tools of the craft are at your command: narrative, dialogue, color, style, pace, syntax, language, grammar, punctuation and all the rest. It's how you mix 'em up that makes for a good read."

"But you think dialogue's important, huh?"

"You'd better believe it, Pilgrim. The more you 'air out' your pages with white space, the more inviting they are to read. Besides, a bit of dialogue can allow you to change viewpoints in your yarn, and allow the reader to see the circumstances through a different pair of eyes. Most valuable, you'll see."

THE QUESTION OF PERSON—FIRST OR THIRD

William Zinsser, widely admired author, journalist and professor of nonfiction writing at Yale (He is Master of Yale's Banford College) writes the following in his splendid book, *On Writing Well* (Harper & Row, 1976).

"A writer is obviously at his most natural and relaxed when he writes in the first person. Writing is, after all, a personal transaction between two people, even if it is conducted on paper, and the transaction will go well to the extent that it retains its humanity. Therefore I almost always urge people to write in the first person—to use 'I' and 'me' and 'we' and 'us.' They usually put up a fight."

I think that Professor Zinsser has it dead right.

The use of the first person in your biographies and company histories lends a sense of immediacy to your writing, and the kind of intimacy which biographies demand. If you, as interviewers and writers, have done your jobs properly, you will have become so well acquainted with your clients that it will pose no problem for you to "write for them in their own voices," using the first person.

As author/teacher Ken M. Symes observed in his book, *Two Voices: Writing About Literature* (Houghton Mifflin Company, Boston, 1976), writing in the first person allows the writer to participate in the action; to become a witness, recorder, or actor in the story. "This voice, characterized by the use of 'I,' may let you see less but more deeply than another storyteller could...Or the first person point of view may serve chiefly to characterize the person telling the story. For instance, if a priest tells you a vicious story about another clergyman's vices, the point of view may reveal the narrator's own lack of charity, possibly a greater vice than any he finds in his fellow priest..."

Use of the third person—"he," "she," "the subject," "Ms. Client"—can also allow the biographer to speak from the standpoint of a witness or recorder to the action, but "once removed" from the immediacy lent by using the first person point of view.

Professor Symes defines the third person as: "...an all-knowing voice who can look into minds, make guesses about the characters' motivations, record conversations, and leap from continent to continent, if necessary, to continue the story. This voice, to insure a kind of credibility, may stay closest to one character and attempt to look at little else outside the main character's mind, conversations, and contacts..."

All well and good, but the third person still does not have the *authority* of the first person. Further, your use of the first person is perfectly justified because you have been appointed spokesman for the very person you have been interviewing—your client. To borrow a baseball term, you are the "designated hitter"—the "designated spokesman"—for the client who is paying your fees. Using the first person carries with it an additional advantage. Although your client tells his story from the first person viewpoint (the young participant), he must perforce regard his past from a third person point of view (the older observer). As he tells his story and you write his book, he becomes, then, at once participant and observer, thereby enjoying the benefits of both points of view.

TRIVIAL PURSUITS—WHAT GOES IN; WHAT'S LEFT OUT

Not long ago, our entire nation was fascinated by a board game called *Trivial Pursuits*. Trivia questions have been the stock-in-trade of television game shows for thirty-five years. Crossword puzzle fans have been dealing with trivialities as well as obscure and arcane words for twice that long. We delight in the trivial because it is so important! As Bertrand Russell once said,

"There is much pleasure to be gained from useless knowledge."

Many of the questions you ask of your clients, and much of the information they volunteer will come under the general heading of "trivia." Your subjects will talk about church socials, family reunions, shivarees and hayrides. They'll speak of playing keep away, tag, marbles, and mumblety-peg. And you're liable to hear about household items long gone from merchants' shelves—Flit, blotting paper, yellow naphtha soap, collar buttons and Sen-Sen. And you'll be treated to a lesson in economics by being reminded of penny candy, nickel cigars, ten-cent movies, fifteen-cent cigarettes, and the three-dollar-and-a-half Arrow shirt.

Who gives a damn about all this trivia? The answer, surprisingly enough, is: almost everyone for whom your books are designed. Trivia about other peoples' lives is just so much nonsense; about our own relatives and friends-of-the-family it becomes the stuff of legend!

Paradoxically, perhaps, but true, it's the "little stuff" that counts. The quirky ways, the mild aberrations, the little eccentricities, the quaint and unusual are the traits which make the people in books endearing or memorable. And often it is the out-of-the-ordinary, the contradictory, and the oxymoronic which leap immediately to mind when we recall distant places, objects of the long ago, and occasions which are indelibly etched in our minds.

We may think of Paris, and of the naive tourist in the group who filled the bidet to overflowing with beautiful cut flowers; an out-of-the-ordinary but trivial happening in a faraway place. We may remember our grandfather's first automobile—an Oldsmobile which came equipped with a buggy-whip holder attached to the dashboard (tradition dies hard!); a contradictory and trivial thing to remember about an object of the long ago. And we remember the sweet sorrow we felt at the funeral of a grandparent: an oxymoronic depiction of an occasion which combined the seeming incompatibilities of "sweetness" and "sorrow": sweetness because of the joy of once again being in the presence of family members and friends of our past; sorrow at the loss of a revered ancestor.

In the grand design of the universe, these incidents and memories are trivial indeed. Of what lasting importance are the recalled memories of flowers in the bidet; anachronistic whip-holders on automobiles; the happy/sad poignancy of family funerals? Of only the most trivial importance, to be sure. Yet it is this kind of *detail* which makes a biography live and breathe; makes it come alive with the vibrance and immediacy of *life*—the life which it attempts to recreate.

Treasure trivia, then. Once you have learned to differentiate between that which is merely dull and ordinary, and that which is trivial but captivating, you will have made important strides toward your goal of literary and artistic discrimination. It was no less a light than Samuel Johnson who said: "The true, strong and sound mind is the mind that can embrace equally great things and small." And nearly two centuries later, Oscar Wilde provided a latter-day echo with this wry observation. "It is a very sad thing that nowadays there is so little useless information."

Just as a pinch of oregano or thyme will add piquancy to a whole stewpot full of victuals, and a hint of garlic will add undefinable (but indispensable) savor to an immense joint of beef, so a *soupcon* of trivia will add greatly to your biographies. Trivia is, perhaps, one of the "secret ingredients" that makes the well-written biography so very palatable. Don't discard it as being too slight to make a difference. On the contrary, learn its value and use it skillfully. Trivia can be that dash of seasoning, that bit of zest, which will elevate the spirit and satisfy the soul.

There are other bits of material which your client may "throw into the hopper" that may cause you some head-scratching consternation. This is the stuff that falls somewhere between the tawdry and meretricious and the clever, cute or candid. Like the response given (by an elderly but vivacious, sometimes devilish, woman client of mine) to my question: "What is the orneriest thing you did when you were of grammar-school age?"

With a glint in her eye, she went on to describe an encounter with a fellow first-grade classmate in which her curiosity about mammalian anatomy got the best of her. My client, when about six years old, enticed her little-boy classmate into the air-well of a basement window, then "propositioned" him with: "I'll show you mine, if you'll show me yours."

I examined that rarefied bit of intelligence from every angle, and after some rather serious-soul searching, included the anecdote in my final draft of the lady's book. I reasoned that most kids *did* stuff like that, and since the mutual boy/girl examination was done in childish innocence and curiosity, there was no venality nor harm in either the act or in my written account of it.

At the time I was writing the draft, I had (as you will have) the benefit of four month's intimate contact with my client, which allowed me to quite accurately "size up" her personality, and to know something of the characteristics of other family members. Thus armed, I calculated that my client and her children would accept the narrative of this innocent little encounter with the good humor in which it was intended. My analysis proved correct, and the anecdote stood as written.

One caveat. It is important that you learn to assess what is suitable and "right" for each client. Had I been writing the formal biography of a distinguished cleric, in a book which would have seen wide circulation, I would have probably omitted the incident. As it was, I wrote my client's book for a tightly circumscribed audience. The book was to be printed in limited numbers for use by family and only the closest of friends. In the context in which the material was written, and considering the client and the small audience for which the book was intended, all was quite fitting and proper.

"CLEARING" THE FINAL DRAFT WITH YOUR CLIENT

The moment of truth!

You have completed your manuscript and are ready to show the finished product to your client. You present the finished draft to the discerning soul who has been paying your bills for the last few months, then depart, wondering how your best efforts will be received. For you, the intervening days will seem an eternity: like waiting for the results of your bar exam, your finals to be graded at college, the jury to come in, and the Academy Awards to be granted, all rolled into one. You can spend these days in an agony of nail-biting suspense, or in the comfortable calm born of knowing that you did the best you were able with the material provided and your own well-developed skills.

Chances are, your client will want some changes. You (and she) got the color of the wedding gown wrong; she and her husband were on the *Rhine* River, not the *Rhone* on that trip in 1966; the way you handled the details of retirement made it sound like the executive was "eased out" of the company (which he was) rather than being ushered out of the fray with all honors; an important incident which occurred on the honeymoon trip was overlooked and should be inserted.

All of these adjustments are minor, are easily put right, and are to be expected. Perhaps I am fortunate, but I have never had a client challenge the way I handled the technical part of the assignment—the way dialogue was inserted; or on matters of chronology, syntax, grammar, punctuation and spelling. Nor have I been put to task because of tone or style.

There have been a few times when clients asked if I thought certain stories or anecdotes belonged in their books, and we have discussed these at some length. Often, these were stories which put the client in (perhaps) "too human" a light, showed petulance, anger, or were otherwise mildly uncomplimentary. Or, the incidents may have revealed an early indiscretion or incident in which poor judgment or lack of maturity played a part, and, these happenings could have been conveniently forgotten or passed over.

In almost every instance, I had already carefully evaluated the worth and propriety of these anecdotes, and had used them for very good reason. I am happy to report, in almost every case I was able to convince my clients that these "questionable" stories belonged in their books lest their characters come across more as plaster saints than as living human beings complete with a full complement of flaws, frailties and fallibilities, as well as the customary virtues. Together, we sought, my clients and I, that elusive and most ephemeral will-o'-the-wisp, truth—which, at best, almost always lay in that uncertain middle ground somewhere between whitewash and denunciation.

However, the client must have the last word as to what is included in his book, and what is omitted. You are entitled to argue your case for the inclusion of this story or that, but you cannot *insist* that any material be retained when the client clearly does not want it in his book. After all, he's paying the freight, and he can ask you to write his story any way he wants it told. You are not an investigative reporter for the *Evening Herald*; you are not a free-lance writer composing your own book on speculation: you are a "hired hand"—a commissioned writer paid to perform a specific job of work which must be to your client's liking. If you are asked to distort the truth, your only recourse may be to take measures to ensure that your name does not appear on the book. By so doing, you will have retained your professionalism and your standing as an honest craftsman without having had to abandon a lucrative contract.

There are certain perils which may arise during the time your client is scanning the draft of your book. Of all the commissioned books I have written, three have never seen print. In the first instance, the book was a company history. The company president ordered my draft of the book to be duplicated, and circulated copies to every member of the board of directors, and to every person who had been mentioned in the book, asking that they critique the manuscript and make any changes in the MS they thought necessary and appropriate. Like many doomed bills in our Congress, the book manuscript "never got out of committee."

The second case involved an elderly and indecisive woman whose eyesight was so poor, and energy level so low, that her endless perusal of the manuscript ended in frustration for both of us. She didn't know what she wanted, and I didn't know how to "fix" a manuscript which wasn't "broken." Since the lady was still handling most of her own affairs, I felt it would have been intrusive and impolitic for me to approach her children with the suggestion that they "take over" from their ailing mother, and make the necessary decisions relative to the manuscript. The manuscript has yet to be approved, and the book will probably only see print after the lady's demise—and then, only if the children, in their turn, approve of what their mother and I put together for them.

The third book manuscript which has not yet been released by the client involved an aggressive businessman whose story I recounted as accurately as I knew how, using the information he provided. When we began the project, I did not know that my client had a friend who was a publisher, and who was interested in bringing out the book. In due course, I delivered the manuscript to my client, he made some minor adjustments (which I incorporated in a second draft), and all was well. He was happy with his book, and I had been paid all my fees. It was understood that he would undertake the details of publishing himself.

Some months went by, and I had heard no more from this man. When I called him to inquire when the book was to come out, he told me that his intended publisher had not liked the manuscript—it was too angry; too belligerent; too abrasive, his friend had said. Moreover, the friend no longer wanted to publish the book. What the publisher had had in mind was a "happy" book which would appeal to a large and varied audience.

Not having been blessed with the gift of prescience, I had no idea (nor, apparently, had my client) what kind of book the anonymous publisher had in mind. But I was off the hook. I had performed everything called for in my contract, and I had done so to the satisfaction of my client. And I had been paid. The only reward I lacked was seeing the book finally in print—the book whose crafting my client and I had both approached with diligence and joyful enterprise. To this day, I don't know whether this book will ever see print.

Shrug.

[Note: A few months later, the client formed his own publishing company, brought out the book with only minor rewrites, and it is now enjoying wide circulation. (RVS)]

We write our books, we use our judgment and skills to the fullest, we "clear" the manuscript with our clients, and then we can only hope for the best. If all goes well, our work is approved, the manuscript goes to the printer's, and (after the passage of much time) we may hold in our hands a beautifully bound volume which attests to the quality of our work and confirms us as craftsmen of high order. And all along we have been paid well to follow that pursuit which, among all others, nourishes and sustains us, and proclaims that we are alive, positive, and contributing members of society, happily chronicling the lives and times in which we live.

Few callings promise greater satisfaction.

CHAPTER 18

PREPARING COPY FOR THE SMALL EDITION

(FEWER THAN 100 BOOKS)

Just how difficult it is to write biography can be reckoned by anybody who sits down and considers just how many people know the real truth about his or her love affairs.

— Rebecca West

You are about to embark upon a remarkable adventure—one, which in some ways, may be likened to the conception, the carrying to term, and the delivery of a child. And the writing of a book takes about as long. You've gone through all the trauma [the morning sickness (when you first contacted your prospect), the attacks of "nerves" (Will you ever forget that first interview?)] and you're now entering your third trimester. It won't be long until you will be able to present the fruits of your labors to a waiting world!

Your client has carefully read your last draft of the manuscript, and has made all the necessary changes and corrections. You have checked your spelling for accuracy, punctuation for correctness, syntax for smoothness and flow, and you have polished your manuscript as carefully as you know how. Perhaps you have even asked a colleague or an editor to examine your work for any errors you may have missed—to perform a kind of literary amniocentesis to warn of any unforeseen birth defects.

At about this time you will consult with your client about the number of copies of the book required and, if fewer than one hundred, will show samples of the typefaces you have to offer (and suggest) for use in the camera-ready copy. If you use an IBM ball-element typewriter, you may wish to show your client an IBM catalog which illustrates the various typefaces available, and select one from among the many 10- or 12-pitch typefaces which would be suitable. If you use a word processor and a printer, show your client samples from several different daisy-wheel printing elements, or a catalog which illustrates different typefaces.

In general, a serif type (as contrasted with a sans serif) is more pleasing to the eye. I have produced several books using, for example, IBM's Letter Gothic typeface. This bold, uncluttered sans serif typeface worked well, and pleased my clients. Aesthetically, however, I believe that IBM's Courier, Prestige Pica, Bookface Academic or Delegate (serif types all) to be more pleasing to the eye.

CAUTION: If you are using a computer/word processor in tandem with a printer, the impact or letter-quality printer (as contrasted with the dot-matrix printer) produces the superior typescript for our purposes. The early, nine-pin dot-matrix printers imprinted fuzzy, unclear letters which were unsuitable for finished work. Recently, however, eighteen- and even twenty-four-pin dot matrix printers have surfaced, and their advocates claim that they nearly equal the print quality of the impact or letter-quality printers. Upon close examination, however, while the print quality has satisfactory density, the clear definition of the letter outlines—the crispness of serifs—typically produced by the impact printer is lacking. Some have compared the quality of dot matrix printers to that of conventional typewriters using old-fashioned cloth ribbons rather than their more modern Mylar ribbon counterparts. Until the technology of the dot matrix printer has been improved even further, I would counsel staying with the known high performance of letter-quality printers.

If your client selects a typeface for which you have no IBM ball or daisy-wheel printing element, don't demur at this point! If the typeface selected is *at all* acceptable for the intended use, just be agreeable to your client—then go out and buy the necessary print element. They aren't expensive; you'll avoid any possible disagreement with your client; and by this small purchase, your arsenal of equipment will swell by the addition of yet another type style which is sure to be useful in the future.

As you are talking with your client about the number of copies of the book required and the typeface preferred, bring up the subject of quality and color of available book bindings. A choice must be made. Velo-bind (the manufacturer of a patented binding system) and, I would assume, other companies as well, offer a variety of colorful hard- and soft-covered bindings. From your printer, obtain catalogs and samples of the binding materials available to him so that your client may make a wise and considered decision about the final "packaging" of his book.

PRINTER vs PUBLISHER

We sometimes fall into the trap of using the two words as though they are synonymous. They are not. For the purposes of this chapter, a printer is the operator of a "quick-print" establishment. Once provided with your "camera-ready" copy (many quick-print outfits use some variation of the photo-offset lithography process), your printer will "shoot" (photograph) your copy, make his planographic printing plates of either heavy paper or thin metal foil, and run your job. Some quick-printers (the ones you want to work with) will provide you with halftone negatives derived from your client's old photographs so that you may illustrate your work, and will also package your finished work in suitable permanent bindings.

This is about all you may rightfully expect of your printer. Your printer takes your money and hands you back the finished product—printed and bound books—for you and your client to do with as you see fit. And, it must be borne in mind that the books provided by your quick printer won't look like conventional library books. They won't cost as much, either. (While a printer of conventional hard-cover books may spend as much as $3,500 setting type and making printing plates before his big rotary presses roll one revolution, the quick printer's "make-ready" costs are but a tiny fraction, pennies, really, of that amount.) The books you will receive from your quick-print shop will be large volumes whose covers measure about 8 5/8 by 11 1/4 inches, and which look much like the yearbooks published by high schools and colleges.

Contrasted to a printer, a publisher purchases a manuscript which will be transformed into a book for sale to the public. And with this, he assumes almost all of the duties attendant, not only to the printing and binding of the book, but to its advertising, promotion, distribution and sale to libraries, book wholesalers, jobbers, and bookstores. Among the many chores assumed by the publisher are obtaining and editing the manuscript; designing the cover; scheduling all steps in layout, typesetting, printing, and binding of the book; sending copies out to electronic media, magazines and newspapers for review; defining the "target" marketing regions; and planning the sales campaigns—distribution, advertising, and promotion.

When a *printer* is employed to produce a book for the writer and his client, and that book is sold, the client keeps the money resulting from any sales. All copies of the book belong to him. He has, after all, paid the writer for his work, and the printer for the finished product. When a *publisher* buys a manuscript and produces such a book for the marketplace, it is the publisher who keeps most of the money, because he has footed the bill from the very moment he signed a contract with the writer agreeing to buy his manuscript.

WORKING WITH YOUR PRINTER

Your role as writer has come to an end; your job as editorial coordinator has just begun. You must now oversee the many and varied details attendant to the printing and binding of your biography or company history.

In 1976, a wonderful book by Howard Greenfeld was published by Crown Publishers, Inc., of New York. The book, *BOOKS: From Writer to Reader* succinctly and interestingly describes the parts played by the various members of the publication team. The print of *BOOKS* is large, and the language straightforward. I recommend this book to any serious writer of biographies and company histories. We should *all* be familiar with the responsibilities of those skilled professionals who will usher our camera-ready copy from the darkness into light.

A partial table of contents of *BOOKS* follows.

The Writer

The Decision to Publish

The Editor

The Illustrator

The Copy Editor

The Designer

The Jacket Designer

The Production Supervisor

The Compositor

The Proofreader and Indexer

The Printer

The Color Printer

The Binder

In the situation which this chapter treats (an edition of fewer than 100 copies), you, the writer, will undertake or assist in many of the jobs listed above. Certainly, you are the writer. In addition, you will also be, in full or in part, the editor, the illustrator (helping your client select the photos to be used), the designer, the production supervisor, the proofreader and the indexer, if an index is to be provided.

If the reader will be indulgent, I will synthesize a dialogue between a WRITER and a PRINTER. By this device I hope to transmit much useful information in a brief but comprehensible fashion.

WRITER: (Entering print shop) Good morning.

PRINTER: (Standing at counter) How can I help you?

WRITER: I'm about to prepare camera-ready copy for a book I have written for a client. I'm looking for a printer and binder who will be helpful in putting out an edition of about 100 books, well printed on good paper stock, and bound in a stout but attractive binding. The book will contain photographs and its title is to be imprinted on the outside in gold leaf. I wonder if you are the man who can best help me.

PRINTER: I think you've come to the right place. We've done a lot of jobs which have called for all the things you mentioned, and they're fun to do. As a matter of fact, I rather like working with writers in helping them showcase their work as attractively and durably as I know how. What's the format of your book to be? Have you a preference on page size?

WRITER: Because I'll be giving you camera-ready stuff, right out of my typewriter, I think that 8 1/2 by 11 inches will work O.K. And I'm assuming that you do most of your work on that size paper stock. Right?

PRINTER: Right you are. And you'll have any headline material—chapter headings, the internal book title as a part of the front material of your book, and anything else requiring larger type—all pasted up and ready to shoot with the camera?

WRITER: Yes. I have all my headline material produced on the headliner machine at our neighborhood newspaper office. I'll have all the large-type stuff done there. And the cost is reasonable. All the headline material I need for a book can be produced in about half-an-hour on the headliner. And half-an-hour's time costs me about $35.00. Then, I just ask 'em to hot-wax the back of the copy, then it's a simple matter to cut out the individual headlines or chapter headings, and press them onto the body copy sheets—the pages of text—which come out of my typewriter. Then they'll be ready for your camera. Here's what my headliner order calls for. (Hands the following copy to the printer) I ordered more headline copy than I needed, and had a number of heads printed in all caps, initial caps, and lower case, even though I knew I'd be using only one of them. I'd rather order more than have to go back for just one headline. One headline or a dozen, I'd still be charged for a minimum of fifteen minutes of the operator's time on the machine—at about $70 dollars or more per hour.

HEADLINER ORDER TO MURRAY PUBLISHING COMPANY

Font 14392, Bodoni Bold Italic, I-36 Point, 7 Count
(1) each:

FROM HERE TO ANTIQUITY
From Here to Antiquity
A FAMILY BOOK
A Family Book

(1) each: I-30 Point, 8 Count

JANICE KERGAN STREET
Janice Kergan Street
A FAMILY BOOK
A Family Book
by BY WITH With with

(1) each: I-24 Point, 10 Count

JANICE KERGAN STREET
Janice Kergan Street

(1) each: I-18 Point, 14 Count

ACKNOWLEDGMENTS

FOREWORD

TABLE OF CONTENTS

LIST OF PHOTOGRAPHS

AFTERWORD

APPENDICES

BIBLIOGRAPHY
THE KERGAN GENEALOGY
THE STREET GENEALOGY
THE NEW GENERATIONS
FROM "The Argonaut" July 7, 1939
SEATTLE, WASHINGTON 1979
Seattle, Washington 1979
OSO, WASHINGTON 1979
Oso, Washington 1979
ABOUT RICHARD SAWYER
Richard V. Sawyer
BY WITH By With with
CHAPTER ONE Beginnings—Our Forebears and the Foundations of the Family

CHAPTER TWO The Immediate Family and my Preschool Years

CHAPTER THREE My Introduction to Grammar School

CHAPTER FOUR The House Near the Lake

CHAPTER FIVE The College Years

CHAPTER SIX William Sherman Street

CHAPTER SEVEN Courtship, Marriage, and Our Own Family

CHAPTER EIGHT The Building Years—Milwaukee and the Boston Store

CHAPTER NINE God's Country—Seattle and the Pacific Northwest

CHAPTER TEN Chicago—1943 to 1946

CHAPTER ELEVEN In the Evergreen State Once Again—This Time to Stay!

CHAPTER TWELVE The House at Sibleywood and the Move to Oso

CHAPTER THIRTEEN Opinions and Observations—Reflections on a Lifetime

CHAPTER FOURTEEN The Legacy of this Volume

(1) each: I-14 Point, 16 Count

Copyright All Rights Reserved 1987
RICHARD V. SAWYER Richard V. Sawyer
BY By by WITH With with
Seattle, Washington

PLEASE WAX BACK OF ALL COPY

PRINTER: (Nodding) Looks like you have your book pretty well organized. And no chance of your headliner operator misunderstanding what you want—you have your typeface specified, the point size (12 points to a pica; 72 points to an inch), and the count—the number of characters required to fill a given space on your copy. And I see that you have typed your headliner order *exactly* as you want them to be printed—all capital letters, initial caps, or all lower case.

WRITER: Yes. You can't just type your print order any old way. You have to let the operator of the headline machine know precisely what you want, otherwise, he'll not know what to print.

PRINTER: Seems like you've done your homework. Now—what kind of binding did you have in mind for your finished books? Did you want a mechanical binding such as spiral or plastic coil, soft cover, or a hard cover?

WRITER: I think we're going to want a vinyl hardcover binding on these books. They are intended to last a long time, and we need something durable.

PRINTER: Something like Velo-bind should suit you nicely. Their hard covers come in a variety of colors and textures, they're very attractive, and the crimped plastic binding should outlast the conventional glued-and-stitched binding used on most hardcover books. But don't forget, you'll want nice, wide side margins to leave room for drilling the holes and inserting the plastic binders. "Gutter allowance," they call it in the trade.

WRITER: What's a 'nice, wide margin'?

PRINTER: An inch-and-a-half all around should do nicely, although you could leave a little more room at the top and bottom to set your page off attractively and not make it look crowded. And you could use flush right margins if you have a word processor and printer that will give you those neat and tidy justified right margins—or ragged right—it makes little difference in the long run. It's all according to what pleases your eye.

WRITER: (Nodding his understanding) What kind of price do you get for printing both sides of the 8 1/2 by 11-inch paper stock, sheets, collating them, and getting them ready to bind?

PRINTER: I get ten cents per sheet for printing both sides, and this will be on a premium quality book paper of 60- or 70-pound text-weight paper. There is an extra charge for collating, but it doesn't amount to much—it depends on how many sheets we must process.

WRITER: How about the inclusion of pictures in my books? What do I have to supply you with so that I can be assured of good illustrations? And how much will photographs add to the cost of these books?

PRINTER: Pictures and illustrations enhance any book, and I would surely recommend their use. All I need are clear, preferably black-and-white, glossy photographs of any size or shape. We can make them larger or smaller, depending upon the page size of your books, and how much space you want to allow for each picture. We make halftone negatives of your pictures, usually 140 to 180 screen. The higher the screen number, the finer the definition on the printed picture in your book. We then make printing plates from the halftones, and run them on special, textured and finished paper that gives the photographs additional dimension. Making the halftone negatives costs about $25.00 each, and there is a slight charge for the special printing paper we use—but that is a small consideration.

WRITER: You specified black-and-white photographs. So many people shoot color today. Can't you handle color pictures as well, using them to make black-and-white illustrations for my book?

PRINTER: Sure! They just don't print quite as clearly or crisply from the halftones, that's all. Heck, I've even made halftones from old tintypes so crinkled and abused that you wouldn't have thought you could get *any*thing off them. And although the scratches and flaws showed, the resultant pictures came out better than we could have expected, and with more detail than you would have believed possible. But the best "raw materials" are still glossy black-and-whites, either contact prints or small enlargements.

WRITER: How about having some color pictures in the books?

PRINTER: Now, you're starting to talk important money. Color separations, necessary for the printing of color pictures, cost a bundle! For a short press-run, like we're talking about here—100 books or fewer—the cost-per-copy for the inclusion of color pictures would really be steep. There are some new processes on the horizon, though, and let's cross that bridge when we come to it. But using state-of-the-art techniques, you would probably have to charge more than it's worth for color. If it comes to that, though, and you have a client to whom money is no great factor, we would prefer to work with color transparencies rather than color prints.

WRITER: How about the cutlines, or captions for the pictures? How do I handle those? What's needed?

PRINTER: When you deliver the original photographs to me, indicate whether you want the pictures in the book to be run in the vertical or horizontal format. That'll tell me how I have to print them from the halftones. Then attach to each picture the identification—the cutline—which will be run underneath the picture. Type your single-spaced copy to fit well within the available space in whichever format is to be used—the vertical or the horizontal. And be sure to number your pictures and their accompanying cutlines so that there is no possibility of confusion. And f'heaven's sake, when you mark on the back of a picture, use either a very dull, soft lead pencil or a wax pencil—and don't press down very hard! Ballpoint pen marks will "trace through" on the emulsion, and felt-tip pens sometimes "bleed through" onto the picture. In both cases, the photograph is either damaged or ruined completely for our uses.

WRITER: How about artwork. You know—diplomas, awards, certificates of appreciation, sketches—that kind of stuff? Is there any way that kind of material can be incorporated into the book?

PRINTER: If it can be photographed, or shot with the halftone camera, we can include it in your book. There's not much we can't do, these days.

WRITER: O.K. I think we've covered most of the bases. Now—about cost. Say I present you with a 300-page manuscript and ten photographs. And my client wants 100 copies of his book, bound in hard vinyl covers, with the title of the book and authorship stamped in gold leaf on the front of the books. What would be your estimate for turning out such a job?

PRINTER: (Talking to himself and punching in numbers on a small calculator) Lessee, now. Ten cents a page for printing both sides, times 150 pages (that's your 300-page manuscript) times 100 copies comes to $1,500 printing costs for all 100 books. Then, 10 photographs (and the making of ten halftones at $25.00 each) comes to $250, plus another $15.00 premium for the special paper, comes to $265.00 for processing your pictures. Bindings at about $7.00 each comes to $700. Collating all the pages of your book will cost $6.50 per thousand pages, and we have 15,000 pages, so that'd be $97.50 for that little bit of work. Then the gold-foil titles on the front. Figuring everything for the gold-foil work, I'd say that about $250 would do the job.

WRITER: Whew! You're coming up with some pretty good-sized numbers, there. What does that work out to on a per-copy cost?

PRINTER: Lemmee see what my electronic abacus says, here. (Again, works with small calculator) Well—your total bill with me would be about $2,812.50. And if you have me run 100 books, that'll make each one of 'em cost about $28.13. And I have to tell you, that's less than you would pay for *just the typesetting* if you were to go to a regular book-printing outfit.

WRITER: When you calculate the per-copy cost, it doesn't sound too formidable. How long will it take you to run such a job?

PRINTER: Well, working it through the shop, along with all the other jobs we have to run, I think I could have it all ready for delivery in ten working days. That will give me time to order your halftones, the right-sized binders, and the special paper stock for the photographs. Does that sound reasonable to you?

WRITER: Sounds good to me. I'll bring in the camera-ready material on Monday.

CALCULATING THE PER-COPY COST FOR YOUR CLIENT

Once you are this far along the road, you may tend to forget that you are still working, and should be compensated for your time in getting the copy ready for the printer. There is the time spent on typing out the print order for the headliner, taking the headline copy to the neighborhood newspaper office, cutting out the headlines and pasting them onto our manuscript copy, preparing and typing (to format) the cutlines for the illustrations—all the detail necessary in doing layout work. There will be a fair amount of time spent running around town in your car during this stage of your production, and you should be compensated for it. It may be that you will spend as much as two or three full days coordinating the printing of your book, and doing the work necessary to that objective. Those are $200-days, and you should not be timid about garnering what is yours.

You may add these hours to the bill you present to your client, or you may increase the per-copy cost of the books. It makes little difference how you charge for these hours, as long as you are paid your established professional rate.

You are too close to your goal to forget basic principles—the first of which is that you are, in every sense, an entrepreneur and a private business-person. You have taken risks, you've invested your capital, your skills and your time. You are performing highly demanding work, and deserve to be paid what you are worth. That's one of the reasons you entered this field in the first place—to perform a needed, heretofore lacking professional service within your community—and to be appropriately compensated for your contributions.

CHAPTER NINETEEN

PREPARING COPY FOR THE LARGE EDITION

(MORE THAN 100 BOOKS)

Like the wheel—which we have learned to make stronger and more cheaply, but which remains unaltered in concept—the book, we may hope, is a unique and lasting invention.

— Dan Lacy, managing director,
American Book Publishers Council,
Newsweek, Nov. 14, 1960

A knowledgeable and understanding printer is the most needed ally at this point. Above all, we need a helpful and skilled professional who will not attempt to intimidate us because we may lack "print-shop savvy." In the world of commerce, sensitivity and compassion are rare commodities, but if a printer may be found possessing such characteristics (along with the requisite skills), we will do well to cultivate the relationship, and cleave like a limpet to this treasure! Such a one can lead us unscathed through the thickets and thornbrakes of printers' jargon and the numerous pitfalls which await the unwary.

How does one find such a gem?—the ink-stained paragon who will lead us from darkness into light.

Persistence, hard work, and a bit of luck thrown in.

We should not be shy about using our friends. Other writers who have trod these byways before us are usually willing to answer our questions and help us over the hurdles of the printing game. A request for advice is often disarming, and the person asked usually responds with the needed information.

Talking with another free-lance writer, you might pick his brain by saying: "John, you've been down this road before, but I'm stumped. Where would I find a printer in this town who can do a good job on my client's book, yet not cost us an arm and a leg? That last book of yours looked great! Mind telling me who did your work for you?"

A colleague so complimented will usually respond with a forthright answer.

And, don't fail to query the printers you contact. Ask to see copies of the books or brochures they have printed for other customers and ask about the costs of these projects. After all, you (as your client's agent) are going to be spending some important money with the printer you eventually choose, and he should be more than willing to produce samples of work he has done for others.

DETERMINING WHAT YOUR CLIENT WANTS

There comes a time when we writers must assume other roles. One of these is that of production coordinator. We must consult with our clients to talk about the "end product"—the printed-and-bound book we are going to create.

Just what kind of a book has your client envisioned? What are you and your printer expected to produce? Are you going to print the book "on the cheap" or go first class? Or do something in between? You will want to examine all the options, both to satisfy your client, and for your own peace of mind in knowing that, together, you have explored as many possibilities as were open to you.

You may want to suggest to your client that before embarking on a journey, one should always have itinerary, routing, and destination clearly in mind. And by the same token, before consulting a printer, certain goals must be set and decisions reached. You and your client must know, within reasonable limits, what kind of book you eventually expect to hold in your hands before approaching *any* printer for that all-important *estimate* of printing and binding costs. You and your client must agree upon what is wanted. Additionally, you, as the writer-cum-coordinator, must be able to transmit that information clearly to the printer.

HOW MANY COPIES OF THE BOOK WILL BE NEEDED?

Does your client intend to distribute copies only to immediate family and close friends, or does he plan to send copies to every shirttail cousin in the land? Will the books be sent to shareholders in his company, and placed in libraries in every major city? Will the books be offered for sale to the general public? Are five hundred books needed? Or five thousand? Whatever the number, the rule of thumb holds that the greater the number of books ordered, the lesser will be the per-copy cost. In other words, one thousand books will not cost twice as much as five hundred books. A large percentage of the cost of printing is incurred before the presses even begin to roll. These are the costs of typesetting, composition, layout, preparing the photographs and halftones, and press make-ready. These costs remain the same whether one volume is printed, or ten thousand.

WHEN MUST THE JOB BE COMPLETED, AND THE FINISHED BOOKS IN HAND?

Urgency commands a stiff price. If your client demands his books in a hurry, it will cost him money. Conversely, if he can allow the printer a normal amount of flow time for the job to go through the print shop, the printer's fees should reflect the non-panic status of the job.

WHAT SIZE OF BOOK IS DESIRED?

That is, what are to be the finished dimensions of the book? How wide and how tall does your client want his book to be? Have him look at the books in his library. Are there one or two sizes more appealing than the rest? For purely economic reasons, it is prudent to remain somewhat flexible on book size. Paper is costly, and an "off-sized" book may be wasteful of the print stock—the paper on which the book is to be printed. This is particularly true of books printed on (sheet-fed) flat-bed presses, which use pre-cut press sheets rather than the roll paper used in the larger rotary, or web presses. Unless you are very well aware of what you are about, it is wise to defer to your printer in most cases, leaving it up to him to get the greatest number of printed pages from the paper stock upon which your book is to be printed, whether run on a sheet-fed or web press. The most popular size for short-run books is 5 1/4 in. by 8 1/4 in.—but again, check with your printer on the most economical size for *his* presses.

WHAT KIND OF BINDING IS WANTED?

The most popular and affordable binding may well be a compromise between the cheapest and the most costly bindings available to you. This is the so-called "perfect binding" with its glued-on cover, used on most paperbacks, whether "trade" or "mass-market." Wire-stitched bindings, or staples, will probably not be satisfactory for your needs, nor will the spiral-wire or plastic-comb bindings. These are inexpensive special-purpose bindings for books whose usefulness and life are predictably of short duration.

Having your books hard-bound (sometimes called "case-bound") with a glued-and-stitched binding and cloth covers is the most expensive binding option, but one which is far and away the best when appearance *and* durability are to be considered. Because of the many options and variables available, close cooperation with your printer or binder will be to your advantage.

QUALITY OF PAPER STOCK TO BE USED?

Paper is paper, right? *Not so!* The bewildering number of available choices in cover stocks and text (or body) paper can be intimidating, particularly to the uninitiated. Again, consult with you printer. The chances are that he buys certain text and cover paper in large quantities, and regularly stocks these in his storeroom or warehouse. Quantity purchases mean lower prices for the printer, and very possibly for you. He will probably recommend one of his regularly stocked papers to you, and if you find it suitable, by all means go with it. Accepting your printer's judgment is frequently better than pawing through mountains of catalogues looking for a paper stock which may be "different." In your naivete, you may select a paper stock so distinctive as to detract from the words (*your* words!) printed upon it.

HOW IS THE BOOK TO BE ARRANGED?

The writer/coordinator should be at least conversant with the parts of a book, and how they may be most pleasingly arranged. Most books have three major divisions: the *front matter* or *preliminaries*; the *text*; and the *end matter* or *reference section.*

In the *front matter* usually appear such sections as the book half-title (bastard title), title page, copyright notice (if any), publisher's agencies, printing history, country where printed, Library of Congress Catalog Card Number (if used), and the ISBN (International Standard Book Number), if one has been applied for and issued.

Other material which rightfully belongs in the *front matter* section are any dedication of the book, the table of contents, list of illustrations, list of any tables used, the foreword, preface, acknowledgments (if not a part of the preface), and the introduction. *A Manual of Style*, published by The University of Chicago Press, is a most helpful volume to the writer/coordinator, particularly when first encountering the complexities of assembling a book-length manuscript into publishable form. Additional books on self-publishing and printing may be found in public libraries, and I encourage their careful perusal. A few hours spent in library research will pay big dividends. A spate of nose-in-book at the library will arm you against (later) anguish and indecision when you begin, with your printer, to put your book together. After a bit of concentrated study, you will probably (as I did), breathe more easily as understanding dawns; the muddy becomes clear; the confused, plain.

CAN YOU TELL A BOOK BY ITS COVER?

Look at a number of books in your own library. What do their covers tell you? How colorful are they? How important is the artwork to the image the book "telegraphs" to you?

The cover of a book usually contains certain basics: the title; a subtitle which says something about the book's subject; the author's name (or the name of your client plus your own, i.e, "By James T. Client, with Alice B. Writer");

the publisher or printer, and perhaps a book jacket bearing an attention-getting piece of artwork which draws the eye.

The back cover (if perfect-bound; otherwise the back of the book jacket) of your commissioned book may be used to convey a word image of your client, or of the company whose history you have written. A photograph often accompanies this short bit of biographical or historical material. This photo may be of your client; your client and his immediate family; or some representation of the company (manufacturing plant, service or product) whose history you have captured on the pages within.

The spine of the book or the book jacket should be imprinted with the title, your client's (and/or your) name, and that of the publisher, or the publisher's distinctive logo.

An effective cover design is no accident: it is the result of much thought and trial-and-error until the right combination of words, colors, and design are reached. After noodling some cover ideas around with your printer, it may be that he will recommend the services of an illustrator or graphics designer who has produced satisfactory book covers in the past. Or you may know someone in the advertising or graphics field who knows the *selling potential* inherent in an effective book cover.

At this point in the proceedings, it is well to remind yourself that the cover or paper jacket of your book is its *best selling tool.* (This is of great importance if your client plans to market his book; of lesser importance, certainly, if the book is intended only for a small, private audience.) What may be an artistic and aesthetic triumph—a composition most pleasing to the eye—can be an inglorious flop when it comes to moving your book off the shelf. What is required of a successful book cover is *drama*, and achieving that tenuous balance between art and color requires the skills of a specialist.

WHAT TYPEFACES WILL BE MOST EFFECTIVE FOR THE BOOK?

Here again, you and your client should look carefully at published books available to you, and decide which typefaces and type sizes are the most pleasing to your eyes. When the decision has been reached, take the sample book to your printer to see how closely he can match the typefaces selected.

Some printers also have available printed booklets illustrating typefaces (body type and headline, or display type) available "in-house." If your printer has such a catalogue, you and your client can examine the various typefaces available to determine which is most suitable for your book. In general, it is not wise to mix serif with nonserif typefaces. It is also usually advisable to stay within the same "family" of types (Bodoni, Gothic, Futura, Garamond, etc.) for both body copy and headline copy.

Again, work closely with your printer on the matter of typefaces. He's been there before, and will know what will look attractive on the page yet be economical to produce.

WILL THERE BE ROOM FOR PHOTOGRAPHS, GRAPHICS, AND ART?

Almost any book is improved by illustrations, graphs, photographs and other artwork. Biographies and company histories are particularly enriched by the inclusion of old photographs. Good quality half-tones (photographs reduced to a pattern of dots for offset printing) can be made even from very old ferrotypes (tintypes) and daguerreotypes, amazingly, often with great enhancement of detail.

Family snapshots and portraits can easily be converted to half-tones, and a scattering of informal photographs intermixed with more carefully posed shots lend an undeniable "lift" to finished biographies. Uncle George clowning at a picnic, attacking a huge wedge of watermelon as though playing a harmonica; kids frolicking at the beach; Aunt Min burlesquing her culinary skills as she ostentatiously presents a perfectly roasted turkey to assembled guests at table. Such examples are of the type that will lend charm and personality to any personal biography.

Crisp black-and-white photographs produce better half-tones than color pictures, so if there is a choice, go with the black-and-white. Color photographs work satisfactorily, but the black-and-whites are usually more "contrasty" and produce sharper images in the finished product. If color slides are the only available medium, prints must first be made from the slides, then the prints reduced to the dot matrix of the half-tone. There is very little appreciable loss in picture quality if this method is used, even though there is one extra step in the process.

In my books, I try to have a minimum of one picture for each chapter. Of course, photos of grandparents, parents, and the principals (your clients) should appear in your book, but photos representative of the pre-school years, the grammar-school years, the high-school years, military service, college, and other distinct eras in your client's life should also be included. As you chronicle your client's growth and maturity through the words in your book, the accompanying photographs will show future readers the changes in appearance we all undergo as we grow older. If you are fortunate, you will be able to find photographs showing your client as he or she appeared as a child, as a teenager, as a young adult, as a mature grown-up and seasoned senior citizen.

Selecting photographs can be an arduous and time-consuming part of your work, and it is always helpful to enlist the aid of your client in making these selections. This is not to say that you should always *defer* to your client's suggestions as to the photographs to be included. Often, he will create an imbalance in the photo section of your book. That is, he may select too many pictures from, say, the college years of his life, and have nothing representing the high-school years or the early years of marriage. It is here where you, the writer/publisher/editor must use some diplomacy and tact, and point out that certain eras in his life have not been documented in the book by photographs. Search through the albums and boxes and envelopes of prints until you have uncovered at least one appropriate photograph for each stage of your client's life. With any luck, you will then come up with a "package" of photographs to complement the words you have written, each chapter with its own photographic accompaniment showing your client as he or she looked at that period in life.

HOW MUCH IS THIS ALL GOING TO COST?

By this time, you will have discussed with your printer/binder all of the elements which will go into your book: paper stock, cover treatment, number of photographs, type of binding, typefaces to be used, the size of your book and the number of pages to be printed. Once the number of copies of your book to be printed has been determined, your printer will be able to give you an estimate of the charges.

This estimate, of course, should be in writing. The estimate probably will also include the terms of the agreement between the printer and yourself—you acting as the representative of your client to the printer. This agreement will list the specifications agreed upon for the book, delivery date of the finished copies, and the terms of payment for work performed. It is also customary for the printer to provide several different options, depending upon the size of the press run—the total number of books to be printed. As mentioned earlier in this book, the greater the total of books produced, the less the per-book cost. Thus your client will want to decide whether he wants 500 books at $2.00 a copy, or 1,000 books at $1.50 a copy.

If you have produced your book on a word processor, be certain to check with your printer about the capabilities of his equipment in handling floppy disks. In many modern print shops, type can be set *directly* (or with some slight modifications or compensations) from the floppy disks you have produced on your word processing equipment. If your printer offers such an option, by all means use it, because it will save the cost of someone else having to "re-keyboard" your entire manuscript.

One important *caveat.* There is a heavy penalty for making any changes in the book after the type has been set! Afterthoughts and last-minute corrections are going to cost your client *big bucks*, and will do little to enhance the relationship you have so carefully nurtured during the months the two of you have been working together. I suggest that you go over your manuscript with a finely-tuned critical eye before it is ever submitted to the printer. Better yet, if you know an editor or a "'script doctor," let that expert go over your manuscript before it goes to the printer, and be prepared to pay whatever fee the editor charges. Better to pay a small fee to a competent editor than making costly last-minute changes at the printers, or worse, finding glaring boo-boos in syntax, construction and grammar *after* the book has been printed!

Make all the changes on your final copy on your typewriter or word processor (or in pen-and-ink, for that matter), before you submit your copy to the printer for typesetting. Oversights and omissions can reduce your profits and your confidence.

With a little foresight you can avoid much agony.

BOOKS TO READ

A Manual of Style, The University of Chicago Press

How to Self-Publish Your Book Successfully, by Jerod Rosman, Snohomish Publishing Company, P.O. Box 499, Snohomish, Washington 98290

Publish It Yourself—A Beginner's Guide to Printing, Murray Publishing Company, 2314 Third Avenue, Seattle, Washington 98121

Breaking Into Print, by Philip J. Gearing and Evelyn V. Brunson, A Spectrum Book, Prentice-Hall, Inc., Englewood Cliffs, New Jersey 07632

Books—From Writer to Reader, by Howard Greenfeld, Crown Publishers, Inc., New York, N.Y.

Any fair-sized public library will have on hand a number of additional books on typography, layout, self-publishing and printing which will be useful to you. The counsel of a seasoned and helpful printer in conjunction with the reference books available should provide all of the information necessary to transform your finished copy into handsome books which you will be able to deliver with pride—and for which your client will pay you well.

SEVERAL ROLES IN SEARCH OF PLAYERS

Up to now, your project has been almost a one-man show. You've done everything from promoting the concept of *biography as legacy*, selling the idea and getting a contract signed, conducting the interviews, typing the rough drafts, organizing and writing your book, and now coordinating the printing.

If your skills are broad ranging and of the highest level, you may be able to continue your solo act. However, shortly before or at about the same time you begin to consult with your printer, you and your client may want to bring in other communications specialists, particularly if a large number of books are to be ordered. As skilled professionals ourselves, we can be many things to many people, but it is the rare bird indeed who can be *all* things to *all* people. It usually just isn't in the cards.

Specialists whose aid you may want to enlist include one or more of the following:

COPY EDITOR: The Copy Editor's job is a difficult one in that it entails examining the finished copy for factual accuracy, consistency of style, spelling and usage.

BOOK DESIGNER: The Book Designer is part artist, part engineer, and part printer. He or she determines what your book is going to look like in its finished form. Typefaces for both body type and display type must be decided upon, book size, color, art treatment and many other variables come under the Book Designer's purview.

JACKET DESIGNER: Many of your clients for self-published books will not find the nicety of a book jacket necessary or within their budgets. However, if your book is to be sold to the public, or given wide distribution, a jacket is probably indicated. A successful book jacket will attract attention and provide information—make it stand out from countless other books on the shelves. And it must reflect the "tone" of the printed material embodied in the book's copy.

THE PROOFREADER: The proofreader carefully checks the final set of proofs (provided by the printer) against the author's manuscript to make certain that no discrepancies exist. He also examines the proofs for errors by the printer—spelling, word division, punctuation, broken or damaged typefaces, etc.

THE INDEXER: If your book is of such a nature as to require an index, the kind of index indicated must first be determined. Some indexes will list only proper names; others will list only the names of people; still others will include ideas and perceptions. It will be up to you and your client to decide how elaborate an index is needed to render the book most useful to the largest number of readers, or, if an index is required at all.

Of course, you, the writer, may feel qualified to undertake at least some of the tasks which, in the trade-publishing world, are assumed by staff specialists in the employ of publishing houses. It is the rare writer who is capable of providing the art for a book *jacket*, although many writers have helped in book *design* with the aid of a competent printer or bookbinder; many have proved to be skilled copy editors and proofreaders; yet others have successfully undertaken the indexing of complex material.

ISBN AND COPYRIGHT APPLICATION

The International Standard Book Number concept was developed jointly by the R. R. Bowker Company, the American National Standards Institute, the Library of Congress and the Association of American Publishers. If your client's book is to be widely distributed, and most certainly if it is to be offered for sale, it would be prudent to apply for an ISBN number.

You may make inquiry of the ISBN Agency, R. R. Bowker Company, 1180 Avenue of the Americas, New York, N.Y. 10036 where a booklet, *The ISBN Users Manual* and the necessary forms for filing an ISBN number are available.

Copyrighting of your work—your client's book—will be your responsibility. And how copyright ownership is stated must be agreed upon by you and your client. Will the client own, outright, the copyright on the work you jointly created (but for which he paid), or will he be willing to share the copyright with you? If your client is hesitant about sharing the copyright with you, it is usually not worth causing friction which could jeopardize the cordial relationship between you and your client. Accede graciously and let your client control the copyright. After all, you have already been paid for your work.

However, if you see that you are creating a book for which there may be the promise of lucrative secondary markets—motion pictures, television, magazine serialization, foreign publication and the like—the agreement about copyright ownership should be reached early on in your dealings with your client. At the outset, if you perceive that secondary markets may indeed develop for your book, copyright ownership should be made a part of your initial contract with the client, and you will want to share in that ownership if at all possible.

The use of a copyright notice on your book does not have to be approved by the copyright office in Washington, D.C. The copyright notice must, however, conform strictly to the requirements of the copyright law.

In the front matter of your book must appear three elements which will assure you and your client of copyright protection. These are:

1. The symbol "C" with a circle around it, or the word "Copyright," or both.
2. The name or names of the copyright owner.
3. The year of first publication.

To obtain more information on copyrights, and the necessary forms for registration with the copyright office, write to the Register of Copyrights, Library of Congress, Washington, D.C. 20559. Ask for any applicable information booklets, and for a copy of Form TX, "Application for Copyright Registration for a Nondramatic Literary Work." Two copies of your published book, plus a small fee, must then accompany the completed Form TX when it is returned to Washington. If all is in order, your copyright will be issued "in due course."

After shepherding your book from the initial interview with your client, through the thickets and quagmires of writing, editing, proofing, printing, binding, to the final joy and relief of seeing it copyrighted, you have every reason to be well pleased with yourself! You have created a valuable thing from whole cloth—something of great intrinsic worth which would never have existed had it not been for your wide range of skills and studied perseverance.

And when you tackle your next book or other writing project, you will be amazed at all you have learned from this *first* big writing and publishing experience. You have grown. You have absorbed new information about fields of endeavor about which you had probably only the slightest inkling before you began your grand project. You now know what questions to ask about book design, jacket art, typefaces, illustrations, indexes, paper weights and finishes, printing-and-binding techniques and materials.

When your successful project has been completed, and you view the fine book you hold in your hands with a mixture of astonishment and pride, you can well afford to sit back and relish your moment of triumph.

You brought the thing off like a professional!

And with good reason. You *are* one!

CHAPTER TWENTY

BIOGRAPHY OF A DIFFERENT SORT:
The Company History

He banged the door on the way out, and out of that bang came eventually the Chrysler corporation."

— Alfred P. Sloan, Jr.,
on Walter Chrysler's departure from General Motors,
"My Years with General Motors," *Fortune*, Sept. 1963

COMPANIES ARE PEOPLE

Wow! What a quotation! Eighteen words have been skillfully juxtaposed to tell *reams* about how one of the most powerful corporations in the world came into being. And that moment of coming-into-being (of Chrysler) all hinged on the anger and the action of a *single man*!

And that one quotation reminds us forcefully that company history is still biography! The actions of *people*!

We've spent a whole book talking about biography and methods for documenting the lives of individuals. When we come to another facet of the biography, the company history, we are apt to mistakenly identify it as a whole 'nuther thing; as a different breed of cat. Not so. Personal *interaction* is still the key. We're still talking about people, and how they interact with one another—only this time in the environment of business rather than in the milieu of the family. (See above for how Walter Chrysler "interacted" with the hierarchy at General Motors.) The company history, then, is just a different kind of biography.

How does the company history *differ* from the individual biography? Let us count the ways:

1. You, the writer, will usually be interviewing more than one person during the course of information-gathering for the company history;

2. The emphasis during interviewing and writing will be more on your subjects' educational and business experiences than on personal and family incidents (although the latter must not be overlooked as contributing to the character and make-up of the interviewees);

3. In the company history, you are free to seek out material which will lend drama, great conflict, and even impart a sense of "mission" to the finished document. When recreating certain incidents in the history of the company you are writing about, and with all the actors playing their parts (and with firsthand information about actual dialogues which took place), you may find yourself functioning almost as a novelist or playwright rather than as a strict documentarian.

4. The creating of a company history permits the writer great leeway, in that complex personal interactions, elaborate schemes, ploys, and (sometimes) even skulduggery can enliven the narrative. Writing the history of a large and dynamic company can become something akin to dramatizing material for a stage presentation. In the real world of business and finance,

faction tugs against faction, while internal conflict inflames emotions to a point where a genuine sense of stagecraft may be demanded of the writer.

(If you think that the "dull" world of business does not engender conflict, drama, and excitement, take a look at some of the nighttime television "soaps" such as "Dynasty," "Hotel," and "Knott's Landing"! While the situations and characters are intentionally overdrawn in these TV dramas, the genesis of these modern-day fairy tales is deeply rooted in the very real worlds—battlefields, sometimes—of commerce and finance.)

5. The history of a large company will usually take longer to write than an individual biography. More people must be interviewed, and more archival material reviewed for the sake of accuracy and completeness of coverage. The sheer volume of available (and necessary) information simply makes the company history a larger undertaking than the personal biography. Then, too, scheduling difficulties may arise, causing your project to take longer than the personal biography. Key subjects, people you *must* interview, and who are vital to the success of your project, may be out of town, retired and living elsewhere, or otherwise temporarily unavailable to you for immediate interview.

6. In creating a company history, you may anticipate that some travel will be involved. When it is necessary for you to travel in the conduct of your work, charge the client company your regular hourly rate for writing, editing, and the like, *plus* all meal, lodging, long-distance telephone and other expenses incident to that travel.

In writing the company history, you may also anticipate a treat. Beneath the surface of those glossy annual reports and cold-as-ice financial statements, often there is a thick, steamy soup rich in complex strategy and intrigue. And sometimes, once on the inside of a business organization, we find the broth not as savory as the menu would make it appear. The aroma may be less than wholesome as we see the wily manipulations and (occasional) questionable tactics which went into the creation and operation of this heady brew known as The Corporation.

While many business leaders are just plain good guys, even as thee and me, you may also expect to encounter the little Napoleons, the reclusive researchers, eccentrics and megalomaniacs. You will come across some businessmen having killer instincts; others with messianic complexes. And you will become privy to family sagas and stories of rags-to-riches, riches-to-rags, and back again. Strife and excitement can be interwoven in your narratives if you but read between the lines and question your interview subjects carefully as you weave the rich tapestry of disparate lives dedicated to a common endeavor, yet entangled in skeins of intrigue, then thrust into the emotional and stress-ridden cauldron of modern business and finance.

It is up to you (and all the skills you can muster) to let as much of the warts-and-all facts of the company's beginnings and current operations *show*! By balancing the good with the bad, the exemplary with the shoddy and suspect, you will probably write a company history (and build a corporate image) which is somewhere close to the truth. This, of course, is your aim. You don't want to knowingly whitewash a company; neither do you want to give it a black eye. One would be a betrayal of your craft; the other a betrayal of your client. You can afford to do neither. Your experiences in writing company histories will redefine and give new meaning to the expression, "tight-rope walker."

Your contact (for which, read *editor*) within the company may well elect to expunge some of what you have written about the company's less-than-savory maneuvers; about power struggles within the corporate hierarchy; about acts and "deals" which would not tolerate the bright light of day. If they want to delete every uncomplimentary account, so be it. The book is, after all, their property, and they're paying you to write it. They can do anything they want with the final product. It is incumbent upon you, the writer, however, to remind your clients from time to time, that you would like to present the company in as truthful a light as possible, and if the book is *too* Goody Two Shoes; *too* glowing; *too* full of praise; *too* free of self censure—then the book will be judged purely as a puff piece, and of little worth to anyone.

PROSPECTING FOR THE COMPANY HISTORY CLIENT

Where shall we begin searching for the likely business client? At this juncture, I will suggest that you reread those sections of Chapter Four of this book which deal with companies and corporations. Particular attention should be paid to those passages which suggest the use of the business section of your local library, and those sections of this book which call attention to directories published by local Chambers of Commerce. Local and regional business directories are rich sources of information, and properly used as prospect mailing lists, they can and will bring you more business than you can ever hope to handle. The wise use of these resources can save you hours of work and a great deal of postage money by helping you separate the wheat from the chaff.

Another rich and readily available source of prospect names is your right-at-hand directory, *The Yellow Pages*. It can be a gold mine for the prudent prospector. The copy on my desk contains 1,800 pages, and a Customer Relations representative at U.S. West Communications told me that this particular volume contains 332,109 individual listings! Each one, of course, is a *potential* client! Now, if that isn't enough to get you started (and to keep you in clients until you choose to retire, for that matter), I don't know what is!

The Yellow Pages also allow you to solicit prospects in your own area of interest, be it umbrella repair or hang gliding. For example, if you are an avid outdoor sports fan, you might want to approach the owners or proprietors of operations dealing in sporting goods, ski instruction, charter-boat fishing, or the manufacture of outdoor equipment and clothing. If you're interested in cars, you would be a natural to contact speed-shop owners, auto repair shops and automobile detailers. It goes on and on. The message remains: Use of *The Yellow Pages* allows you to cleave to whatever specialty you prefer, and to operate in areas in which you are comfortable and most familiar. Kinda nice when you can pick your own line of work and your own "boss," every time!

There are certain *caveats*, however. It is foolish to waste time and money attempting to make local contact with a company whose home offices (and all the executive decision-makers) are headquartered 2,000 miles distant. Franchise retail outlets, small operations only a few years old, and branch distributorships of out-of-state companies are equally poor prospects. The wise use of your public library and Chamber of Commerce publications will guide your footsteps and show you where you may best spend your time, money, and efforts.

You are looking for locally owned companies, closely held corporations, family owned or sole proprietorships all of which have been in business long enough to have built reputations—histories, if you like—for themselves. It (probably) would be presumptuous to spin your wheels trying to get an interview with the president of IBM. And it would be profitless to interview the proprietor of some little hole-in-the-wall doughnut shop that's been in business for six months, and whose credit rating is nonexistent. It is in that vast, rich territory somewhere in between those two extremes where your best prospects will be found.

For example, that oh-so-very-proper little jewelry store that's been down on Main Street forever and ever, and whose small gold-leaf sign in the window quietly proclaims, "Since 1906"—now *that's* another story! (And probably a story you would enjoy helping the owners tell for the benefit of their heirs and customers!) This is the kind of prospect that should set your gears in motion!

On a busy thoroughfare in Seattle there's a small muffler shop. It doesn't look like much, but every time I pass, I see all kinds of activity, and cars come and go at a great rate. The shop's small sign tells the world: "Three generations. In the same location since 1926." May not be anything—but again, those three generations of grease-besmirched mechanics may have a family enclave in Palm Springs and a luxury condo in Kailua Kona. And when they drive home from work at night, they may be driving in Rolls Royces or Bentleys, for all I know. Lessee, now—the next time I'm down that way, it wouldn't hurt to drop in, introduce myself, chat for a minute, leave a brochure and...

Just because a company isn't the size of Ford, Boeing, or Weyerhaeuser, we must not get the idea that it doesn't have its own unique story to tell, nor sufficient capital to pay a writer to tell that story professionally and well.

Gail Nelson, a Seattle free-lance-writer colleague, has, within the last three years, completed company histories for a well-known regional optical company, prescription opticians with more than a score of locations; a company dealing in illuminated signs and awnings; and a local iron company whose employees are specialists in structural steel fabrication and erection. To the uninitiated, these clients—for whom books now have been written—might have seemed unlikely prospects. But the people who founded and operated these companies had stories worthy of documentation; had audiences they wanted to address; had heirs they wanted to tell their stories to. And they were delighted when Ms. Nelson approached them, saying, "Here is the kind of book I can write for you."

The old aphorisms are true: Appearances can be deceiving; Beauty is only skin deep; Never judge a book by its cover, etc. The company or business you may mentally write off as an unlikely prospect for the services you offer, may well become a valued and lucrative client. Much depends upon you. You may convert a NO-SALE proposition into a signed contract if you but demonstrate sufficient skill in showing present corporate officers or owners how a company history will benefit not only current management, employees, and shareholders, but their successors as well.

It makes little difference whether your prospect is a big fish in a big pond; a big fish in a little pond; or a guppy in a mud puddle! Your hourly rate is the same; your work techniques are the same; and, it is to be hoped, the end product will be the same: a book or other package of work of which you and your clients may be proud.

This word of counsel may be unnecessary, but for you "world burners" out there, those of you who intend to take these ideas and set the world on fire, let me suggest that you take it a bit easy at the beginning. Just to get your feet wet, first go after a couple of the "guppies" or the "little fish" in your corporate community. Leave the IBMs and the AT&Ts for later in your career.

The owners and proprietors of small- to medium-sized companies will be more accessible to you than the moguls of gigantic corporations, and the job you cut out for yourself won't be quite as daunting. Everything will be on a smaller scale: fewer people to interview; less travel involved; not so many old company archives to wade through; not such a mountain of interview typescripts and company documents to boil down to manageable size.

Old aphorisms again: Don't bite off more than you can chew; Walk before you run; Rome wasn't built over a long weekend, etc. You have all the time in the world, and you'll be paid handsomely while you serve your apprenticeship, no matter how long it is extended.

SMALL, FAMILY-OWNED BUSINESSES

These are naturals! *Because* these businesses are family-owned, heirs and successive generations of the founding family have a great deal of interest in what has gone before. The level of cooperation from such clients is usually splendid. The owners are as eager as you are to "get it right," and the amount of volunteered information can be expected to be high.

One of my most pleasant and rewarding commissions involved producing tapes and rough-typed transcripts for a well-known local glass company in Seattle. In this case, it helped that the owners were neighbors, and long-time friends of *our* family, but this fortuitous happenstance was not *necessary* to the production of good documentation. The close familiarity merely eased things along.

Our regularly scheduled interview sessions became almost social occasions, and we gleefully rooted through stacks of old annual reports, newspaper clippings, promotional literature about the company and its products, and drafts of speeches given by the company's executives to civic and industry groups. It was a treasure hunt in which all could participate, and in which we all delighted. (It's not against the law or moral principle for work to be *fun*!)

We approached our project in a businesslike manner, but there was also a lot of room for good humor. There had been some *characters* who had figured importantly in the company, and we weren't about to overlook them. The founder (from whom the present owners had bought the company) was a bit of an eccentric, and we documented how the peculiarities of this man had influenced the beginnings and growth of the corporation. And early on, we decided to eschew the "executives only" viewpoint which mars so many company histories. I was given a free hand to talk with whom I pleased, and as a result, I found myself interviewing retired shop foremen, salesmen, loading-dock workers and installation people, as well as board members and present-day managers.

The resultant typescript of historical notes about the company make delightful reading in themselves, and all those who participated in the project felt that we recorded not only the nuts-and-bolts essentials about the company's founding and growth, but preserved something of the character and personality of the *people* who made the organization come to life and flourish. Years from now, if someone decides to write a formal and very "proper" history of the glass company, all the vital details will have been preserved—and derived not from revisionism or hindsight, but first-hand from men and women who had *been there* as company history was being made.

Several of the people I interviewed for this document, including the then-president of the company, have since died. But the president's son, who is now an officer in the company himself, speaks of the hours we worked together almost every time we meet or talk on the telephone.

"I played some of those tapes again just recently," he told me not long ago. "And you know, I wouldn't take anything for those recordings of Dad as he talked about his company and the people he gathered around him who made it work. They were all his friends, and the company was a big part of his *life*! And now I have, and my kids will have, in Dad's own words, just what all that meant to him."

We are "Life Preservers" indeed. And we do valuable, important, and lasting work.

MID-SIZED AND CLOSELY HELD CORPORATIONS

Like the small, family-held businesses, many middle-sized and/or closely held corporations may be dominated by one or two people. (Even some megacorporations can be so typified: Would Chrysler be Chrysler without Lee Iacocca?) Just because a company is a large and important factor in your business community is no sure sign that its executives are unapproachable; no reason for you to be timorous about approaching them with a valuable idea.

It would not be fair or accurate to suggest that all the CEOs of these larger companies are vain, egocentric and boastful. But they *are* important figures in their community and in their industry, and rest assured that they know it. And they have something of value to contribute (or have convinced others that they have), and it is a pretty safe bet that they would not be averse to having their achievements documented in books about the companies whose fortunes they direct. To be blunt, it is certain that each of these executives nurtures (perhaps privately) at least a small bump of pride, and we would do well to recognize this all-too-human trait, and capitalize upon it. By writing a book about this fellow and his company, we can bolster his ego—not always a bad thing to do.

A man and company for which I wrote such a book comes to mind. And because in so many ways the man *was* the company, the bulk of my interviews were with him alone. I talked briefly with three or four other men, but so closely identified was the man with his company that the story of one was essentially the story of the other.

Mr. Alaska—The Chuck West Story; 40 Years of Alaska Tourism, 1945-1985, epitomizes the self-made and self-directed man. Chuck West was a dashing young aviator who came out of World War II, after having flown 153 missions over "The Hump" between Karachi, Pakistan, and Kunming, China, in the China/Burma/India Theater of War. Upon his separation from the Flying Tigers, from China Chuck West went immediately to Alaska, first to become a bush pilot, then as a contract pilot with Wien Air. Eventually he was to cast off on his own to plant the seeds of what was to become modern Alaska tourism.

To boil a whole book down into a sentence, West parlayed his own skills, enthusiasm, and a beat-up 1936 Plymouth sedan (his first "sight-seeing" vehicle) into a world-renowned travel organization which eventually boasted a fleet of modern tour buses, three cruise ships, hotels, aircraft, and hundreds of employees. That West later lost control of his organization (Westours) is secondary to the story of its creation, although Westours was later purchased by the Holland-America Line, and became the jewel in Holland-America's crown.

Gathering the information for this book and writing the story for Chuck West was a hoot! Chuck was a marvelous storyteller, and our weekly interview sessions sped along, the hour-and-a-half interviews over all too quickly. West was one of those remarkable raconteurs, who, when telling a story, would speak both sides of a dialogue—perform a whole scenario, taking the parts of several players, if need be—to provide the proper ambience for the scene he was reenacting.

The book was a joy to write; I was paid my fee; and West formed his own publishing company to produce the several thousand copies of the book he had printed. The book went on to do rather well in sales from local outlets, chief among them, Chuck West's new company, TravAlaska, which he formed after selling Westours to Holland-America Lines. West's name is on the cover of the book; mine is not. West owns the copyright; I have no part of it. While there is no indication that I wrote the book, there is an acknowledgement of my contribution on the ISBN/copyright page. And this is O.K. too. I had my fee; West had his book: and he could do with it anything he saw fit.

I include this information for a very good reason. The writer/biographer/company historian comes close, though not by design, to being a ghost writer. Your client has paid you to do a job, has paid you for your efforts, and what the client does with the material you created for him is quite beyond your control. Most, but certainly not all of your clients, will be gracious enough to acknowledge your authorship on the cover credits, albeit obliquely. As in: By Josephine Client, *as told to* Jill Scrivener. Or: By Tommy Tycoon *with* Sam Scribe. And that's enough.

Very seldom can we have it both ways. If it's glory we crave, we had best follow in the footsteps of those authors who write novels and nonfiction books on speculation, and hope to snag the big contract and the Hollywood offers. We contract writers may not rate the spotlights and the talk-show interviews by doing what we do, but at least writing commissioned biographies and company histories is a sure way to our own financial solvency.

STOCK COMPANIES AND MAJOR CORPORATIONS

As mentioned earlier in this chapter, writing of the history of a large corporation is a major undertaking which should not be assumed lightly. The bigger the company, the more elaborate the protocols which must be followed; the more people interviewed; the greater the bulk of interview and archival material to be condensed; the more travel involved; the more *every*thing.

The most important corporate commission I ever assumed involved one of the largest conglomerates in the Northwest. The work went well. I made trips to Canada, Iowa and California to interview key figures in the company. I waded through dusty file after dusty file to track down the histories of the 30-odd corporate entities which eventually were consolidated into the company as it is today. After nearly two years of work, I presented my completed draft manuscript, and sat back awaiting the approval of management. Once that was granted, we would do whatever rewrites or modifications were necessary, and could complete our plans to have the book printed and distributed.

After several weeks had gone by, and I had heard nothing from the conglomerate, I called my principal contact at the home office. Was something amiss? No, I was assured, my work had received high praise by most of the executives who had read all or part of it. But it seems that there was some slight disagreement about who had done what to whom and when they had done it. Also, there were differing ideas about which incidents should be emphasized and which downplayed.

To curtail the agony, to you, the reader, let me say that the book MS was completed nine years ago, and it has yet to see print. During the months following my delivery of the manuscript, repeated contacts with the company revealed that the MS was still "being reviewed." I learned only many months later that the draft of my book manuscript had been duplicated, and copies distributed to almost everyone I had interviewed, as well as to members of the board of directors! I envisioned perhaps thirty copies of a book-length manuscript floating around, in various parts of the northern hemisphere, being "blue-penciled" by scores of would-be editors.

In its present form, it is doubtful that the book will ever be published. In the ensuing nine years, there have been major organizational and executive changes within the company. Some corporate entities have been sold; others acquired. Were it to be published today, the book manuscript would have to be largely rewritten to reflect the company's current status.

So much for editing by committee! That was one job I was glad I had not taken on a pay-on-publication basis!

BIG FISH THAT GET AWAY

Try as we might, we can never land 'em all. And, I must admit that I'm still haunted by some of the big ones that got away. To this day, I wonder if I had but used more subtle or convincing suasion, I might have coaxed some of those "biggies" to the net. Two important failed efforts come immediately to mind.

One was a quiet man from a modest background. In his youth, his family had made its home in the woods of Ballard, today a thriving community which long since has been swallowed up by Greater Seattle. But when my prospect had been a boy, more than once he had been pursued by *bears* along what is now a bustling four-lane thoroughfare! Bears in Ballard are rather like cougars in Hollywood or coyotes in the outskirts of Chicago—hard to imagine.

As this fellow was maturing, he worked in his family's bakery, which, by the way, made a ton of money during the Alaska gold rush of 1897-'98. When the young man took over the management of the family business, he expanded it, adding one bakery after another, until he consolidated his operation to become one of the largest commercial bakers in the Northwest. He built a luxurious family home on Highland Drive, in the Queen Anne district of Seattle, and the house became the talk of the town. (The mansion was purchased by the Japanese Government in 1979, and today serves as the official residence of the Japanese Consul General.)

That the man thought highly of his family, both his forebears and his heirs, there could be no doubt. When I talked with him informally in his lovely home (before it had been sold to the Japanese Government), I noted what amounted to a family shrine positioned prominently at the side of the great fireplace and hearth in the living room. The "shrine" was a tilt-top table which held numerous family pictures, the family bible, and other memorabilia.

But I couldn't get him to sign the contract! He was interested in telling me stories of his youth—but not for publication. Too self-serving, he said. Too much a mark of vanity, he protested. This, in spite of the fact that his three children and *their* children were begging and cajoling him to undertake the project. All of this was to no avail, in spite of several months during which family members and I used every manner of persuasion.

Fate soon took the problem from our hands. My prospect suffered a massive stroke and died only a few days later. It was a situation in which there were no winners; only losers. And it was a dratted shame that the man's falsely placed modesty prevented his leaving what would have been a priceless legacy to his children and grandchildren.

Then there was the outdoor-clothing tycoon.

This fellow had come into Seattle during the Great Depression of the 1930s. His arrival was unheralded and inglorious, inasmuch as he rolled into town riding the rails of a boxcar! He may have been cold, dirty, tired, hungry, broke and wet—but he didn't want charity, and he didn't know the meaning of the word 'quit.' In a literal rags-to-riches story, he parlayed hard work and an indomitable spirit into one of the most successful outdoor-apparel companies in the world.

This man and his two sons, who operated the business with the father/founder, responded favorably to the proposition I placed before them. Yes, they were interested in documenting the story of the company, and (perhaps more importantly) the story of how the corporation had come, Phoenix-like, into being.

But, there were industry shows to attend and a big sales promotion coming up which would take all their combined energies. Would I please come back just four months hence? *Then* they would sign the contract and we'd all get down to work.

"I know how busy you are, particularly at this time," I told them, "but surely you could set aside just two hours a week so that we could at least get to work on the project. There will always be *some*thing which is going to interfere with our getting together, and I'd feel much better about it if we could begin work soon."

All to no avail.

"Time is the enemy," I reminded the sons. "Today, your father's memory is sharp and clear, and his recall about the early years of the company is nearly total. But we can't know what tomorrow is going to bring. Why don't we at least begin the interview stage of information gathering, then, if anything untoward happens, we'll at least have most of the vital information on tape."

No soap.

And three months after our initial interview, the old man was dead. Coronary occlusion. No brave stories to leave the grandkids; no wonderful document to inspire shareholders, employees and friends of the company; no lasting record of individual achievement with which to enrich the annals of Northwest business.

I ground my teeth in impotent disappointment. In that three months' time, I could have had it *all* on tape! An astounding amount of information can be chronicled in eighteen hours of interviews! And I (and the family) had *nothing*!

As Kurt Vonnegut says, "And so it goes."

LOOK AROUND YOU

We, as writers of company histories, are not breaking new ground. We aren't pathfinders or adventurers heading off into the unexplored wilderness. Others have been there before us, but their numbers are relatively few, and for the most part, they have kept the secrets of found riches to themselves.

Even in my own modest library, I find the following titles:

Firstbank: The Story of Seattle-First National Bank, by Shelby Scates (North Pacific Bank Note Company, 1970)

The National Bank of Commerce of Seattle, by Elliott Marple and Bruce H. Olson (Pacific Books, Publishers, 1972)

The Story of Western International Hotels, by Sid Copeland (Frayn Printing Company, 1976)

The Safeco Story, by Sid Copeland (Kingsport Press, 1981). Insurance company

Crescent—100 Years, 1883-1983, by Archie Satterfield. Spices, food flavorings

The O. W. Fisher Heritage, by Herman Steen (Frank McCaffrey Publishers). Flouring mills, food manufacturing and distribution, radio/TV stations, industrial and business properties.

T*he Green Years*, by Gordon Newell (Superior Publishing Company, 1969) Transportation, trade, finance, and the founding of Peoples National Bank

Telephone, The First Hundred Years, by John Brooks (Harper & Row, 1975,1976) History of the American Telephone and Telegraph Company

Out of the Cracker Barrel: From Animal Crackers to ZuZu's, by William Cahn (Simon and Schuster, 1969) History of the National Biscuit Company

From the Captain to the Colonel, An Informal History of Eastern Airlines, by Robert J. Serling (The Dial Press, 1980)

The Only Way to Fly, The Story of Western Airlines, America's Senior Air Carrier, by Robert J. Serling (Doubleday, 1976)

Vision, A Saga of the Sky, by Harold Mansfield (Duell, Sloan & Pearce, 1956) A history of the Boeing Airplane Company

Give the Lady What She Wants! The Story of Marshall Field & Company, by Lloyd Wendt & Herman Kogan (Rand McNally, 1952)

The Plywood Age, A History of the Fir Plywood Industry's First Fifty Years, by Robert M. Cour (Binfords and Mort, 1955)

Bryant's—1928-1978, by Eileen Crimmin (Privately printed, 1978) Marina operation

Time, Tide and Timber, A Century of Pope & Talbot, by Edwin T. Coman Jr. and Helen M. Gibbs (Stanford University Press, 1949) Timber, shipping and real estate operation.

These are just some of the titles of company histories which I am fortunate enough to own. If I can boast of this modest collection of company histories, just think what must await you in any well-stocked metropolitan library! There will be examples by the score, I can promise you. Withdraw some of these books from the library. Take them home with you. Read them critically; thoughtfully. Study them for content, writing style, arrangement of material, use of anecdotes, tone and voice. Have the writers used dialogue to enliven and give a sense of immediacy to their books? Did most of the authors include an index in most of these books you have read? Will an index increase the usefulness of the book *you* intend to write?

The company history is not a great deal more difficult to write than the biography of a single individual. And by keeping one or two company histories bubbling on the fire, you will not only assure yourself of a continuing and dependable income, but will grant yourself the freedom and independence to pursue the more esoteric (and financially risky) pursuits to which most writers seem to aspire—writing the novel, the short story, the play/television drama, or the speculative nonfiction book.

Just think! This is a case of having your cake and eating it too! By going after those commissions to be earned in writing company histories, you may continue to practice your craft and hone your writing skills, while enjoying the comfort of a steady income—*and* the heady luxury of being able to "take a flyer" at writing that novel you have been putting off all these years!

Go for it!

CHAPTER TWENTY-ONE

SUCCESS!
And Spending Your Life <u>Your</u> Way!

"There is only one success—to be able to spend your life in your own way."

— Christopher Morley

RECOGNITION, AND THE SWEET SAVOR OF SUCCESS

Success and recognition, and how to attain them through writing. That's what this "how-to" book has been all about. In a sense, *Biographies and Company Histories* is a recipe book. It provides a sequence of steps which, if taken, will provide the writer with a lifetime of employment, a comfortable income, and a legacy of satisfaction both to himself and to those he has served.

To wish for more would be downright greedy.

I compared this volume to a recipe book, and I believe the analogy to be apt. If we pick up a cookbook intent on finding a recipe for chocolate brownies, for example, we seek out the page, assemble the ingredients, and put them together as directed. If we follow the instructions, we have every right to expect to turn out a batch of palatable cookies. And just because we know a little bit about cooking, we aren't tempted to substitute sauerkraut for the cocoa. To do so would result in a culinary disaster, and an end product not resembling brownies at all.

And when attempting to assemble the material for a biography or a company history, the same kind of careful sequencing should be followed. Just because we know a little bit (or a lot, for that matter,) about writing, we should not substitute a telephone call for the personal interview; an oral description of our services in place of the carefully worded brochure; hastily scrawled notes on a 3 x 5 card in place of the list of carefully-thought-out and cleanly typed list of interview questions. For just as surely, as with the substitution of the sauerkraut, we would have a disaster—only this time, we would have a creative disaster, not a culinary one.

WHAT WE SEEK; WHAT WE SHOULD EXPECT

If it is JOB SATISFACTION we seek, writing commissioned biographies and company histories will let us reap bounteous rewards. This is work we can *do*, and when we have completed our tasks, there comes a marvelous exhilaration at having done something well. I know nothing of the "rush" described by users of hard drugs, but I know the "rush" of holding a finished book in my hands, and the "highs" must be similar—and can be addicting. Once a book or job assignment is completed, I find myself immediately looking forward to the next!

If it is assured INCOME which is paramount, we can look forward to a secure future. It is now possible for us to spend all the rest of our days earning our livelihoods by practicing our craft. And we may expect honest, even generous, compensation for our efforts. With more than 35 million people in the United States aged 65 and older, all the writers in the land could turn to writing personal biographies, and we would never exhaust our supply of prospective clients. The field is wide open, and the possibilities almost limitless.

PUBLIC ACCEPTANCE is assured. As a matter of fact, the concept of *Biography as Legacy* has such universal appeal that in social gatherings I am sometimes reluctant to tell others what I do for a living! To introduce the subject of biography is to invite a long discourse on the subject. If I don't want to be stuck, when questioned about my work, I simply say that I write nonfiction books. There are usually a couple of polite questions, and the whole exchange is over within two or three minutes. But if I admit to writing commissioned biographies, and introduce the idea of *Biography as Legacy*...Wow! I have been (pleasurably, to be sure) tied up for the better part of an evening sharing ideas with people hitherto unknown to me. Barriers drop, and even in a party setting, confidences are willingly shared. Bring up the subject of biography, and everyone has a story to tell; everyone has friend or relative (now gone, sad to say), they wished I had talked to. And the evening slips by as animated conversation eats up the hours.

Once the concept of the biographical legacy has been grasped, it seems that *everyone* knows of a potential client I should contact, or someone whose fascinating story should have been captured before that debilitating illness struck, or before the poor subject died. Anecdotes, stories, and whole sagas come tumbling out of perfect strangers, and countless times I have found myself at the center of a previously unacquainted group of people, all animatedly talking about *biography*!

Strangers pouncing hungrily, nay, *voraciously*, on a fresh idea is in itself, a fascinating phenomenon to observe. More importantly, this instant acceptance attests to one undeniable fact: There is *interest* out there, friends! Sufficient interest to keep us all just as busy as we care to be, and for as long as we care to interview clients and write their stories.

We, as biographers of everyman, are even publicly praised for what we do! Can you imagine that? Newspaper columnists and feature writers have written a number of highly complimentary articles about my work, and I can assure you that I am no "personality" whose flamboyance has captured the hearts of the press. Nope. I'm dull as grass. But the Biography as Legacy *idea* has tremendous power, and this the reporters instantly recognize and seize upon.

If you yearn for PEER RECOGNITION, writing biographies and company histories will put you in a comfortable position. After all, it isn't every free-lance writer who completes two to four books a year, and makes his full-time living practicing his craft! With peer recognition may also come just a hint of peer *envy*, as well. And that's all right too. After all, before you stumbled onto this idea of Biography as Legacy, there had been some pretty lean times, eh? And there were times when you were (admit it, now!) envious of others—the "known" writers in your region, whose names and new titles were frequently in the papers, or members of your writers' group who were forever talking knowingly about agents, and the sale of paperback and foreign rights. Right? Now that you have "paid your dues," it's *your* turn to be recognized by the members of our writing fraternity.

If you are striving for SELF-ESTEEM, providing this kind of commissioned writing service to your community should pay big dividends. No need to be apologetic to anyone about the kind of writing you do. After all, putting together a detailed company history or adroitly assembling the facts and emotional ups-and-downs of a long life require the same skills demanded of the writers of fiction and nonfiction books alike. Research, sensitivity, an awareness of drama, organization, the creation of realistic dialogue, character delineation, continuity and narrative thrust are *all* demanded of the biographer and company historian. Make no mistake about it, you are not "playing" at writing, nor are you some sort of marginal pretender to the title of "writer."

The one *big* element missing from the catalog of similar characteristics shared by trade-book and commissioned-book authors is that of *risk*. Thousands of writers and would-be authors have squandered tens of thousands of man-years, writing books and manuscripts which will never see print. Other thousands of (marginally more successful) writers have slaved over their typewriters, agonized over rewrites, sold their books, had them printed and marketed—only to find their compensation for years of work to be a paltry few hundreds of dollars.

This element of risk I gladly leave to the trade-book writers. SELF-ESTEEM need not be based on the writer's willingness to take risk or ability to walk financial and emotional tightropes.

If you would build LONG-RANGE GOALS, STABILITY and CONSTANCY into your professional life, biographies and company histories are your meat. By removing yourself from the trade-book milieu and acting as your own promoter, agent, and jack-of-all-trades, you automatically obviate some of the more familiar writerly ills and pitfalls.

For example, there shouldn't be any squabbles over rate of pay or promptness of payment: you determine your *own* salary, and send out your *own* statements.

There won't be any beefs with your agent, because you won't have one.

There will be no struggle with the chain of command, nor will suggested manuscript changes have to trickle down from publisher to editor to assistant editor to agent to (finally), you, the writer. In writing biographies and company histories, the producer (you, the writer) is in direct and intimate contact with the consumer (your client). With the removal of all the middlemen, and you and your client talking face-to-face, there is little room for misunderstanding. Additions, deletions, and suggested changes may be incorporated into the manuscript quickly and painlessly.

There won't be any complaints about distribution and publicity, because these details (if there is any reason for them) will be handled by the owner of the property (the book), who is is your client.

And there won't be that gnawing fear that plagues many first-time authors: the haunting suspicion that they may be "one-book" writers. If you follow the plan stated so clearly in this book (send out the letters; make the phone calls; ask for the appointments; sign the contracts), you'll be writing books for as long as you have the strength to punch a keyboard.

Finally, if you must have INDEPENDENCE, you must view the promise offered by commissioned writing as a fervent wish granted. By following the plan of attack here set forth in detail, you may write a different way, and for a different market, and thus free yourself of the agent-editor-publisher complications endured by most writers. Writing one or two commissioned biographies or company histories a year will provide enough income so that you are free to experiment with other, more speculative forms of writing. You may experiment, then, with the confidence and certain knowledge that if your experiments in speculative writing are *failures*, all you must do is return once more to the well, write another commissioned book, and *grant yourself* another spate of freedom during which you may once again try to break into writing fiction, poetry, or for radio/TV and the legitimate theater.

INDEPENDENCE (and the accompanying extra income) may mean many things to many people: the freedom to travel; the ability to upgrade living standards; college educations for children; the security of a few more dollars of discretionary income. I envision many a retired or semi-retired person of seasoned years, undertaking the writing of just one biography a year—or one every *two* years—to "keep her hand in"; to inject a little "fun" money into an otherwise stringent budget; to keep flowing those productive juices which otherwise might dry up with inactivity.

And, if STIMULATION turns you on, curiosity is a great stimulator of the intellect! Probing the inner *sancta* of other people's lives can quicken your *own* interests and endless fascination with the process of living! While writing biographies doesn't exactly give us a license to pry, we *do* become privy to the secret lives of our clients—and we live vicariously the lives of others, even as we document them. As we go about our work, we celebrate *life*! There is a vitality about biography that rubs off on all connected with it: on the writer; on the subject; on the readers of our books. Seeing a biography through from first interview to finished book is a tonic for everyone involved!

One final, heartening word.

COURAGE!

Because each step of the process detailed in this book depends upon the success of the *preceding* step, no stage of the orderly progression should be slighted. But at no time should the goal—tapes-and-transcripts or a finished book—be lost sight of, either.

The very thought of sitting down to write a book is almost more than most of us can visualize. It's like trying to visualize a billion dollars.

But we can write a sentence. And a half-dozen sentences make a paragraph. And four or five paragraphs make a page. And a dozen pages make a chapter. And a chapter is five percent of a book! Five percent, then ten percent, soon fifty percent—and we're halfway to our goal.

Using the same analogy, it is no trick to develop a short, descriptive brochure—doing it a word at a time, a sentence at a time, a paragraph at a time. Neither is it any great challenge to compose a simple cover letter to accompany the brochure. We know how to mail letters; we know how to make telephone calls; we know how to arrange appointments. And we know how to ask questions, and how to write, otherwise we would never have gone this far.

Have, then, the COURAGE to take the information you now have at hand to craft for yourself a rewarding and fulfilling lifetime career which will be yours, and yours alone!

GOOD WRITING, AND MAY YOU HAVE LONG AND REWARDING CAREERS!

INDEX